FREEDOM'S RING

FREEDOM'S RING

Literatures of Liberation from Civil Rights to the Second Wave

JACQUELINE FOERTSCH

RUTGERS UNIVERSITY PRESS
NEW BRUNSWICK, CAMDEN, AND NEWARK,
NEW JERSEY, AND LONDON

Library of Congress Cataloging-in-Publication Data

Names: Foertsch, Jacqueline, 1964- author.
Title: Freedom's ring : literatures of liberation from civil rights to the second wave / Jacqueline Foertsch.
Description: New Brunswick, New Jersey : Rutgers University Press, [2021] | Includes bibliographical references and index.
Identifiers: LCCN 2020031105 | ISBN 9781978822719 (paperback) | ISBN 9781978822726 (cloth) | ISBN 9781978822733 (epub) | ISBN 9781978822740 (mobi) | ISBN 9781978822757 (pdf)
Subjects: LCSH: Civil rights—United States—History. | Liberty—History. | Equality—United States. | United States—History—1945- | United States—Politics and government.
Classification: LCC JC599.U5 F63 2021 | DDC 323.0973—dc23
LC record available at https://lccn.loc.gov/2020031105

A British Cataloging-in-Publication record for this book is available from the British Library.

♾ The paper used in this publication meets the requirements of the American National Standard for Information Sciences—Permanence of Paper for Printed Library Materials, ANSI Z39.48-1992.

www.rutgersuniversitypress.org

Manufactured in the United States of America

CONTENTS

Introduction: Freedom's Ring throughout the Post-WWII Decades 1

1 Talking First and Shooting Later in the Black Power Era 31

2 Nothing Left to Lose: Maximizing Liberties in the Late 1960s Free-for-All 65

3 Tools of the Trade: Working Women and Radical Women in the Liberation Era 109

Conclusion: Postscript from the Present Day 150

Acknowledgments 155

Notes 157

Works Cited 161

Index 175

FREEDOM'S RING

INTRODUCTION

FREEDOM'S RING THROUGHOUT THE POST-WWII DECADES

The advertisers sponsoring Fox News's daytime lineup are a niche cohort, to say the least. In spot after spot, products few outside the Fox-viewing context have ever heard of (e.g., silver and gold in solid weights, to best navigate the postapocalyptic economy) tempt the core Fox demographic—elderly white men with sufficient time postretirement to nurture their most exaggerated hostilities and hysterias. One ad from the recent past promoted the Freedom Male Catheter, whose cynically opportunist attachment to the original American value is distinguished from examples abounding in the post-9/11 cultural spectrum only by the bathos of its circumstances. No right-wing politician completes a speech today without a dozen genuflections at the altar of Freedom,[1] and audiences scream their assent as if ghosts of the last democratic administration were coming to take their guns. Though once a seeming eon ago, freedom was just another word for nothing left to lose, it has in recent decades become little more than a flag-draped excuse for selfishness and greed—freedom to make as much money as I want without caring whether you can put food on the table; freedom to shoot if I don't like your looks without spending a day in jail. So bombarded have we become with the infantile caviling of liberty-lovers in every echelon of politics, media, and the marketplace that I recently remarked to a colleague at lunch, "I hate freedom"—and I almost do.

In that long-ago era when Janis Joplin wailed her soulful anthem to "Me and Bobby McGee," freedom indeed lived another life in the American imagination and defended another agenda altogether. As frequently as *freedom* is applied to right-wing causes today, the term played a key role in the motivating mission of numerous progressive interests from the mid-1950s to the mid-1970s. Civil rights protesters began the tradition most honorably with their moving appeals for voter rights; access to education, housing, and public accommodations; and freedom of movement across the segregated South. Their cries of "Freedom now!" inspired countless protest marches and sit-ins during the early civil rights era, while in 1961, the Freedom Riders took a harrowing journey on integrated interstate buses through the South for the purpose of enforcing their constitutional right to do so.

The Mississippi Freedom Democratic Party (MFDP) was a delegation of black voters who arrived at the 1964 Democratic Convention with the aim of unseating the conservative whites officially sent. And on Berkeley campus the following fall, the arrest of Jack Weinberg for distributing civil rights literature led to a three-day showdown between the police car holding Weinberg and hundreds of surrounding demonstrators. One of these, Mario Savio, leapt on the hood of the vehicle and inaugurated the Free Speech Movement (FSM) with his inspiring words. A sit-in at Berkeley's Sproul Hall led to eight hundred arrests but eventually resulted in revised policy that created new space on that campus—and those nationwide—for political information-sharing, controversy, and debate.

Notably, MFDP's failure to win any more than two seats on the convention floor—a compromise they staunchly rejected at any rate—resulted in a bitter disappointment that turned many in this group, and their advisors in the Student Nonviolent Coordinating Committee (SNCC), toward increased militancy. The disappointments of Freedom Summer therefore led to the death of freedom as the universal desire of the civil rights movement; as SNCC leader Stokely Carmichael announced in the bitter aftermath, "We've been saying freedom for six years—and we ain't got nothing. What we gonna start saying now is Black Power!" (qtd. in Lytle 228). Mark Hamilton Lytle observes, "The difference between 'freedom now' and 'Black Power' was unmistakable. The one spoke of the trials and tribulations of long-suffering African Americans. The other was fraught with racial pride and self-assertion." From his diverging, nonviolent standpoint, Dr. Martin Luther King Jr. countered that "'Black Power' was inflammatory because it suggested 'black domination instead of black equality'" (qtd. in Lytle 228). Referring to the controlled, decorous, but perhaps ultimately limited approach that King trademarked in that era, Todd Gitlin remarked that upon his assassination, "nonviolence went to the grave with [King] and the movement was 'free at last' from restraint" (*Sixties* 305–306).

Freedom through Violence in the Civil Rights Context

In fact, freedom had freed itself from the constraints of passive resistance a decade before King's death in the remarkable but undercredited example of Robert F. Williams of Monroe, North Carolina. Williams, a working-class ex-Marine, was an NAACP chapter president committed to integration but also to armed self-defense. He thus clashed frequently with the nonviolent, middle-class demographic constituting NAACP national leadership at that time, facing a six-month suspension at one point and an utter lack of support during later travails: in 1961, Williams was subjected to a trumped-up charge of kidnapping, placed on the FBI's Most Wanted list, and forced to seek asylum in Cuba and then in China for most of the rest of the decade. As all understood, he was targeted by federal authorities, ironically, for his staunch adherence to the Second Amendment, specifically his ownership of numerous firearms and his training of other armed activists (who eventually formed their own NRA chapter) in Monroe, resulting in late 1957 in a shootout with the Klan. His story and his influential treatise *Negroes with Guns* (1962) are credited with inspiring militant groups such as the Deacons of Defense and Justice based in Jonesboro, Louisiana, in 1964 and the Black Panther Party of Self Defense of the late 1960s. To be sure, the Panthers burst onto the national scene in May 1967 when they entered the California State Capitol armed to the teeth as legislators debated the Mulford Bill, written to curtail arms-bearing in public places. As the ironies of history would have it, Governor Ronald Reagan was making a speech to a group of teenagers as the Panthers approached, and his frightened scamper into the recesses of the Capitol might have done more to establish their cultural cachet than their ultimately failed protest against the bill. In retrospect, Panther cofounder Bobby Seale regarded the apocalyptic spectacle of "niggers with guns" (153) as igniting both black revolutionary fervor and hysterical white backlash.

From Cuba, Robert Williams and his wife established "Radio Free Dixie," a weekly program exhorting its listeners to fight racist oppression at home and support the efforts of freedom-loving persons of African descent worldwide. As the Missile Crisis reactivated the U.S. military, including its African American members, Williams advised them over the airwaves, "While you are armed, this is your only chance to be free" (qtd. in Dobbs 182). In China, he congratulated his hosts on their acquisition of nuclear weaponry, referring to "a people's bomb, a freedom bomb of the oppressed" ("Speech: Delivered"), and as opposed to many others in the national black leadership in this period regarded the right to bear arms as essential to the attainment of other rights. Williams's call for persecuted African Americans to "defend themselves on the spot when they are attacked by whites" (qtd. in Tyson 557) thus promoted the avoidance or preemption of law enforcement and the courts; while the courts were the very arena in which civil rights leaders achieved landmark rulings throughout the period, Williams came to assume that waiting for justice to prevail was a fool's errand.

Though he at times professed great faith in the Constitution, he declared at a lower moment that "there is no Fourteenth or Fifteenth Amendment or protection of Negro rights in the court" (qtd. in Tyson 557). Later, "A Civil Rights Bill will have no more effect than the US Constitution" ("USA" 5). As he advocated the preemption of legal proceedings with forceful self-defense, so he advocated the preemption of the loftier, perhaps ultimately illusory Civil Rights Amendments from the Reconstruction era with the more immediate results guaranteed in the Second Amendment from the Bill of Rights.[2] Though Williams recognized a place for both "pacifists and nonpacifists" in the civil rights movement, his compliments to the former group were backhanded, to say the least, and fraught with the cynicism that frequently clouded his view of the U.S. justice system: "Self-defense is a reflex action to a Marine [like himself]. People like Rev. Martin Luther King have been trained for the pulpit. I think they would be as out of place in a [violent] conflict . . . as I would be in a pulpit praying for an indifferent God to come down from Heaven. . . . I believe if we are going to pray, we ought to pass the ammunition as we pray" ("Can Negroes" 73).

Ironically, Williams's faith in arms-bearing is thus readable as the ideal means by which to integrate into white society; anticipating a famous statement by the late-1960s SNCC leader H. Rap Brown that "violence is as american [*sic*] as cherry pie" (144), Williams's ready resort to shooting it out with his white adversary is in some contexts entirely preferable to King's nonviolent direct action, which King himself frequently acknowledged as a foreign import—that is, inspired by the examples of Jesus and Gandhi.[3] Since American society is practically built upon the bedrock—though more accurately, the ever-shifting tectonic plates—of gun-slinging self-assertion, Williams would have been correct in his assumption that the best way to communicate with its white majority was to speak a language it understands and to gain its respect by laying claim to the fundamental right to defend home and family. When Williams's widow Mabel remarked years later that Williams as a young man had "discovered the American tradition of freedom through guns," she both commented upon America's broader mythography of "regeneration through violence" (Slotkin 10) and solidified an assumption as fundamental to American identity as the lofty aspirations of the Declaration of Independence: that freedom does not simply grow on the trees of the American paradise but can only be claimed at the expense of the freedom of others—by violent force whenever necessary.

In 1964, Malcolm X traveled U.S. cities with his equally attention-getting statement regarding "The Ballot or the Bullet"—that is, his own take on violence as a means of shoring up the exercise of political rights. In that election year, when African American voters in the North and would-be voters in the South looked with dismay upon the choice between the overtly anti–civil rights agitator Barry Goldwater and the Dixiecrat Lyndon Johnson, whom many regarded as clearly aligned with archsegregationists in Congress, Malcolm in his speech equates "freedom" with the right to vote racists out of office and African American leaders into their places; in his modern, liberation-minded translation of Thomas Paine, "it'll be liberty or it will be death. The only difference about this kind of death—it will be reciprocal . . . [W]hen I go, you go" (32). Although this book will stress the ideal of equality with respect to equal *opportunity* and all that entails, Williams and Malcolm engage the long American tradition of reading guns themselves as "equalizers"; they envision if nothing else a state of final equality resulting from mutually assured destruction between the American races.

As Williams and Malcolm were early advocates for a militant stance on minority rights, so in other contexts freedom mutated into an equally militant quest for "liberation": women, gay men, Chicanos, and Native Americans each promoted their own liberation movements, while the Symbionese Liberation Army, the Black Liberation Army (BLA), and numerous other radical/anarchist groups from the late 1960s based their names (and goals) on North Vietnam's National Liberation Front and professed a doctrine of liberation to politicize (and thus justify) every criminal offense from looting to murder. If shoplifting a candy bar now became "liberating" goods from the clutches of capitalist pigs, we had entered the era when freedom itself became liberated from its attachment to respectable, legitimate efforts to attain constitutional rights, spinning out into the context of unfettered radical, cultural, and lifestyle liberalism that resulted in the conservative backlash (and the co-opting of freedom's rhetorical arsenal) of 1980 to the present day. Weinberg and Savio's Free Speech Movement, for instance, enjoyed support from student groups across the political spectrum; in the words of FSM alum Michael Rossman, "It was really a United Front, very strange bedfellows. Because after all, here was a Constitutional issue" (102). The relative ease with which the privileged, gifted, and largely unfettered Berkeley cohort achieved significant campus reform—no heads cracked nor bombs thrown and the goal reached in a single semester—indicates the shift from committed, embattled Left activism to a more diluted and amorphous antiestablishment mindset that undergirded every late-1960s phenomenon from navel-gazing hippiedom to any-means-necessary Black Nationalism. The women's liberation movement moved along a similar knife's edge, as its several legitimate bids for sexual freedom resulted in social changes that only fitfully increased women's own agency while enlarging the liberties taken by men in every instance.

Lifestyle Liberalisms in the Freedom Era

The liberal lifestyle manifested itself in numerous ways from the mid-1960s to the mid-1970s. After the deprivations of the 1930s, the sacrifices of the 1940s, and the conformity of the 1950s, little escaped the onslaught of freedom during the swinging '60s: music and dance styles, hair and hem lengths, bras and girdles, sexual mores, and access to all manner of drug technologies—from the prescriptions of the suburban medicine cabinet to the hallucinogens of the Haight. A large youth sector high on both LSD and the mesmerizing concert sets of the Grateful Dead likewise felt free not only to turn on and tune in but also to drop out; freedom from completing a college degree, entering the workforce (or especially the military), or joining political movements such as civil rights or Vietnam War protests characterized the hippie lifestyle. Though there may have been little difference to Establishment outsiders, in fact, the purposeful going limp enacted by nonviolent resisters in the civil rights, antinuclear, and anti-Vietnam contexts was to be sharply contrasted with the stupefied inertia instigated by the typical psychedelic trip. In the words of Martin A. Lee and Bruce Shlain in their exhaustive history of LSD in the postwar decades, "The radicals disagreed with the acid eaters who . . . rejected the possibility of revamping the social order through political activity, opting instead for a lifestyle that celebrated political disengagement" (164–165). Ken Kesey infamously told an antiwar rally attended by fifteen thousand to "look at the war, turn your backs and say . . . Fuck it" (qtd. in Wolfe 224), and as Lytle phrases a thesis moment, "Many people in the sixties passed off self-indulgence and arrogance as moral and political commitment" (xiii). Like the well-heeled Berkeley cohort of FSM, those seeking lifestyle freedoms were often those who had always enjoyed the most freedom in U.S. culture to start with—white middle-class, college-ready young people whose foray into the counterculture secured personal freedoms but left little that was constructive in its wake (see also Gitlin, *Sixties* 353). Of course, maximized personal (instead of collective) freedom is the point of today's conservative rallying cry, and in the book commencing here, the confluence and divergence between political and personal liberties, as well as the conceptual fight to death between (political) freedom and (economic) equality in U.S. culture, will be ongoing issues of concern.

Hippie high points (pun intended) like the Human Be-In in San Francisco's Golden Gate Park in January 1967; followed by be-ins, love-ins, and rock, folk, and jazz festivals around the country in ensuing months; and culminating in mass events like San Francisco's 1967 Summer of Love and Woodstock in August 1969 are recognizable as having been largely to entirely underwritten by the remarkably relaxing properties of hallucinogens. Thus one comes to question the legitimacy of the fellow feeling produced in these contexts, whether "peace and love" were anything other than chemically induced moods created by pot and LSD. Remarking upon the drug charge that landed him in Soledad Prison in 1954, Eldridge Cleaver averred that he had been caught with "a shopping bag full of marijuana, a shopping bag full of love" (*Soul* 4). Though hippie counterculture contrasted itself with the hypocritically militant and violent antiwar movement, was the love and pacifism exuded by tripping hippies any less cynical in origin or effect? And when historian Charles Perry reports that "the dealing economy . . . made the original [late-1960s Haight-Ashbury] community possible" (261), the many ways in which hippie-related progressive values depended upon drug culture comes into fuller view. The fatuous suggestion that turning on LBJ would be the quickest way to end the war (Lee and Shlain 162) pales in comparison to the most political use to which LSD was likely ever put, when Vietnam soldiers "were dropping acid and tripping out on the battlefield. . . . taking LSD voluntarily to incapacitate themselves" (235) during battle.

Giving Freeness and Taking Liberties

The Diggers of late-1960s San Francisco and later New York were a collective of advocates (including the San Francisco Mime Troupe and the Artists Liberation Front) for a "Free City," whose agenda straddled the divide between faux-radicalism and true countercultural effect; per Gitlin, they were "a quasi-ghettoful of the hip in search of their liberated space" (*Sixties* 315). Just as antiwar protesters, second-wave feminists, beleaguered Chicano crop-pickers, and all those seeking rights in this era copied the nonviolent-resistance and direct-action methods of the civil rights movement, so counterculture adherents from the white middle-class borrowed into the African American experiences of poverty, repression, and social marginality by purposely adopting behaviors anathema to public order. If African Americans were barred from gainful employment, hippies (the Diggers included) simply refused to work; if their racial difference stigmatized African Americans and caused fear from whites in daily interactions, hippies dressed in outlandish, sexually provocative, or otherwise uncouth ways to draw negative attention from the well-dressed establishment; if ghetto-dwelling African Americans turned too frequently to marijuana and street drugs to escape psychic pain and social discrimination, their white wannabe contemporaries indulged in paralyzing marathons with psilocybin, mescaline, and

LSD in search of personal enlightenment. Yet while pot and heroin could be very expensive, including costs involved with arrest, bail, and incarceration, the Diggers' LSD (especially before illegalization) was freely distributed by the ubiquitous and eccentric millionaire Owsley Stanley, whose homemade batches kept the party going at numerous Digger, Dead, and "acid test" events.

Abbie Hoffman, who regarded himself as a Digger before he was a Yippie, set up a free store on New York's Lower East Side. He repeatedly—with a "making free" of word choice universally off-limits in the more politically sensitive present day—insisted, "Spades and Diggers are one. Diggersareniggers. Both stand for the destruction of property— . . . [to] give it away. The free thing is the most revolutionary thing in America today" (*Revolution* 28; see also Cannato 221). Espousing the same philosophy for all hippiedom, before uniting with Hoffman in the Yippie cause, Jerry Rubin remarked, "Our long hair is our black skin" (94) and "For us, empty pockets means [*sic*] liberation—from draft cards, checkbooks, credit cards, registration papers" (232). Digger founder Emmett Grogan writes critically of Hoffman and the Yippies in his memoir, deriding Hoffman as a fake radical and "street theater director" (344) and calling out the broader white Left for slumming as "the 'new niggers'" (325; see also 438), having an "adventure of poverty" (316).

Grogan undercuts "the New York Diggers [as] . . . publicity-seeking cronies" (386). He critiqued Hoffman's hippie guide to free goods and services throughout New York, *Fuck the System* (which will be discussed later), as "outrageously selfish" (455) and as "snitching" (456), since it published the secrets poor people used to game various official systems, giving the system a chance to close vital loopholes. Yet Grogan is just as guilty of taking liberties that read now as racist insensitivity; at a conference where he and Stokely Carmichael share the stage, Grogan "simply refused to smile back and shake the hand of a man he disliked extremely" (429). When addressing the audience, Carmichael "yelled so goddamn loud that the tone finally became the point of his speech rather than his words" (430). At the Students for a Democratic Society (SDS) meeting that famously generated the Port Huron Statement, Grogan and fellow Diggers interrupt the proceedings by running onstage and abusing the audience. Grogan "throw[s] a black cat out the front door because he was the only black person there. You goddamn nigger, you shouldn't be *here*! Your people need you!" (402).

Grogan's fellow Digger Peter Berg, founding member of the San Francisco Mime Troupe, reached for the perceived cachet of danger surrounding civil rights protesters throughout the period: "[The Troupe] is a group of performers (actors, mimes, and dancers) dedicated to *actional* theater and confrontation. The troupe has . . . created *A Minstrel Show* to put-on Jim Crow and get beneath the skin of the civil rights issue," later shut down by officials at Olympia College in Washington. Though one could debate the merits of the Diggers' controversial performance on a college campus, their resurrection of blackface, no matter how politically left-leaning the intention, reiterates the appropriations committed by Hoffman's hip and "integrationist" terminology; by fellow Yippie Jerry Rubin, who declared hippies the "white niggers of Amerika" (80); and by numerous other writers of the counterculture (see chapter 2). Berg's telling phrase regarding his desire to "get under the skin" of the civil rights issue suggests the general trend of white radicals' attempt to adopt the posture, legitimacy, and national spotlight then accorded to African Americans pressing for the vote and other rights in this period. Responding to a memoir by a member of San Francisco's drag troupe The Cockettes, Malik Gaines notes this group's influence by the mime troupe and its own satiric use of blackface: "It was a black audience member who asserted his own agency by intimidating the white performer into giving up the practice" (154).

The San Francisco Mime Troupe's own manifesto, "The Post-competitive, Comparative Game of a Free City," lists the components of urban culture demanded for immediate liberation from city surplus, including free public spaces, housing, food, clothing, medical and legal assistance, car repair, tinkers and gunsmiths, radio and TV frequencies, and education—even money. They insist on top-quality goods and services; in the Free Stores, for instance, "important that these places are first class environments with no trace of salvation army/st. vinny de paul charity rot. Everything groovy. Everything with style . . . must be first class. *It's all free because it's yours!*" (16). Grogan echoes this sentiment in typically acid tones: "People who tried to deposit their refuse at the Free Frame of Reference were told to go and recycle their garbage someplace else" (249; see also Hoffman, *Revolution* 148–149). This rather naive insistence upon a boutique atmosphere in each outlet was ultimately belied by the disorganized, low-quality items offered in the few Free Stores established, on display in the photographic record ("Digger Free Store" and Perry). Early in Huey Newton's career as a community organizer, he visited a Free Store and remarked, "The store was incredibly disorganized. After fighting our way through the piles of garbage, we managed to have a discussion with some of the Diggers" (144).

Hoffman biographer Marty Jezer remarks that "unfortunately, the [Free Store] publicity also attracted other secondhand clothing dealers, who emptied the shelves to stock their own profit-oriented used-clothing emporiums" (88). Jezer adds, "In the deliberate structurlessness that was part of the hippie philosophy . . . there was no way for the organizers to insist that the store was properly run" (88). As a dismissive report from a 1967 *New Yorker* "Talk of the Town" column remarked, the staff "worry about relatively long-range problems as how to raise enough money to pay the rent . . . meet the gas, electric, and telephone bills," while Hoffman's partner in early organization efforts, Jim Fouratt, felt that one media event, an attempted clothing giveaway inside Macy's, "like the Free Store, was a lesson in how difficult it was for people to change their thinking" (Jezer 89–90). How many actually poor (instead of "actional" poor; see also Perry 96) the Diggers ever helped is difficult to determine; their own tendency to turn on and drop out created a self-fulfilling population of needy, hungry welfare recipients—including, most regrettably of all, their powerless underage children—in hippie enclaves such as the Haight-Ashbury and numerous rural communes in northern California in this period.

Despite the questionable effectiveness of the Diggers' cultural interventions, there is a revolutionary aspect to their deployment of the word *free*, the prospect of a society awash in "free stuff": freeness, if not freedom, is a blueprint for the social equality terrorizing to those (literally) invested in the privileges of class hierarchy since national inception. In some remarkable footage from the Digger film *Nowsreal* (1968), shot from the steps of San Francisco's city hall, Berg reads from a list of free goods and services demanded for immediate release (see also Grogan 464–465). As he speaks, the camera pans over the consternated faces of the conservatively dressed men and women in his audience; as if they were pellets from a BB gun, his every utterance of the word *free* causes another furrowed brow or pained grimace. Per Lee and Shlain, for the Diggers, "FREE was 'social acid' that blew apart conditioned responses and called into question prevalent cultural attitudes about class, status, morality, consumerism, etc." (174). Clearly their manifesto elicited this audience's worst trip imaginable; freely available goods would curtail the limiting, containing effects of income inequality, of money itself, and open the door to unprecedented social mobility. In the album *Dick Gregory's Frankenstein* (1970), the beloved stand-up performance artist Dick Gregory told a student group at Bronx Community College that the revolutionary act of "feeding poor, hungry black . . . and white folks" was the best way to "get your door kicked in and your brains blown out."

Grogan's critique to the side, most revolutionary of all Digger statements might have been Hoffman's widely circulated *Fuck the System* (1967), expanded into *Steal This Book* in 1971, which exploited capitalism's own tendency to overproduce and waste with abandon. Hoffman advised readers on where to be when butchers, bakers, and fishmongers got rid of their day-old wares; on diverse scams ("Free Bus Rides: get on with a large-denomination bill just as the bus is leaving" [9]); on goofy giveaways (free buffalo from the Department of the Interior); and once or twice on outright theft (e.g., syphoning gas). Most cleverly, he taught his unwashed readership to take advantage of the complimentary offerings unique to genteel retail and cultural settings, such as bars with heavily marked-up liquor but free buffets and museums with free days each week. Counting on polite society's disinclination to confront freeloaders or the otherwise outré, Hoffman locates undefended terrain in the class war with true economic value. He tells his reader that if he even paid for *Fuck the System*, he "got screwed" (back cover), while ironically, a rare original of this ephemeral work now sells online for $899.99. The value of Hoffman's advice aside, his own and the Diggers' insistence on free stuff should always have been questioned as a legitimate substitute for the *right to earn* attendant upon meaningful work for a living wage—an issue I will explore throughout this project. Work's radical prospects emerge in Frank Wilderson III's demoralizing summation regarding African American rights: "We were never meant to be workers; in other words, capitalism/white supremacy's dream did not envision us as being incorporated or incorporative. . . . We are meant to be warehoused and die" (238). After thirty years of bitter exile in Cuba, Assata Shakur echoed these sentiments in an essay for *Crisis*: "When it came to jobs, I was never 'most wanted'; when it came to economic opportunities I was never most wanted. . . . It seems like the only time that Black people are most wanted is when they want to put us in prison" ("Assata" 25). Much more valuable than free stuff is a decently paying job, which provides not only salary and purchase power but the intangible, invaluable benefits of personal dignity and national belonging.

Freedom's Highs and Lows

The Black Panther Party (BPP) emerged next door to the San Francisco Diggers in Oakland, California, but prior and inspiring to the Digger troupe as well as to other white Left groups in and around the Berkeley environs, including SDS and the Peace and Freedom Party (PFP). This latter group mounted a slate of national candidates in 1968, including many prominent Panthers. Like Robert Williams's gun-toting NAACP chapter in rural North Carolina a decade before, the Panthers appealed to a lower-class black population in northern California and nationwide; their militant stance and ready recourse to loaded weapons touched a nerve among the most politically beset and economically underresourced among all African American groups. Like the Diggers, they staged various theatrical demonstrations—though again, with guns overtly displayed and state penal codes at the ready—such as police patrols in black neighborhoods and their 1967 visit to the California State Capitol, referred to above and in detail in my next chapter. As the Diggers would, they ran a social support program for poor local families, most famously a children's breakfast program, and also as the Diggers would, they issued various position statements, most notably Executive Mandate #1, declared from the steps of the Capitol, in which they enjoined their black audience to join the revolution. Their famed Ten-Point Program demanded a series of freedoms (e.g., exemption from military service, release from prison, and freedom from police oppression); freely accessed jobs, education, and housing; and yet more free stuff (health care, financial reparations, land, and "bread"—the synecdoche for "food" since at least the Bolshevik era [e.g., D. Bell 283] and perhaps also slang for "cash" in 1960s-era lingo). Remarkably, the points conclude by quoting the first two paragraphs of the Declaration of Independence; while the Panthers thus present themselves as the vanguard of an emerging nation of the black oppressed, their ten points indicate the contradictions—legitimate demands for national separatism colliding with legitimate claims to full rights as U.S. citizens—that replicated tensions elsewhere within the BPP.

Notably, the Party found its motivating cause in a dramatically particularized quest for freedom—that of Party founder Huey Newton, who waited in a California jail for his trial in the 1967 shooting death of police officer John Frey. The "Free Huey!" campaign gave rise to a cottage industry of buttons, flags, photographs, and signage bearing Newton's image or the "Free Huey!" slogan and promised the incendiary event—either Newton's release or sentence to the gas chamber—that would ignite the fight to the death between "the people" and "the pigs." When Newton was sentenced to a limited term, then released on a technicality in 1970, the freedom so avidly sought—either total vindication or release from all restraint at the hour of his execution—was mired in conflicting details, meanings, and attitudes. As historian Hugh Pearson notes, it was impossible for Newton to live up to the messianic role he was vested with by his hopeful followers; soon after his release, he was addicted to powder and then crack cocaine, lived a life of violence and paranoia, and was gunned down by a contract hitman, as Ronald Reagan soared through the final phases of his first successful presidential campaign, in August 1980.

If the liberating, revolutionary effects of LSD on white middle-class youth from the late 1960s are open to question, the freedom sought after in the use of street drugs including the cocaine that enthralled Newton and especially heroin, mainly by impoverished residents of America's inner cities during the postwar decades, is all the more so. In various terms pertinent here, a remarkable fifteen-year-old writer, Gary Blue, declared in the November 1970 issue of *Essence* that he "refused to get drafted into the drug-polluted army." Blue argued that "all addicts are traitors" to the black nationalist cause and asked, "How can you rap about freedom and then imprison yourself with drugs? What kind of freedom is that? Freedom to become a drug capitalist. Freedom to destroy the minds of younger brothers and sisters. . . . [Y]our habit oppresses everyone." He regarded addicts as latter-day overseers who sold their unwitting young victims into a modern form of "slavery" (40).

As Blue concedes that many in his community view street drugs as, if nothing else, their most immediate avenue of escape from intractable poverty and oppression, he suggests the dilemma between freedom and enslavement that postwar drug technologies of all kinds posed: did the "dolls" so eagerly consumed by the heroines of Jacqueline Susann's best-selling novel from that period symbolize women's radical embrace of the personal and professional fulfillment enabled by modern drug technologies? Or did these pills simply provide a modern, chemically engineered palliative to the limitations women had always faced? Did the hippie's LSD and other hallucinogens constitute the revolutionary shot in the arm (or tab to the tongue) that usefully moved the entire country to the left? Or did it cynically substitute for the "beloved community" that the civil rights and antiwar movements attempted but ultimately failed to mobilize into real change? Did the heroin that truly enslaved a generation of inner-city residents find at least partial justification in the "street capitalism" that Blue decried as an alternate economy to beleaguered urban neighborhoods in the wake of massive deindustrialization? Like LSD, heroin had its own golden, somewhat innocent age in the immediate postwar period, when it enlarged the mystique of major jazz and bebop artists and was said to play a key role in their creative abilities. Of course, many of these major figures (Billie Holiday, Charlie Parker, Sonny Clark) wound up hopelessly addicted and meeting early death, and heroin quickly lost its allure within the African American community as anything other than the most desperate "fix" to numerous personal and collective crises. Heroin's only other finest moment, if the term can even apply in this context, was when it served (as did LSD) as a coping mechanism for beleaguered Vietnam soldiers, most of whom remarkably walked away from their habit—notably mainly smoked instead of injected—once released from their stressful combat roles (see Schneider 160–161, 181).

If LSD proponents favored the outlandish dress, paisley swirls, peace signs, and Day-Glo palette of the "psychedelic," this cheerful, even juvenile aesthetic contrasts meaningfully with the myriad indicators of recession-era urban decay that characterized heroin-afflicted neighborhoods in this same period: abandoned buildings (shielding drug deals and shooting galleries); graffiti-covered walls, bridges, and subways; and spiraling crime and corruption rates among citizens and police, respectively. As Eric C. Schneider in his history of heroin in New York observes, "Crime overwhelmed New Yorkers in the 1960s. Between 1960 and 1968, robbery increased over 825 percent and burglary 480 percent. . . . Homicide—generally the most reliably counted crime—doubled in this same eight-year period" (117). Schneider adds that "robbery played a particularly important role in New Yorkers' perception of safety" and was, notably, interracial in nature about half the time: "Robbery thus fueled racial and ethnic tensions with white New Yorkers blaming African Americans and Puerto Ricans for the increasing volume of street crime" (117). Schneider regards the 1962 Metcalf-Volker Bill, which allowed for hospitalization and aftercare for narcotic addicts in lieu of jail time, as "the high point of liberalism" but a moment that was soon undermined by the rampant crime rehearsed earlier and the basic breakdown between good intentions and hard realities: "Liberal activists forgot that addicts too had agency, and that the life of a street addict was . . . also a choice, for many a better choice than living under state supervision. . . . [F]ew completed [commitment's] terms and 80 percent were rearrested subsequent to their hospitalization" (132).

The argument presented here casts no favor on the recent-day Disneyfication of Times Square or any gentrification trend that prices low-income residents out of home neighborhoods. But it does read the gritty, all-but-unpoliced, 1960s-era expression of urban cultural liberalism as a "making free" (or as outlined earlier, taking liberties) with one's own rights against the rights and sometimes physical bodies of others: violent crime itself is a manifestation of maximized personal freedom; crime aimed specifically at a member of the white privileged class is an even more radical, effective, and economically expedient maximization of same. Describing his famed concept of "negative freedom" in 1958, the Oxford philosopher Isaiah Berlin remarked, "When I induce someone to make room for me in his carriage, or conquer a country which threatens the interests of my own," unjust, violent, even enslaving though these acts may be, "it can scarcely be denied that thereby the agent is able in the most literal sense to increase his own freedom" (140). Though surely many of the robberies and murders in late-1960s New York were heroin-related, they were also readable as the ultimate attempt to correct egregious economic imbalance at the expense of the oppressor class's sense of safety, security, and power.

The graffiti that covered late-1960s to early-1980s New York subways inside and out did nothing to support the vandal's heroin addiction, overdue rent, or underfed children, yet this trespass against city property was another manifestation of personal freedom—vandalism for its own sake and performed with the understanding that its commission in this liberal era would go entirely unchecked. Such graphic displays—of anger, frustration, or simply adolescent bravado—surely increased the fear and despair of nonvandalizing, nonaddicted, low-income New Yorkers, who had no choice but to ride vandalized buses and subways and walk through graffiti-covered underpasses on a daily basis. Such spectacles of liberty-taking in this period tell the story of an urban citizenry and an urban infrastructure that had been all but abandoned by those with the resources to improve things and chose not to, or to remove themselves to distant suburbs, which they did in droves. John Carpenter's campy, dystopian blockbuster *Escape from New York* (1981; see chapter 2) is a time capsule from the era of unbridled liberalism, which presents a scene in which America's middle and upper classes have fled the urban environment, locking the doors behind them as they go and leaving the beleaguered underclasses remaining there to fight it out to the death among themselves.

Inspired by the 1965 Watts uprising in his home state, Eldridge Cleaver considered the larger national environs from Folsom Prison and deplored the fact that "in America, everything is owned. Everything is held as private property. . . . There is nothing left over" (*Soul* 134), and urban blacks, surrounded everywhere by "branded" establishments and the security force (the police) that keeps these from their own possession, "feel alienated from the very sidewalks on which they walk" (136). Like the mugging incidents referred to earlier, Watts and successive urban uprisings in the period are thus meaningfully readable as an effort to "expropriate the land from the former owners" (135), including gutting showrooms and resorting to arson as a means by which to take blighted urban neighborhoods back to the unencumbered land itself. Cleaver adds, "The sanctity surrounding property is being called into question. The mystique of deed ownership is melting away" (135). He trenchantly defines freedom as a bid by American blacks to hold their own things and spaces, in the face of the fact that neither of these has ever been free for their owning before. Indeed, the only shift since national inception has regarded African Americans' own status as property: having once themselves been listed as "assets" on the inventories of white slave owners, "in this day of rage against the costs of welfare, blacks are listed amongst the nation's liabilities" (134). Finally, can massive black disaffection and disinvestment in the American enterprise be any kind of surprise, when "the only way they know of making withdrawals from the bank is at the point of a gun"? (136).

Freedoms Found, Equalities Essayed

Numerous histories of the civil rights movement have traced the meteoric rise of King's campaign across the Deep South in the 1950s as this crashed and burned when it moved to the urban North in the 1960s and shifted focus from political rights to economic equality. Exploring King's career-long commitment to shared national prosperity, Thomas F. Jackson observes that "few Americans recall the discordant notes with which King began his legendary speech at the March on Washington for Jobs and Freedom" (1); indeed, few even recall that the March on Washington had anything to do with *jobs*, so intent was the tendency, which I will question throughout this project, to prioritize the political over the economic (freedom over employment) in the liberation era. King's posthumously staged Poor People's Campaign, taken to the doorstep of power in Washington, DC, has been widely branded a failure for doing little if anything to improve the lot of America's lower classes or even distract the Johnson administration from its all-consuming focus on the war in Vietnam. Remarkably, the vote had been won, school integration was the federally enforced law of the land, and African Americans had made modest gains in the realm of accommodations throughout the cultural landscape. And yet none of these achievements on the balance sheet of *freedom*, some fought and died for throughout the South, had done much if anything to improve this oppressed minority's access to America's twin ideal of *equality*. Though patriots of a sufficiently enthusiastic stripe (and King himself in many-an-inspiring speech) hail these concepts in one breath, as if they were two inextricable sides to the same coin of democracy, in fact, freedom *opposes* equality: if you have as much money as I do, I can't have all that I want (nor can I free myself from the prospect of your buying a house in my neighborhood); if your rights are equal to mine, I may have to pay a debt to society if I exercise my Second Amendment impulse to shoot you in the head. In the trenchant summation of Nikhil Pal Singh, albeit arrived at via the opposite approach,[4] "the principles that apply to the market and those that apply to the nation-state . . . are in direct conflict much of the time" (25). In the civil rights and second-wave feminist contexts that are two focal points in this project, the relationship between the two ideals was less adversarial than fantastical: "Freedom now!" had nothing to do with access to employment tomorrow, and the women's movement was not societally transformative enough to effect the Equal Rights Amendment (ERA)—let alone equal pay for equal work—to this day. As Barbara Ehrenreich et al. observe, "Orgasms [courtesy of the sexual revolution] . . . were easier to achieve than equality" (72).

To be sure, the feminist movement divided (and perhaps conquered) itself over this very ideological split: "Radical women saw feminism as more about [political/sexual] liberation than equality" (Lytle 273), while liberal feminism was accused by radical spokespersons of "seeking for 'women to have the same opportunity to be oppressors, too'" (274). Per Lytle, Betty Friedan "missed few opportunities to denounce radicals as 'man haters' who waged 'sex warfare' . . . [and] diverted feminists from what was the essential battle for equality in the public sphere" (274). Gitlin is correct that "with the help of affirmative action, women broke into politics, law, pulpits, occupations, sports; to varying extents they changed the habits of speech, of the household, and of the bedroom" (*Sixties* 432; see also MacLean, chapter 4). Notably, however, "they won their greatest victories on the American path of least resistance: individual rights. Because men and institutions resisted radical [read: costly] challenges, [women] accomplished far less in the realm of economic equality" (*Sixties* 432). With respect to civil rights, "blacks became police chiefs and bankers, and could drive across Mississippi in the same cars as whites without risking death; but proportionately at least twice as many blacks were out of work as whites, and ghettos were training grounds in desperation" (435).

As Robert F. Williams phrased the situation in 1962, "The fundamental core of racism . . . can be measured in dollars and cents and unemployment percentages" (*Negroes with Guns* 38). Although Williams is most famous for statements and actions regarding armed self-defense, in August 1961, he somewhat quixotically approached the Monroe County Board of Alderman with his group's own ten-point petition, whose first three and last two specifics addressed economic issues. In addition to calling for the immediate desegregation of the town swimming pool and the removal of all signs designating "white" and "colored" areas in public spaces, Williams also pressed for nondiscriminatory hiring practices, equal treatment at local employment agencies and in welfare offices, and equal employment for skilled black workers in the municipal sector. In fact, "our demands for equal employment rights were the most important of the ten points" (39), especially given the demographic and industrial shift from the rust belt to the Sun belt taking place at this time: "We must consider that in Montgomery, where Negroes are riding in the front of the bus, there are also Negroes who are starving" (qtd. in Tyson 551). Two years later, the noted civil rights activist Tom Kahn observed that "the single-demand approach associated with lunch-counter sit-ins gave way to package demands." But "the closer the movement came to the real needs of the Negro community, the more it encountered obstacles that were not purely racial in character" (10).

Historian Nancy MacLean observes that in fact, Williams's Piedmont region, which housed the nation's textile manufacturers, made remarkable gains in industrial desegregation in this period, and one African American textile worker agreed with Williams that a good-paying job was essential to "full-fledged citizen[ship]." This worker added, "You can't even pretend to be free without money" (qtd. in MacLean 88), while movement leaders such as James Farmer and Martin Luther King Jr. questioned the newly gained freedom to spend money (e.g., at lunch counters) without winning the commensurate right to earn same (in MacLean 53 and 59; see also Kahn 10). The noted labor organizer A. Philip Randolph published his "Freedom Budget" in mid-1960s movement literature, a $100 billion proposal that included a nationwide jobs program involving valuable skills such as home- and road-building. Though it was never mirrored with any seriousness by budget-planners in Congress, Randolph's Freedom Budget had the backing of numerous movement luminaries (see MacLean 104) and like the other examples here recognized freedom traditionally construed as only fully realized in the context of total economic equality.

Though, as noted above, freedom in the civil rights period was an ideal seemingly so difficult to come by that many risked and lost their lives in its attainment, a federally guaranteed form thereof was eventually quite easily bestowed upon all those seeking it. Ultimately, this is because in almost all substantive circumstances, freedom is *free*, costing officialdom little if anything to implement and maintain, while equality shall forever be the much more expensive nut to crack: if the cost of printing additional ballots, for instance, to allow for an influx of African American voters to the polls, is ultimately negligible; if even the cost of opening one's lunch counter to a whole additional sector of the population is ultimately much more profitable than keeping these customers away; guaranteeing this same oppressed minority equal access to quality schools, jobs, salaries, and housing is a proposition that U.S. society has never deemed affordable enough to achieve. Defending "social" discrimination—in schools, jobs, and broader rights of association—Hannah Arendt in her now infamous "Reflections on Little Rock" defends with equal vigor the low-cost freedoms referenced here: voting rights, integrated public transport and hotel accommodation, even interracial marriage. As Anne Norton remarks, in Arendt's view, "African Americans are properly concerned with affairs of the body, whites are properly concerned with education" (257–258). Per Hanna Fenichel Pitkin, "Noting the derivation of the word 'economics' from the Greek term for household, [Arendt] holds that for the Greeks, economics was private" (54) and thus regrettably has been brought into the public, welfare sphere only in the modern day.

As King himself remarked around the time of his shift from South to North, "It didn't cost the nation anything to guarantee the right to vote. . . . but we are dealing with issues now that will cost the nation something" (qtd. in Lytle 251; see also Boggs 271). Thus while Singh, critiquing the "King-centric account of the civil rights era" and its attendant "mythology of racial progress" (5), writes in part to emphasize King's "complex, worldly, and radical politics" including "currents of democratic socialism and black nationalism into his thinking" (3), my own debt to King regards the radical nature *of* his liberal insistence on full access for African Americans to America's capitalist employment enterprise. Singh critiques overemphasis on the "short civil rights era" (8) replete with the political victories that I also put into perspective here, yet notably, this shorter era coincided with and may have been importantly enabled by an apogee in U.S. market prosperity: even the political freedoms at last recognized for African Americans in this period are readable as resulting from the postwar boom—the opening of new American frontiers (industrial, suburban, and otherwise) that relaxed tensions among groups in many regions of the United States and fomented even greater hopes, however illusory, for economic progress.

Describing Randolph's presentation of the Freedom Budget at the first of two White House conferences on civil rights early in LBJ's term as "the most controversial of the opening speeches," Kevin L. Yuill observes that "delegates were faced with the relatively new problem of massive funding being necessary to further civil rights progress—something that had not occurred when civil rights problems were restricted to the South" (266). Elsewhere in the realm of political breakthroughs, even historic black election victories such as by New York's Rep. Shirley Chisholm in 1969 and Newark's Mayor Kenneth A. Gibson in 1970 had little impact on the poverty, despair, and general lack of opportunity that shaped the majority of African American lives. The individual freedoms sought and gained by the civil rights movement could have been (and ultimately were) granted by the stroke of a presidential or judicial pen, while the equalities pressed for just as vigorously for almost as long remain a dream deferred.

Moynihan's Faulty Scissors

Back in June 1965, the Johnson administration had indeed grasped the vital difference between freedom and equality; still enjoying the afterglow of a landslide presidential victory, with both houses of Congress in political concert and a slate of progressive legislation already to his credit, Johnson in the final hours of the post-WWII economic boom delivered a commencement address to Howard University regarded as significant to this day. Therein, he uttered the oft-quoted proclamation that "freedom is not enough," then added, "We seek not just legal equality . . . but equality as a fact and equality as a result." He made a now famous analogy: "You do not take a person who, for years, has been hobbled by chains and liberate him, bring him to the starting line of a race and then say, 'you are now free to compete with all the others'. . . . [I]t is not enough to open the gates of opportunity. All our citizens must have the ability to walk through those gates." Giving the impression that "opportunity" itself was limitless—plenty of good-paying jobs and newly built housing to go around—Johnson spent much of the rest of the Howard speech piling up the grim statistics that left mid-century African Americans at a disadvantage. He argued that their poverty was of a special nature, based on the "antique [yet unrelenting] enmities" of white Americans that, without using Kennedy's term *affirmative action*, would therefore need a massive and well-focused effort to eliminate.

Although the speech was warmly received by its Howard audience and hailed by commentators the following day, its popularity waned sharply in the coming weeks as pundits studied its more controversial particulars. The lightning rod of debate was Johnson's focus on the family. Assuming the worst about even the middle-class members of the graduating class, Johnson described "an ability . . . stunted by the family you live with, and the neighborhood you live in, by the school you go to and the poverty . . . of your surroundings." He concluded, "The family is the cornerstone of society. . . . So unless we work to strengthen the family, to create conditions under which most parents will stay together—all the rest: schools, and playgrounds, and public assistance, and private concern will never be enough to cut completely the circle of despair and deprivation." Commentators soon took issue with the intrusive, finger-pointing, misdirected nature of the family theme and launched a campaign in defense against such cultural critiques that remains strong to this day.

The Howard speech's spotlight on family structure came directly from the eventually just-as-controversial "Moynihan Report," which started out as an internal memo to the secretary of labor and presidential advisors, gaining notoriety when its seventy-six pages were leaked to the press and later published in book form. Throughout the report, officially titled *The Negro Family: The Case for National*

Action, its author, Daniel Patrick Moynihan, at the time an assistant secretary of labor and from the mid-1970s to the mid-1990s a Democratic senator from New York, provided the full range of Census-Bureau charts, tables, and percentages forming the basis of Johnson's statistical run-through in the Howard speech. Per Daniel Geary, "The report's heavy use of statistics suggested a technocratic faith in the ability of elites to engineer solutions to social problems" (12). Most infamously, its thesis that the broken home was the key to the "tangle of pathology" troubling the African American community exploded in the public sector, creating the distraction that, in Moynihan's reassessment in *Commentary* in 1967, destroyed the prospects of the economic agenda Johnson had also pressed for in this speech. According to Moynihan, the upset likewise doomed the indeed acrimonious and ineffectual White House conference, "To Fulfill These Rights," on the race issue taking place in early 1966 and more or less permanently derailed the integrated drive for economic equality.

In Moynihan's view, "Negroes . . . now have enforced legal rights as never in their history, but they remain terribly weak in economic and social terms" ("The President" 33). Later, "just as almost everyone was free in 1863, almost everyone was able to vote a century later. On the other hand, no one had the 'right' to own a farm in 1865, and no one had the 'right' to hold a job in 1965" (33). In the report itself, Moynihan closes in on an idea central to my own project: "Liberty and Equality are two ideas in American democracy. But they are not the same thing. . . . nor are they always compatible" (*Negro Family* 2). In addition, "by and large, liberty has been the ideal with the higher social prestige in America. It has been the middle-class aspiration par excellence. . . . Equality on the other hand has enjoyed tolerance more than acceptance" (2). As on-target as these observations are, Moynihan soon shifts from these broader issues to the personalized pathologies surrounding the family per se. As Geary observes, "Moynihan felt his 'personal history' of being raised in a 'broken family' with economic hardship allowed him to understand African Americans who came from 'mostly the same world' as he did. His Catholicism . . . prompted his belief that 'family interests [especially the male breadwinner's family wage] were perhaps the central objective . . . of social policy'" (12; second ellipsis in original). Geary adds that Moynihan's coauthorship with Nathan Glazer of another sociological best seller from this period, *Beyond the Melting Pot* (1963), led both authors to hypothesize that "American ethnic groups' success owed to deeply rooted cultural institutions such as family structure" (Geary 13).

Moynihan later remarked that his breakthrough came when he observed crisscrossing lines on a graph, later famously defined as "Moynihan's scissors": "In the '60s employment began to improve, but family conditions did not. *The possibility was real that the situation had begun to feed on itself*" ("The President" 36). Though it is hard to imagine that Moynihan, an advanced degree-holder with expertise in sociology, would so impatiently assume problems installing themselves over generations would reverse themselves in half a decade, this in fact was his assumption, and he spends the remainder of *The Negro Family* inverting chicken and egg to deleterious effect: following the long discourse on the perceived pathology of

African American family structure, "unemployment" shades imperceptibly but incontrovertibly into unemployability. Later, a statistic regarding "nonwhite family income slip[ping] from 55 to 53 percent of white income" between 1960 and 1963 (*Negro Family* 24) comes to be explained not by entrenched institutional racism but by the absence of Father from the home (see also Geary 43). By the time we approach the report's discussion of "The Failure of Youth" (34–37), the report's moralizing effects are unmistakable. Its summation makes no return to the equality trumpeted in the opening pages; instead, like a peeping Tom in striped pants and top hat at the tenement window, "national effort towards the problems of Negro Americans must be directed towards the question of family structure" (*Negro Family* 47). And with a final libertarian flourish anticipatory of Moynihan's later role as advisor to Richard Nixon, "after that, how this group of Americans chooses to run its affairs, take advantage of its opportunities, or fail to do so, is none of the nation's business" (*Negro Family* 47–48).

In his survey of the Moynihan Report's scholarly context, James T. Patterson cites numerous thinkers (including Gunnar Myrdal, E. Franklin Frazier, Stanley Elkins, Kenneth Clark, Nathan Glazer, and Charles Silberman) who had already analyzed in-depth the damage to African American culture and family due to long-standing economic exclusion and diversely manifested attacks on political freedom (see Patterson, chapter 2). What was likely so explosive about Moynihan's report—his own boss, Labor Secretary Willard Wirtz, called a summary of its findings "nine pages of dynamite" (qtd. in Patterson 43)—was the national platform, that is, LBJ's commencement address to Howard graduates, these ideas had at last achieved. No longer the theories of pointy-headed (however best-selling) intellectuals but the talking points of national leadership in a high-profile media context, these decades-old demoralizing views intersected with a rising tide of black militancy to create their own crisis-inducing scissor effect. In Patterson's phrasing, the report "suffered from three especially large liabilities: its messenger was white, the report focused on sex and family life, and the timing could hardly have been worse" (77). With the hindsight of a couple of literally riotous years, Moynihan relocates his focus on the economics of the issue: the tab for the programs that never got sponsored, due to controversy over the "family" issue, would have been "$5 to 10 billion per year. . . . *But we had the money*" ("The President" 36), and Moynihan in these remarks—and often over the next several years—blames misguided naysayers for snatching defeat from the jaws of victory. In Geary's assessment, Moynihan's 1967 *Commentary* essay "established the neoconservative narrative of the controversy" (173), and Moynihan himself, Geary posits, was a key figure in the shift from late-1960s white liberalism to the neoconservatism of the 1970s and 1980s.

Indeed, critics understandably challenged the paternalist blame-the-victimism of both the Moynihan Report and Johnson's speech at Howard University, which pinned the problem of entrenched urban poverty on not only the absent breadwinner but also the resulting "matriarchy," "illegitimacy," and "delinquency" among youth. Although Moynihan blames the reaction to his report and Johnson's speech for stealing essential thunder from the equalizations that might have otherwise taken place, one is equally justified in blaming Moynihan's/Johnson's own misguided focus on family problems and their wishfully naive assumption that massively expensive U.S. inequalities (once more, regarding jobs, education, health, and housing) would take care of themselves once black couples renewed their vows. In the estimation of Patterson, "Neither then nor in later years . . . did the United States come close to securing the egalitarian racial goals Johnson called for in his speech at Howard" (xii) due to the Moynihan controversy. But in the earlier and notably divergent assessment of Lee Rainwater and William L. Yancey, two on-the-scene sociologists who covered the Moynihan Report and reaction in exhaustive detail, "The controversy, then, was a kind of lucky break for the Administration, since it served to distract from and conceal the fact that the Administration was not really ready to assume the independent role it had reached for at Howard University" (294).

Though in the Howard speech the president complimented the civil rights movement upon the "impressive restraint" displayed in all confrontations with white intransigence thus far, the rioters in Watts, California, in August 1965 (as abysmal historical irony would have it, mere days after Johnson had signed the Voting Rights Act of 1965, regarded by all as his crowning legislative achievement) hardly showed this same restraint. The later, largely exonerating Kerner Report aside, the 1965 uprising was regarded by Johnson and much of liberal America with profound hurt and stunned disbelief, and white backlash followed swiftly, with strong Republican gains in both houses and many new Republican governors in the midterm election of 1966. But the long view clearly indicates that the Watts riot—or more correctly, the altercation between a white LA police officer and a black motorist that sparked it—was just the next explosive incident of summer 1965 to follow the Moynihan controversy: like the preceding Harlem riot of 1964 and other uprisings nationwide in its wake, Newark and Detroit in 1967, the MLK assassination and tumultuous national reaction in its aftermath, and the entirety of the war in Vietnam, Watts was one of many agonizing 1960s-era political derailments from the complex and expensive project of true economic equality. White America (liberal and conservative), and a president just turning his attention to a soon-to-be astronomically costly war, was never entirely inclined to undertake such a project in the first place, and to this day, every time a white police officer shoots a black citizen, the nation is plunged once more into political upheaval, and the impossibly difficult task of redressing widespread, deeply slanted economic disparity is once again necessarily but conveniently deferred. Per Robin D. G. Kelley, "We are constantly putting out fires, responding to emergencies, finding temporary refuge, all of which make it difficult to see anything other than the present" (11).

Our Rightward Listing Constitution

In his important mid-1960s treatise on the nature of ethnic group life in the United States, sociologist Milton Gordon noted a constitutional conundrum of significance here: "The American political and legal system recognizes no distinction among its citizens on the grounds of race, religion, or national origin. From the legal point of view, there are simply 190 million discrete American individuals" whose "communal life as Negroes, Jews, Catholics, or Protestants . . . is not recognized or delineated by law" (4–5). As Gordon goes on to prove, however, ethnic belonging is momentously important to Americans of all kinds, all of whom tend overwhelmingly to flock together in the management of any scarcity, real or imagined. Even though, as Arendt, Singh, and many others observe, all Americans ostensibly enjoy equality before the law, in the social and economic registers, in Arendt's arrestingly simple formulation, "people group together, and therefore discriminate against each other" (51). Gordon trenchantly adds that while all groups—Jews, Catholics, African Americans, and so on—may model a certain clannishness in their political, professional, and personal activities, Protestant clannishness stands apart for its unique invisibility in U.S. society. As the dominant culture, WASP ways are frequently misrecognized as "the American way" or "general American society" (Gordon 221), and white Protestants "can afford to be relaxed about their own communalism, indeed, as seems frequently to be the case, can even afford to be unaware of it" (Gordon 222; see also Singh 19–20). Engaging Gordon in his own landmark work from a few years later, Harold Cruse remarks that "political institutions recognize the reality of ethnic groups only during election contests," when the "hyphenated-American vote" (6) becomes highly sought after.

In accord with Gordon, "the individual in America has few rights that are not backed up by the political, economic, and social power of one group or another" (Cruse 7–8). Cruse's point is that only within a culturally homogeneous society can rights as individuals be truly enjoyed, and America has only experienced such homogeneity in its earliest decades—when it hypocritically restricted citizenship to white males of a certain age and social class. Philosopher Horace Kallen's defense of the framers' pluralist outlook—that as they wrote, they took into consideration the presence of Scottish, Irish, French, German, and Dutch immigrants in their midst (in Gordon 146)—hardly speaks to the actual diversity constituting the American populace then or now nor to the rights persistently denied to various American outgroups (see also Singh 21). Thus, despite the Enlightenment-era, thoroughly modern Western democracy the U.S. Constitution was designed to realize, in fact, its framers were (and its framers' descendants remain) as tribe-minded as the primitive societies they proudly believed themselves to have superseded; their founding document is thus less a description of law as practiced than a blueprint for a Utopia yet to be located (see also Gordon 25). In the optimistic terms of King, who half a century ago saw much of what this book presents today, "America is essentially a dream . . . a dream of a land where men of all races, of all nationalities, and of all creeds can live together as brothers" (qtd. in Zepp 221).

In the main, the Constitution is a long list of guaranteed individual rights, privileges, and freedoms, more or less offset by the Reconstruction Amendments, which introduce eighty years after the document's inception the divergent, often competing if not cross-canceling concept of equality. As Donald Grier Stephenson Jr. observes, the Fourteenth Amendment's insistence on equal protection under the law was "new to the Constitution" (91). That is, in the 110 years since the Declaration of Independence had stated (with no legally binding authority) that all men were created equal, the principle of equality made its first appearance in a national document in 1866 and has been more or less anchoring that side of the balance sheet on its own ever since. It is especially the Fourteenth Amendment's equal protection clause that is regarded by many an originalist as the wrench in the works of the Constitution's freedom machinery. Notably, this amendment was so radical a prospect in 1866 that it was only enacted by an all-Union Congress, who had ejected the Rebel cohort a year earlier for having gone to war against the United States; ratification, completed in 1868, was the condition upon which former Confederate states gained reentry into the Union (see Foner 276 et passim). Stephenson notes the equally strong arm it took to impose the Fifteenth Amendment onto the national statute: "Ratification . . . came about more as a result of Reconstruction and partisan politics than because of any large-scale change of mind in the general white population about the desirability of political equality for blacks. This revolution . . . originat[ing] not at the grassroots [as had the campaign for female suffrage], but at the highest levels of government . . . would succeed only if the national government were prepared to commit sufficient resources" (Stephenson 186).

Also notably, the equal protection clause was included for the express purpose of making constitutional the Civil Rights Act of 1866, which was reissued following ratification of the Fourteenth Amendment as the Civil Rights Act of 1870. This act, which guaranteed African Americans free access to the polls and federal protection in the event of any challenge to this access, was one of three "Enforcement Acts" passed by Congress between 1870 and 1871, the third of which sharply curtailed the activities of the KKK and seems the specific target of D. W. Griffith's *Birth of a Nation* forty-five contentious years later. The last Reconstruction law of this nature was the Civil Rights Act of 1875, which guaranteed African Americans unrestricted access to public accommodations, public transportation, and jury service. It was the Fourteenth's equal protection clause that was infamously misinterpreted in the Supreme Court's *Plessy* decision of 1896 and this clause that was restored to its original dignity when it enabled the 1954 finding in *Brown v. Board*. Thus we may observe the repeated necessity of congressional law to help realize the ideals described but rarely sufficiently enforced in constitutional amendments, and we may be astonished at the evident need for the several Civil and Voting Rights Acts of the 1960s, as if these Reconstruction-era acts had never been placed on the books. Floyd McKissick deeply doubted the Johnson-era bills, declaring them "all unnecessary. . . . These civil rights bills did more for Congressional public relations than for Blacks" (*3/5* 80).

As William F. Buckley framed the issue in 1957 in the *National Review*, "The Fourteenth and Fifteenth Amendments to the Constitution are regarded by much of the South as inorganic accretions to the rest of the document," and his like-minded colleague Willmoore Kendall described "the post-Civil War 'equality' amendments" as the opening salvo in the "war of aggression launched . . . by the

Liberals" (qtd. in MacLean 48). In conservative publications such as *Modern Age* and *National Review*, writers forged a sharp distinction between the Constitution "originally conceived" (qtd. in MacLean 47) and the "pro-black Amendments" (MacLean 47) of the Reconstruction era. Reflecting on Little Rock, Arendt felt that school desegregation had nothing to do with constitutional freedoms and therefore never should have been forced into the social spheres of racist whites. Per Arendt, African Americans "had never [even] been included in the original *consensus universalis* of the American republic" (qtd. in Norton 254) and thus "only an 'explicit constitutional amendment, addressed specifically to the Negro people of America' might (but only might) have served to invite them into the nation" (Norton 254–255). As with Moynihan, Arendt is so certain that "social, economic, and educational equality for the Negro . . . shall [be reached] in the foreseeable future" (48) that she now regards it as part of the problem: "The more equal people have become in every respect, . . . the more will differences be resented, the more conspicuous will those become who are visibly and by nature unlike the others" (48).

Even liberal Arthur Schlesinger, reacting along with Arendt and many other thinkers of the immediate postwar period to the totalitarian threat per se, agreed that, ultra-Right Nazism now being vanquished, the main enemy was ultra-Left Communism. Schlesinger's liberal heroes are accountable aristocrats like Winston Churchill and "responsible conservatives" (42) like Teddy Roosevelt; his seven "tests of freedom" boil down those rights (e.g., "free expression of opinion, courts free of violence") guaranteed by the Constitution, and as in the Constitution, Schlesinger's one question regarding equality—"Will there be fair play for the poor as well as for rich, for private persons as well as Government officials?" (8)—must be answered equivocally at best. Schlesinger discerned a crisis of freedom in the immediate postwar period, as (quoting Kierkegaard), the "dizziness of freedom" (52) drove modern, industrialized, anxiety-ridden men into the arms of totalitarian dictators like Stalin. Schlesinger's firm opposition between freedom and totalitarianism made the former little else than a synonym for America—and thus a natural originating byword for the civil rights movement, which was making its first gains (including the desegregating of the Armed Forces and interstate train travel) just as Schlesinger published *The Vital Center* in 1949. But as unassailable as was this distinction between the free world and the totalitarian bloc, just as ambivalent (verging on schizophrenic) was Schlesinger's ultimate prescription: "Big government, for all its dangers, remains democracy's only effective response to big business" (182), and yet "the state must *not* . . . put much stock in the interminable enterprise of government regulation" (185). Elsewhere, "no one should be allowed to starve for lack of food, or die for lack of doctors . . . but the state must *not* place its main reliance on a static program of welfare subsidies" (185). Schlesinger both decries (194) and defends (201) anticommunist witch hunts and lambasts Franklin Delano Roosevelt's one-time vice-president Henry Wallace (209), whom he evidently loathed as much as he adored FDR. Comparing "civil rights and civil liberties" (189), Schlesinger indicates where his main interests lie by treating the former in two paragraphs (190–191), then moving on to broader questions regarding "our libertarian faith" (191). Even the "equality amendments" to the Constitution Schlesinger reads as a corrective to our "crimes against freedom" (192).

Title VII of the Civil Rights Act of 1964, like the Reconstruction Amendments, sought to bestow equal opportunity and was thus likewise a lightning rod for conservative backlash in the civil rights era. Cruse trenchantly observes that "most vocal opponents of the Civil Rights Act of 1964 *cite* the American Constitution," which also guarantees "rights of individual and private property" (7). The presidential run of ultra-Right Arizona senator Barry Goldwater, which inaugurated the modern conservative movement, stemmed directly from Goldwater's pronounced opposition to the Civil Rights Act, and the noted conservative James Kilpatrick declared Title VII "the antithesis of freedom" (qtd. in MacLean 67). His laying claim to "freedom" here marks the intersection where the term began its move to the Right and where progressive African American, women's, and social protest groups adopted the more militant language of "power" and "liberation" instead. Per the contentions of Buckley, Kilpatrick, and others, the long view reveals that equality guarantees are rare exceptions in the centuries-old procession of U.S. laws passed in the name freedom diversely defined and that each such equality gesture exhibits its own history of local resistance, questionably effective court battles, and egregious underregulation and underfunding by governing bodies. Finally, the maximizing of political rights during this era may have only intensified the necessity, controversy, and final bitter disappointments involved in the concomitant bid for equal economic opportunity. Separatist-era writers focused on this dilemma came to critique the hollow ring of the movement's earlier calls for freedom—and the hypocrisy, myopia, classism, "benign neglect,"[5] and malignant individualism that echoed throughout the 1960s to the present day.

Terminology: An Apology

The concept of liberalism is complex, even contradictory, and has both an economic and a political guise. From its roots in the Enlightenment period, Revolutionary-era America adopted liberalism's (political) credos of rule of law and individual rights and both personal and (economic) market freedoms; ideas regarding liberalism are thus heavily entwined with the birth of modernity (especially modern democracy) itself, and yet the ever-shifting political contexts to which it may be compared bespeak the conceptual shifts unavoidable in the project commencing here: compared to the monarchies and tyrannies that inspired the French and American Revolutions, liberalism's left-leaning qualities shine forth, while liberalism's emphasis on private, individual rights and freedoms even more easily gives way to the self-interest and violence of late-stage capitalism/neoliberalism, critiqued in my opening paragraph and distrusted by radical activists throughout the liberation era. In the immediate post-WWII period, Arthur Schlesinger decreed liberalism "the vital center"—simply and starkly opposed to the totalitarian threat, but a threat that emanated from both Far-Right Fascism and Far-Left Communism. Further into the freedom era, liberalism displayed more Janus-faced relativity, which needed pinning down in each cultural context: relative to the conservative (often virulently racist and sexist) mentalities on display in the period, liberalism took up its still most-often recognized position on the political left; relative, however, to the even further-left intentions of postwar radicals, liberalism looked like conservatism in sheep's clothing. In the liberation era, liberalism was leftism for the establishment, while radicalism was leftism for the counterculture, and radicals frowned—vociferously—upon the hypocrisies and contradictions perceived to constitute the liberal position. Recalling girlhood days on New York's Upper West Side, then as now a bastion of the left-leaning white middle-class, Assata Shakur remarked that "'liberals' express every conceivable opinion on every conceivable subject. . . . As far as I'm concerned, 'liberal' is the most meaningless word in the dictionary" (*Assata* 132; see also Boggs 277).

Meanwhile, a crystalizing example of *liberal* feminism, to be referenced again in chapter 3, regards Betty Friedan's "integration" of the Oak Room of the Plaza Hotel on 12 February 1969. By official policy, the Oak Room was a men's-only midday meeting place where great wealth and power were brokered over three-martini lunches; Friedan and other members of the National Organization for Women (NOW) stormed the barricades for access to those economic opportunities. *Radical* feminists, notably Germaine Greer, also discussed in chapter 3, eschewed such buying in / selling out to the system and embraced principled, however impoverished, gender separatism instead. In the civil rights / Black Power context, the "blue-eyed liberal" (Malcolm X's epithet; see chapter 1) also prioritized integration into the nation's economic structure, seeking educational and professional opportunity even if only for the educated elite best suited for success in the middle class. Malcolm and other radical race separatists preached a gospel of economic self-sufficiency and divorce from white institutions. The Black Panthers' last chairman, Elaine Brown, has advocated in both modes in the recent past; in a 2005 run for mayor of a majority-black town in Georgia, she campaigned for "full employment for the 16,000 residents" (Watson 1; see chapter 1), while as recently as 2017 she challenged, indeed mocked, an audience of prison-reform activists—"go and get yourself a job and be happy in massa's house" (qtd. in Harrison 1B)—in operative terms: "There's only one way for us to be free and that's revolution in the United States" (qtd. in Harrison 2B).

Surveying the state of feminism from the early 1990s, Zillah R. Eisenstein sees "the neoconservative attack" against "liberalism itself [to stem from] the presumed demand during the 1960s and 1970s for too much racial and sexual equality" (xv) and associates liberal feminism with the bid for equality throughout her project (e.g., 180, 193). Concurrently, in *Freedom Dreams*, Kelley makes the equation between visions of "freedom" and "the black radical imagination" explicit: as I have begun my project, so Kelley begins his by observing that "freedom today is practically synonymous with the free market" (xi) and thus casts back into civil rights history to consider various African American liberation movements that construed their freedom goals in terms of "pure poverty" (32), "revolution, socialism, and self-determination" (62), and the "advocating [of] strident acts of violence" (79), among others. Kelley contrasts co-optation "by the marketplace" and "getting paid" as the goal of the mainstream civil rights movement (7) with the counternarrative of black radicalism in the postwar period; although my own study focuses on the revolutionary aspects of "getting paid" in its own right, Kelley's dichotomy illuminates the liberal/radical divide in the late civil rights era. Thus the race liberals and the liberal feminists of period, in their staunch insistence on *equal* access to economic and professional opportunity, defied traditional definitions of liberalism as imbricated with personal and market-based *freedom*. The race and gender radicals of the era, in their pronounced antipathy to capitalism in every form, sought both personal and economic *freedom* from such entanglements and thus ultimately challenged the status quo much less forcefully. The conceptual framework based on this vital liberation-era dichotomy—liberal/economics/equality versus radical/politics/freedom—is key to my discussion in chapters 1 and 3.

Meanwhile, in chapter 2, and in keeping with the shifting liberation-era use of this term, I will refer to liberalism more broadly defined as the ideological opposite to conservatism: if liberals in the civil rights and feminist contexts struck radicals as overly disciplined, capitalist-oriented, and simply too conservative to countenance, to the garden-variety right-winger of the period, the liberal was everything and everyone to the left of Barry Goldwater: Betty Friedan *and* Germaine Greer, Martin Luther King *and* Malcolm X, hippies *and* antiwar protesters, never mind the sharp ideological differences that divided these pairs. In chapter 2, I will read liberalism in gestures of personal liberty-taking as an ultimate maximizing of the political freedoms gained by civil rights and feminist movements that now ring hollow to the degree that they have reconfigured the inequalities of American life not at all. While race liberals and liberal feminists reliably pressed for economic equality, "liberals" broadly defined (with Yippie Abbie Hoffman as a useful crystalizing example) were often essentially motivated by economic redress but "made free" to correct such imbalance via looting, theft, or extortion instead of the legitimate channels advocated by King or Friedan. In chapter 2, I will read *making free* as so suffusing of political and popular culture in the liberation era that rioting prison guards, corrupt cops, and striking garbage workers will themselves figure as right-wing "liberals," clearly anticipating the modern-day freedom-lovers critiqued in the opening of this introduction. "Full circle" in this project is in fact a Möbius strip that reflects the complicated path traveled by freedom and liberalism since national inception.

Chapter Outline

Freedom's Ring is divided into three sections, each focused on a major rights movement from the liberation era: Black Power and related African American separatist movements; antiwar protest, urban uprising, and lifestyle liberalisms from the mid-1950s to the mid-1970s; and women's liberation concurring with the sexual revolution. In each, I will trace the career of freedom, liberation, power, and related political themes in major texts pertinent to each context as well as consider the ways these themes vied with or substituted for the expensive economic propositions related to providing equality—that is, equal access to education, housing, jobs, and wealth; equal pay for equal work—for all Americans. My introduction has emphasized the freedom calls of the civil rights era, since these inspired and instructed freedom-seekers from many groups throughout the period. Chapter 1 continues this narrative by tracing the transition from "freedom" to "power" insisted upon by charismatic leaders such as Malcolm X, radical SNCC leadership from the mid-1960s, and the founders of the BPP—all of whom drew large audiences and fomented great social energy through spellbinding occasions of public address. This chapter thus explores the divergence of "talking" (electrifying speechmaking with its vital political outcome) from "walking" (old-style actions such as marching, picketing, and boycotting; confronting police or other figures of security/authority; or community organizing such as breakfast programs, health clinics, etc.). Criticized by many in the outgoing SNCC leadership for lacking specific programs, young African American spokesmen for radical separatism exploited the political payoff of a galvanizing rally: the campaign to "Free Huey!" Newton, for instance, was fundamental to the visibility and viability of the BPP throughout the late 1960s. Other famed leaders from the Black Power era were celebrated for their rhetorical gifts but also hounded into silence when their free speech was deemed too incendiary to tolerate—the constitutional equivalent of yelling "Fire!" in a crowded movie theater. As indicated in this introduction, the tensions between politics and economics manifest in the black separatist context as well: the rights demanded by talented leaders through both inspired speechmaking and various direct actions (e.g., the Black Panthers challenging police or bearing arms in public) succeeded to an admirable extent, while the economic equalities sought after—even attempts so well-meant as the Panthers' Breakfast for Children program extending beyond sporadic donations by local businesses—met with resistance and ultimately failed.

Chapter 2 regards instances of liberty-taking and lifestyle liberalisms broadly defined, departing from the modern-day tendency to define *liberal* as left orientation or membership in the Democratic Party: in the 1960s and 1970s, freedoms maximized took so many forms that narrow political definitions must be temporarily set aside. Certainly, progressive voters (or dissenters) protesting the crisis in urban America, the Vietnam War, or the moral failings of U.S. presidents undertook varying measures of left-wing politicking recognizable in the present day. But chapter 2 considers the lives and writings of not only urban rioters and antiwar protesters but also those leaders of the counterculture (e.g., Abbie Hoffman and Jerry Rubin) roundly dismissed by outspoken "politicos" of the era, even as Hoffman and Rubin regarded themselves as both committed, political, standard-bearers *and* as fun-loving street theater–makers whose stunts and "put-ons" had their own revolutionary import. Theatricality is in fact an important subtheme in chapter 2: it opens with readings of some brief but trenchant "street" pieces by the Black Arts dramatist Ben Caldwell, discusses urban-themed plays from several of his fellow Black Arts practitioners, and considers the diverse examples of maximized freedoms that made up city life in the period: rioting, looting, vandalism, graffiti, and littering, all of which, according to some, were meaningful strikes against an oppressive system; drug-taking (both acid-dropping and opium-shooting) with its many uncanny and tragic theatrical qualities; and varieties of white working-class running-amok. These include violent police "rioters" at scenes of urban and prison rebellion throughout the period; corrupt police shaking down rich, poor, black, white, guilty, and innocent with such abandon that the context can only be theater of the absurd; and belligerent strikers (from garbage collectors to teachers) who greatly impacted city life in Lindsay-era New York. This chapter closes with a reading of John Carpenter's *Escape from New York* (1981), a slice of dystopic futurism that yet comments directly on 1970s-era urban decay, interracial conflict, and spiraling crime rates for New York and all U.S. cities.

Chapter 3 examines the second-wave women's movement, built upon the writings of movement leaders (and once again the speeches, stunts, and theatricality of its street-level practitioners) and mainly affecting the lives of women from the white middle class. Although Betty Friedan's *Feminine Mystique* (1963) is credited broadly (and here) as a founding document, in fact, the liberal feminism espoused by Friedan—job opportunities and equal compensation in all professional spheres—was a minority view in a radical/separatist environment calling for disavowal of the capitalist workplace and even of children, marriage, and men, depending on the stripe of radicalism in question. Throughout chapter 3, the conflicts between political radicalism and sexual freedom complicate many early feminist writings and actions; for some, these two go hand-in-glove, while many suspected the sexual revolution (and the birth control pill or other pharmaceutical technologies) to be weak substitutes for authentic rights or, worse, cynical ploys to create an atmosphere of liberation in which men wound up on top yet again. This chapter discusses the intellectual context of radical feminist thinking, then explores popular novels, films, and memoirs that claimed for themselves standard-issue feminist credentials or, belonging not at all to the feminist canon, commented meaningfully nevertheless on the plight of the liberation-era sexual or professional woman, whose dilemmas were uniquely embodied in the figure of "the working girl."

One way to gauge the transition from 1950s to 1960s U.S. culture is to consider the national move from indoors to out: privatized, domesticated "togetherness" (including a frantic search for single-family housing after the war and a boom in consumer goods-purchasing to feather the suburban nests of the white middle class) gave way to vital public displays of solidarity, protest, and indeed new freedoms. If the homebound 1950s bespeak both the atomic fears and the zeal for baby-making that preoccupied millions, the rush to the streets of the 1960s bespeaks the boredom and alienation of that 1950s-era isolation as well as the pent-up energies and desires (sexual, professional, and political) of various contained national groups: African Americans of the rural South and the urban North; white middle-class adolescents; and their repressed mothers. Although Martin Luther King Jr. deserves credit for taking it to the streets (in theater parlance, for taking his act on the road) as early as the Montgomery Bus Boycott in 1955/1956, in general, the examples of street-level organizing and street theatricality boomed with the turn of the next decade: even the social protest that occurred in the late 1950s is less associated with the city street than—quoting a popular civil rights anthem from Phil Ochs—"that southern road." Meanwhile, urban-based leaders of the later civil rights / Black Power movements went directly to the "brothers off the block" for their constituency, and all protest groups of the 1960s resolutely moved their rallies, patrols, and demonstrations off the safe and socially sanctioned sidewalk.

Important scholarship such as Todd Gitlin's review of the antiwar movement, *The Whole World Is Watching* (1980), Patricia Bradley's *Mass Media and the Shaping of American Feminism* (2003), Jane Rhodes's *Framing the Black Panthers* (2007), and Amy Abugo Ongiri's *Spectacular Blackness* (2010) consider not only the look-at-us (and listen-to-us) theatricality of protest participants but also the role of mass media in shaping these groups' images and legacies. The project commencing here continues in the vein of these and other valuable inquiries as I interrogate both the spectacle of rights protest in the late 1960s and the role played by the groups' own and mainstream media. Chapter 3, however, examines the special dilemmas related to women in the spotlight, as these women sought to create visible, political, even sexual selfhood unpoliced by the male gaze and freed from the stigma and censure that have dogged "the public woman" for millennia. Notably, the Happy Hooker Xaviera Hollander took pains throughout her career to distance herself from the ordinary streetwalker and was at one time the wealthiest and most powerful of all those public figures whose lives and writings are discussed here. Closing a rather odd circle, she insisted upon the comforts (and increased profitability) of the private, domestic interior and succeeded in her aims until the long arm of the state absconded with her hard-earned savings and showed her the national door. In general, however, street theatrics and street life were, respectively, the bread and butter and the life's blood of many liberation-era rights-seekers; in the representative view of the inimitable Abbie Hoffman, "I loved it on the street. I ate there, panhandled there, sometimes even made love there. . . . As a kid I was taught that everything bad happened on the street. Disease lurked in the gutter. When you got fired you were 'out on the street.' . . . [But] just being there was liberating" (*Autobiography* 95).

In addition to its focus on street theater, *Freedom's Ring* traces the conflict between liberal and radical versions of the era's major rights movements, noting the repeated inclination toward the latter in all cases. By the late 1960s, a generation of young activists regarded the liberal alternative (integration, peaceful protest, equal access to the workplace or military) as antithetical to the agendas of separatism, rebellion, and revolution important to each. To be sure, as the Vietnam War ground on, as rights for oppressed rural and urban African Americans were promised by the courts and then withheld in real life, and as the national mood moved further from Kennedy-era idealism to fear- and war-mongering conservatism from 1966 on, the radical alternative seemed the only one. And yet this book's inquiry into the complexities of political and personal freedoms broadly defined—as valuable gains in their own right but also, ultimately, as affordable if not cost-free substitutes for the expensive equalities U.S. society has never aggregated the budget to provide—creates a thesis in favor of what was once dismissed as liberal reform but emerges as a radical alternative: meaningful work, sufficiently compensated, and the education, housing, and personal safety essential to quality of life were in the liberation era and remain to this day priceless (however pricey) social goals. The long view suggests that overemphasis on rights and freedoms not only distracts the well-meaning Left but also excuses the self-interested Right, from facing, paying for, and solving complex national economic problems. My conclusion will elaborate on the meaning of this thesis for present-day politics, specifically regarding the plight of the forgotten, addicted, underresourced but overvalued U.S. worker of both the American "heartland" of recent years and the urban inner city since the end of World War II.

CHAPTER 1

TALKING FIRST AND SHOOTING LATER IN THE BLACK POWER ERA

Although likely deserving regard as the most effective civil rights president of the twentieth century, Lyndon Johnson was reviled by militant black activists in the mid- to late 1960s, who reacted as negatively to his failed legislation as to his elderly, slow-talking, southern-fried mien. In the grimly comic summation of SNCC field secretary Julius Lester, "When Lyndon Baines Johnson became president . . . [and] asked for the nation's help and God's in that cracker drawl, black people began pulling out road maps and train schedules and brushing up on Spanish. They had always wanted to see what Mexico was like anyway" (15). As Bernice Reagon remarked to historian Bradford D. Martin, "Johnson's use of 'We Shall Overcome' [in a landmark speech to Congress] marked 'a decline in the use of songs and singing' in the movement in general and 'ended the effectiveness' of that song in particular" (45). Whither the Black Power, Black Muslim, and Black Panther movements had the dynamic East Coast scion whose assassination opened the door to LBJ's presidency survived into a more militant era? Would a long-haired Kennedy dropping acid and flashing the peace sign have redone the East Wing in psychedelic colors, extricated the nation from Vietnam under less shameful circumstances, and encouraged the opportunity that would have headed off the explosive racial rhetoric and actions of the late 1960s? Lester adds that "Old Big Ears . . . fooled everybody" (15), strengthening the civil rights bill and "giving Martin Luther King competition as to who was going to lead 'the movement'" (15), and perhaps only a "cracker" like Johnson could have bent the southerners in Congress to his own and his better nation's more egalitarian will.

To be sure, Johnson could not have been a less suitable president for the revolution his young and radical nation was in the process of working itself through. The vituperations of Malcolm X and SNCC's new leaders Stokely Carmichael and H. Rap Brown, as well as the 1965 Watts riots and successive summer uprisings across America, were as much a rebuke to Johnson per se as to the ultimately meager payoff from civil rights, voting rights, and fair housing laws of the period. Notably, all of the figures leading the late-1960s Black Power movements started out not as churchgoing devotees of peace and patriotism (such as King, Bayard Rustin, and elder statesman A. Philip Randolph) but as rougher-hewn "brothers off the block" who by both hook (an innate talent for speaking, crowd-pleasing, and street theater-making) and crook (assorted crimes and stretches in jail prior to and during their leadership careers) rose to renown in the eyes of spirited college studensts and urban underclasses alike. In an early issue of the *Black Panther* newspaper, Eldridge Cleaver's poem "Crackers to Spare" mocks "Super Cracker, Lady Cracker, Lynda Cracker, and Luci Cracker / [who] Farted in the kitchen of the American Dream" (23 November 1967, 10), among other indignities. Johnson was an irresistible foil to young militants throughout the cultural spectrum whose distrust and rancor energized not only Black Power but antiwar and related protest movements.

Broadly considered, the shift from liberal/integrationist to radical/separatist phases in the civil rights struggle manifests at the onset of LBJ's presidency; in the introduction, I described the movement's early bids for political freedom largely achieved, followed by much less successful attempts to win economic equality. As the new generation emerged in the mid-1960s, the once-radical cries for freedom voiced by King echoed in younger ears as weak and futile. The vanguard read integrationism as a bid for equality—equal access to a "white" world that they themselves wanted no part of. While early civil rights workers sought the right to integrate a neighborhood, later radical groups demanded ownership of the entire apartment complex; Carmichael insisted "that an exploiting landlord or storekeeper sell [to the community], at minimal cost, a building or a shop that they will own cooperatively, [lest this community] back their demand with a rent strike or a boycott" ("What We Want" 8; see also Carmichael and Hamilton 172–173). While such proposals faced long odds with policymakers, black business ownership fell afoul of even more militant leaders such as, for instance, SNCC's James Foreman. He "was ambivalent about such efforts to divert blacks from revolutionary strategies, complaining that many black nationalists . . . had been the first to 'jump on the bandwagon of black capitalism'" (Carson 294).

King envisioned his last great national action, the Poor People's Campaign (PPC), as a mass demonstration with its own "march" element: "Wave upon wave of the army of the poor, descending on the Mall, setting up their makeshift camps, and preparing for arrest until District jails were overflowing. King and his SCLC lieutenants expected to be among the first protesters hustled off to jail" (McKnight 112). When after King's assassination the SCLC "pulled back from launching a campaign with arrest-provoking tactics and settled instead on erecting a semipermanent camp" (112), the "walking" (old-style pickets, bus boycotts, and marches—*movement* as a literal term) that radical young firebrands had already grown impatient with slowed to a crawl. Famously bogged down in thick mud after days of heavy rain, the PPC's somewhat ironically named Resurrection City was trapped in a stalemate with an uncaring Congress and finally left Washington humiliated and empty-handed. The campaign's benighted attempt to "integrate" the National Mall all but cried out for the corrective measures of King's more militant successors, who would counter the cold, rain-soaked entrenchment of the PPC with lightning-fast moves across urban America, using hot rhetoric to dramatically ignite public unrest.

Malcolm X preferred the southern "wolf" to the northern "fox": "Under the steady lullabies sung by foxy liberals, the Northern Negro became a *beggar*. But the southern Negro, facing the honestly snarling white man, rose up to battle that white man for his freedom" (*Autobiography* 381). He described the liberal-in-chief, LBJ, as "a fox who could have [African Americans] half-digested before they even knew what was happening" (381). Carmichael, too, looked with the radical's skepticism upon the integrationist agenda of his movement's liberal wing: "the goals of the old civil rights leaders—open accommodation, housing, education, and job opportunities" (Stewart 437)—were unacceptable because they were aimed only at the "executive-level" talented tenth (that is, the gifted, assimilated *individual* instead of the large, poorly educated, diversely needy, and thus much more expensive-to-accommodate *group*; see also Cruse 311–312). Carmichael describes the upshot of the typical integrationist scheme—"the man who 'makes it' leav[es] his black brothers behind in the ghetto as fast as his new sports car will take him" ("What We Want" 6)—while H. Rap Brown similarly describes the talented (or light-skinned) Negro's mode of exit: "a Thunderbird" (9). In her memoir, Assata Shakur called the "petty bourgeois upward-bound 'Negroes'" (*Assata* 156) with whom she once worked "professional escape artists" (155), and activist Grace Lee Boggs named the annexation of black leadership into the U.S. middle class "Operation Co-optation." After this, "the Black community from coast to coast would be balkanized into little Black bailiwicks resembling the tiniest neocolonial nations" (274) with no political or economic power. No such co-optation, said Boggs, "can incorporate or contain the . . . deepest and fastest-growing layer inside the black community, the layer of Black city youth" (274). Most of what has been gained by African Americans since the 1950s has gone indeed to those willing or able to adopt the liberal mode, and radical leaders of the mid-1960s decried these meager gains.

In fact, *liberal* connoted a specifically white mindset in many civil rights and Black Power contexts, be this the well-meaning ally of the integrationist years or the "blue-eyed" hypocrite challenged by radicalized youth of later days. In journalist Loren Miller's incisive estimation from 1962, "The liberal sees 'both sides' of the issue, the force of the Negro's constitutional argument and the existence of customs, sometimes jelled into law, that justify the gradualist approach. He is impatient with 'extremists on both sides.' The Negro is outraged at being called an extremist . . . [since] there is only one side: his side, the constitutional side" (235–236). Malcolm X and Stokely Carmichael critiqued the emphasis on programming characteristic of the early movement—the sit-ins, marches, and related campaigns that bloodied the heads of many protesters yet brought insufficient returns. Later in the 1960s, the Black Panthers returned to community organizing but added a defiant rhetorical stance and had guns at the ready. We thus might characterize this transitional period—between the dignified movement leadership represented by King and the mass organizing achieved to some degree if under completely different circumstances by the Black Panthers of the late 1960s—as a moment of *free* speech incendiary enough (pun intended) to challenge the boundaries of the First Amendment.

The Power of Words

King's legacy is constituted equally by his landmark statements such as "Letter from Birmingham Jail," "I Have a Dream," and several best-selling books *and* his widely publicized mass-actions including the Montgomery Bus Boycott, the March on Washington, the March to Selma, and the Poor People's Campaign. The "Letter," of course, is both a famous piece of rhetoric and the result of his own daring activism, and many of his most famous speeches were not simply public statements but send-offs to eventful, often violent direct actions. Near the end of his life, King was criticized by the mainstream press and even movement membership for absence from the trenches where his lesser-known compatriots still marched, struggled, and faced mortal risk. As he joined leaders from SNCC and the Congress of Racial Equality (CORE) to complete James Meredith's March against Fear in June 1966, he appeared on and off during the lengthy walk through Mississippi's blistering heat. In Memphis in late March 1968, he was hustled off-site in the midst of a disrupted march on behalf of garbage workers days before his assassination; he was mocked in the press after that incident as "chicken a la King" (see, e.g., McKnight 62).

But the long arc of King's career, not to mention his tragic early death, indicates a life of principled, often death-defying action inspiring to the millions who admired him worldwide, while the younger men who followed in King's wake (although Malcolm was criticizing both "blue-eyed liberals" and "handkerchief-heads" like King as early as 1963) questioned the virtues of walking per se: marching, picketing, crossing a whites-only threshold just to eat a hamburger. In speeches from his most strident period of 1963 to 1964, Malcolm castigated sit-ins as the action of "chumps," pointing out that old women and cowards can "sit down" and asking his audiences why they sought proximity to the white man when he in fact wanted no part of them. He criticized pickets and boycotts as asking whites for jobs when blacks should create their own businesses and enjoined listeners to "stop singing and start swinging." Though he eventually broke with the Nation of Islam (NOI) over their "non-engagement policy"—that is, their pointed lack of "action" (*Autobiography* 295)—even during the final months of Malcolm's indeed-momentous life, amanuensis Alex Haley heard this on the streets of Harlem: "Malcolm X only talked, but other civil rights organizations were *doing*. 'All he's ever done is *talk*, CORE and SNCC and some of Dr. King's people are out getting beat over the head'" (Haley 427; see also Quashie 58). For good or ill, there came following King's victories of the early to mid-1960s a period of disaffected disinclination toward "walking" diversely defined, replaced by the giving of speeches that indeed gave a generation its voice and, by the end of the decade, resurrected a "movement" that rarely marched a step without firearms in tow. If silent stoicism was the posture of the early movement, the noisy spectacle of the young firebrands involved not only powerful words but the weapons display or threat of violence that carried their voices all the farther.

Stokely Carmichael was an obscure but courageous freedom-rider, teacher, and political organizer in the SNCC South just as Malcolm mocked these very actions; in a recollection aptly focused on "walking" instead of "talking," Carmichael notes that when SNCC leader Bob Moses "asked me to be coordinator of the Second Congressional (Delta) District that summer [of 1964]. I was floored. Ah means *speechless*, almost. . . . Had Bob and the folks in Mississippi asked me to organize West Hell, I'da packed my bags" (*Black Power* 357; emphasis added). Some of the best writing in Carmichael's archive records his period of organizing with the Lowndes County Freedom Organization (LCFO); the very title of one essay—"Black-Belt Election: New Day A-Coming"—indicates the optimism Carmichael yet felt, even following the lost bid of all seven LCFO candidates due to white machination. As Carmichael closes this moving account, "November 8, 1966, made one thing clear: some day black people will control the government of Lowndes County. For Lowndes is not merely a section of land and a group of people, but an idea whose time has come" (120). This essay belongs to a collection cowritten with sociologist Charles V. Hamilton, *Black Power* (1967), and both authors define Black Power in terms of political power. Per Hamilton's assessment of the mid-1960s situation in Tuskegee, Alabama, "The blacks [of this community] had achieved education and economic security—both of which are still projected throughout the nation as cure-alls—but the whites continued to lay and collect taxes, rule over the school system. . . . The reason is obvious enough: blacks did not have *political* power" (134). In their conclusion, and in contradistinction to the thesis of my own project, the authors assert, "Our basic premise is that money and jobs are not the final answer to the black man's problems . . . but the inclusion of black people at all levels of decision-making" (183).

But Carmichael was later bitterly disillusioned by the failures of the MFDP at the 1964 Democratic Convention (see the introduction) and the LCFO in the following midterm elections. He is a pivotal figure in this moment for the pivot he publicly enacted from action, which he had come to regard as futile, to speech: his famous declaration to an angry crowd in Greenwood, Mississippi, during the resumed Meredith march—"This is the twenty-seventh time I've been arrested. I ain't going to jail no more" (qtd. in Carson 209)—marked both his own and the national black community's turn from the seeming inefficacy of organized walking to the unscripted possibilities touched off in reaction to fiery talk. By February 1968, at a famous rally in Oakland on behalf of the recently jailed Black Panther leader Huey Newton, Carmichael dispiritedly told his audience, "The vote isn't anything but a honky's trick" (*Stokely Speaks* 116, 117). Instead, Carmichael averred a year later, "power is defined by the amount of violence one can bring against one's enemy" (166).

Organizer Anne Moody is another important figure in the shift from activism to cynicism affecting numerous leaders in this period. While Carmichael came south from the sophisticated and relatively privileged environs of New York and

Howard University, Moody was born to the stark poverty, oppression, and limited education opportunities that radicalized her at a young age. She joined the original sit-ins to desegregate Woolworth lunch counters in Jackson in early 1963 and suffered humiliating inundations of ketchup, sugar, body-blows, and arrests that credential her own version of walking the walk with those most celebrated in the movement. As she ran often singlehandedly voting, clothing, and food drives out of a storefront in Canton, Mississippi, she endured surveillance, prosecution, and vigilantism. Perhaps unsurprisingly for women in this context, Moody's frustration turned not outward in angry speeches or violent retaliation but inward toward a near nervous breakdown and overreliance on sleeping pills (302). Although Moody feels that "we have to take certain positive actions to work on the problem" (259), by the end of her narrative, she will question the efficacy of action of any kind.

Moody alone of those discussed in this chapter attended the March on Washington, but for her, speechmaking, even nationally inspiring orations by the monumental King, means even less than failed grassroots organizing: "Martin Luther King went on and on talking about his dreams. I sat there thinking that in Canton we never had time to sleep, much less dream" (275; see also McKissick, *3/5* 37). Later, in an angry prayer to God, Moody avers, "I have a good idea Martin Luther King is talking to you, too. If he is, tell him that nonviolence has served its purpose. . . . If you don't believe that, then I know you must be white, too" (285). During her one public address, following her ordeal at the sit-in, she lectures fellow activists on the futility of speech itself: "Some of us believe, . . . all we gotta do is walk up to Mr. Charlie and say, 'Man, I want my freedom.' Do you think Mr. Charlie is going to dish it out to you on a silver platter?" (259). Although most famously associated with the late-1960s BLA, Assata Shakur came up (as did Claude Brown; see chapter 2) as a footloose child of the streets of New York and, like Moody, did a stint with the civil rights movement in her native South.

There she, like Moody, casts a cynical glance at the movement's early rhetoric: "I believed we could get our freedom just by appealing to the consciousness of white people." Back in Harlem, she delightedly serves in breakfast and Liberation School programs with the Harlem Panthers because "i [*sic*] was really tired of adults at the time" (227); comparing the writing of Shakur, Angela Davis, and Elaine Brown, Margo V. Perkins singles out Shakur's as "repeatedly alluding to her sense of solidarity with others" (10–11). As she shifts from freedom dreams to the more militant, gun-toting stance of the BLA, she shifts the issue from politics to economics: "Those who believe that the president or the vice president . . . run this country are sadly mistaken. The almighty dollar is king" (*Assata* 139). Only at the end of the Panther heyday did the group's first spokes*woman*, Elaine Brown, mount the stage with soulful "psalms" (*Taste of Power* 310) to the Party's male leaders and a bold declaration regarding guns and money as she assumed Party leadership in 1974. Her initial reliance on tough talk and subsequent shift into organized politics and prison reform will be discussed in the final moments of this chapter. Finally, the young radicals deeply doubted the organized activism in the older movement tradition. Congress of Racial Equality leader Floyd McKissick warned that if younger leaders "begin to offer 'programs' according to the white man's specifications, they will have lost part of their potency and part of their claim to truth" ("Book Reviews" 549). Primarily, it was the fiery *words* of Malcolm, Carmichael, and his SNCC successor H. Rap Brown that sparked within listeners new measures of self-respect and justified indignation whose value lasts to this day. In other words, their "free" speech freed audiences as they had never been released before from self-doubt and self-restraint; Carmichael called it "entertaining ourselves . . . publicly saying what we always privately felt but were afraid to say" (*Stokely Speaks* 146). By turn, these spokesmen's talents at the podium freed themselves (or cut themselves adrift) from the organizations that had sponsored their rise to fame. Yet if in a 1966 debate at Hunter College "Rustin dared Carmichael to provide a blueprint for racial uplift that went beyond slogans" (Joseph 172), at this moment of transition from liberal to radical views within the African American rights struggle, "just sayin'" was its own end and its own strategy for change.

Malcolm's Marvelous Rhetoric

With his sharp wit, rhetorical skill, and blazing indifference to white opinion, Malcolm X galvanized listeners in speeches challenging not only the white enemy but also cherished community leaders from the recent past. Often he established solidarity in his prologue, stressing to his audience how each of them, regardless of religion, wealth, skin tone, or social class was to "catch hell" on a daily basis because they were all black; often he enjoined the group to therefore "differ in the closet" if at all when uniting against the common white enemy. Yet he notably spent most of the rest of these same speeches differing vociferously from established leaders, heaping insults upon even his own listeners as he did. He criticized his audience's "dumb vote, your ignorant vote, your wasted vote" in past elections and laughed at the Christian ideal embodied in "turn the other cheek" ("Ballot" 3 April 1964). In a more strident version of this speech he told his audience, "you will let anyone in and take control of the economy of your community . . . under the pretext that you want to integrate. No, you outta your mind" ("Ballot" 12 April 1964). The March on Washington was to Malcolm a joke on those who less than a year earlier may have regarded it as the milestone of a lifetime: "He ['the man'] made a fool out of you. He made you think you were going somewhere and you end up going nowhere except between Lincoln and Washington" ("Ballot" 12 April 1964).[1] In his famed *Autobiography of Malcolm X, as Told to Alex Haley* (1965), he mocked the event as "the Farce on Washington" and "a one-day 'integrated' picnic" (287).

Even when employing the accusatory "you," Malcolm surely generated allegiance in his audience by moving them with his very words out of an integrationist "Tom" mentality into an enlightened separatism. His audience had a hearty laugh perhaps less at themselves than at the benighted fools who were seconds behind their own coming to consciousness, and in this way his painful lessons were a baptism, however fiery the terms. To be sure, Malcolm's exhortations belong to a tradition of congregational rebuke, more broadly, "the rhetoric of the jeremiad"

(Bosnicova), at least as old in America as Cotton Mather; with his harsh words, Malcolm called his listeners to repent the sin of integration-mindedness and walk the path of righteous black consciousness thenceforward. Too, audiences could take immense satisfaction from Malcolm's own tall, proud, handsome, sharp-eyed, well-spoken, impeccably dressed example of untrammeled freedom. He spoke boldly and without fear and was willing to occupy the solitary role of one-step-ahead for as long as necessary. When he freely criticized the "white devil," the "tricky blue-eyed liberal," and that "old cracker" in the White House, these were rhetorical shots heard around the world, the opening salvos in a revolution that was understood to require violent action in a rapidly ensuing phase.

Malcolm, Carmichael, many in the Black Panther Party, and black leaders around the nation in this period looked with delight upon the freedom struggles being won worldwide as Africans, Southeast Asians, South Americans, and Cubans threw off colonial power; they regarded newly liberated persons of color as more reliable allies than white liberals had ever been (see, e.g., Hartnell 215–216). As Melanie McAlister observes, in this period was forged "a vision . . . of blackness as a *trans*national identity, and African Americans as players on a truly global stage" (649). Malcolm was especially impressed (as would be the Panthers at the end of the decade) with the example of guerrilla warfare fought in small, scattered groups to do in the efforts of massively organized colonial armies. In this book's introduction, I suggested that the ultimatum Malcolm delivers in "The Ballot or the Bullet" might be read as a warning to white America to make the black vote count in 1964 or face mass violence. Yet frequently throughout that speech, he paints a picture in which the hope for such political change is a "chump's" dream, such that the revolutionary bullet, aimed guerrilla-style at the army or the police, was now African Americans' only option.

Ironically, however, many in the Black Power pantheon whose lives were changed by long walks of another kind—their own travels abroad—realized that internationalism was a double-edged sword; members of Malcolm's post-NOI organization, the Organization of Afro-American Unity (OAAU) expressed "a growing disillusion" (Haley 427; see also Hartnell 217–218) in Malcolm's long overseas visits, and SNCC members would later question the lengthy peregrinations of Carmichael; both he and the Black Panthers' Eldridge Cleaver would be accused of running away from domestic difficulties when they established long-term bases in Africa. Discussing a film deeply inspiring to Black Power movements throughout the period, *The Battle of Algiers*, Francee Covington remarked that "general talk on the subject [of guerilla-style revolt] has been in excess" (315): due to myriad cultural and logistical differences between the warring Algerians and African Americans both firmly entrenched and broadly dislocated in urban enclaves throughout the United States, "importing the techniques of revolution that were successful in one place may prove disastrous in another place" (322). Covington's call for Harlem to take on "those elements of the Mafia who control the drug traffic in our communities" (320) as an "apprenticeship" (321) or dry run for national action indicates the difficulty of the challenge.

To be sure, Malcolm's marvelous *Autobiography* narrates a life packed with action, revolutionary and otherwise. One of its many enduring gifts is its scintillating portrait of black Boston and New York in the early twentieth century—its clubs, entertainers, and inimitable street-corner personalities, all of whom Malcolm engaged with as he lived his early days to the fullest, if always on the razor's edge. Similar to several in the Black Panther leadership who will write memoirs at the end of the decade, Malcolm engaged in dope-peddling, numbers-running, prostitution, and burglary as a street hustler in Harlem in the early 1940s. Becoming a reefer salesman with "fifty or sixty dollars" a day in profits, "I felt, for the first time in my life, that great feeling of *free*!" (102). If economic self-sufficiency leads at first to personal freedom, he is caught during a breaking-and-entry in 1946 and does six years in Charlestown State Prison. His own pivot from (criminal) action to a career of principled public speaking began at this moment, again recollected in meaningful terms. Rediscovering literacy at Charlestown, "months passed without my even thinking about being imprisoned. In fact, up to then, I had never been so truly free in my life" (176). Later, "I don't think anybody ever got more out of going to prison than I did. In fact, prison allowed me to study far more intensively than [if I] . . . had attended some college" (183). Thomas Doherty locates in the *Autobiography* "an almost religious reverence for the redemptive power of the printed word as a path to salvation and self-transformation" (31), adding to the equation between speech and freedom solidly forming at this moment.

Malcolm's prison-time conversion to Elijah Muhammad's Nation of Islam not only curtailed the underworld "action" he had engaged in freely throughout his wild youth but sanctioned only the kind of activity that Malcolm turned out to have a supreme gift for—speaking to, debating with, and ultimately converting one benighted soul at a time. Despite their devotional constraints, as several (e.g., Alghawas, Benson, Eakin) have pointed out, Malcolm's conversions—first from atheism to the NOI, then later from NOI to orthodox Islam—were also gestures of expansion and self-liberation. Yet ironically, "the best-conditioned audiences for Mr. Muhammad's teachings [were from] the Christian churches . . . usually Southern migrant people, usually older, who would go anywhere to hear what they called 'good preaching'" (*Autobiography* 223). Despite their radically different approaches, Malcolm X thus found his own early success with MLK's same constituency—more settled, disciplined joiners from the churchgoing South, open in their newly acquired Harlem environs to Malcolm's radical, anti-Christian approach to black consciousness. As would King when he himself came to the urban North, Malcolm had difficulty persuading the careworn "brothers off the block," who would be much less inclined to give up their hustles and inebriations for the asceticism imposed by the NOI.

As Malcolm's talents on the dais drew more and more followers to NOI's message, so the middle sections of his *Autobiography* begin to reflect his life in the spotlight and cannot but pale in comparison to the lusty, swashbuckling reminiscences of his earlier days (see also Eakin 235 and D. Miller 679). Long sections of his memoirs suffer from verbatim rehashes of his (and even Elijah Muhammad's) speeches, his comments to reporters, his religious philosophies. Though well aware of the "power of words" (qtd. in Houck 287; see also Ohmann 139), Malcolm after his break with NOI described himself as "a zombie then—like all Muslims—I was hypnotized" (qtd. in Haley 437). His famous critique of the NOI's "non-engagement policy" (*Autobiography* 295) led to his silencing and eventual split from the group; yet like the SNCC and Panther spokesmen who will follow—and despite his own intent to trade talk for action through the OAAU—Malcolm was never able to relinquish the podium. Following from his tremendous enjoyment of debating in prison, Malcolm relished every opportunity to engage his public: "Except for all-black audiences, I liked college audiences best," since they "never failed to be exhilarating and . . . showed me ways to improve my presentation and defense" (288). Not at all surprisingly, "I got so I could feel my audiences' temperaments. . . . Like a doctor, with his finger against a pulse, is able to feel the heart rate, when I am up there speaking, I can *feel* the reaction to what I am saying" (288).

Quite simply, Malcolm was too good at public speaking for his own literal well-being; his massive success attracting NOI followers, first lauded by his less magnetic mentor, eventually turned Elijah Muhammad jealously against him. When eventually cut loose from the NOI's institutional support, Malcolm embarked on constant speaking tours to promote first his Muslim Mosque Inc., then the OAAU, exhausting himself in the process. As Haley reports, Malcolm's serious financial shortages demanded the never-ending series of speaking engagements, although by the end of his life, it seemed practically a compulsion: he left to speak in Europe as he and his family were being evicted from their NOI-owned home on Long Island and for another trip to Detroit immediately after they were gas-bombed off the premises, likely by NOI enemies (435). Yet notably, this ninety-minute Detroit speech, delivered a week before he met his demise and regarding his new agenda for activism under the auspices of the OAAU, fails for the most part as a *speech* per se: clearly exhausted and shaken by his night surviving the blast to his home, Malcolm in his lengthy remarks on the need to unify with Africans worldwide seemed not even meant to stir the crowd; except in rare moments criticizing the white adversary, this speech of February 14 had little of the humor, rhetorical flourish, and audience energy that characterize his many more famed early addresses. It exemplifies the challenge to his legacy outlined in an early analysis by Thomas W. Benson, that "near the end of his career . . . [Malcolm] was without audience or program" (2); per Carol Ohmann, Malcolm's final challenge, unfulfilled due to his untimely death, was "to translate his, now, deeply humanistic conviction of universal brotherhood into practical action" (148–149).

As an early figure in this chapter, Malcolm in his OAAU speech provides an object lesson in what his several successors went on to discover: that one might talk the talk or walk the walk, but any attempt to "talk the walk" (use speech to outline policy or programs) could cause an audience to question that leader's resolve or simply put them to sleep. Of course, Malcolm died in his speaker's role, as he was tragically gunned down onstage on 21 February 1965 at the beginning of a speech to OAAU supporters, allegedly by partisans from the NOI. Though he did not live long enough to convert his talk into the action he described in his final speeches, his OAAU's Ten-Point Program directly inspired the Black Panthers (see J. Morgan), whose own Ten-Point Program signaled their activist intentions from their first days.

Carmichael's Incendiary Speechmaking

In Stokely Carmichael's speechmaking heyday, SNCC's core membership—deservedly proud of their long record of civil rights activism—looked upon their chairman's fame with misgivings and a longing for the earlier days of sustained program development. Executive Secretary Ruby Doris Robinson worried that Carmichael's angry speeches invited too much negative attention from the press and the police (Carson 230); John Lewis, Carmichael's predecessor before a difficult power shift, criticized SNCC's failure "to provide 'on-going' programs to meet the needs of blacks. 'To have a program is one thing, to have a sort of speech-making public relations thing is another'" (qtd. in Carson 231). As SNCC founding member Julian Bond remarked, in the months following his own resignation from the group, "SNCC did not 'have a program to match its rhetoric'" (qtd. in Carson 232). In his essential history of the organization, Clayborne Carson remarks that by 1967, most of SNCC's attempts at programming, such as incorporating black sections of LA as "Freedom City" and developing a Free DC Movement (233), had failed, while "SNCC began to rely almost totally on speechmaking and its New York office, manned by professional fund-raisers and veteran staff members, to provide funds for payroll expenses" (234). Despite the lucrative visibility Carmichael may have brought the group, things came to a head when he was required by the Central Committee to "stop making speaking engagements after December 10 [1966]," though "he found the limelight difficult to resist. A few months later, the Central Committee forbade his appearance on a television show and decided that he should always be accompanied by another staff member at his engagements" (Carson 230). A modern commentator has phrased the question in terms especially pertinent to my own themes: "Carmichael provided abundant symbolic satisfactions but few tangible ideas and no tangible plans for accomplishing societal perfection through black power. What was to replace integration efforts in housing, education, employment, and government?" (Stewart 443).

The tension between talk and action is on display in a speech Carmichael delivered at Morehouse College in 1970. Here he strains to justify his own recent history of protracted inaction in the cossetted care of African heads of state: "Because revolutionary theories are based on historical analyses, one must study. . . . At the correct historical moment, you make your historical leap and carry the struggle forward" (*Stokely Speaks* 185). Ironically, in the midst of this lengthy speech, Carmichael criticizes those who "think revolution is about yelling and screaming. . . . that they can . . . rap their way out of the trouble we find ourselves in" (185). His critique of tenured radicals "sitting up in an office, jiving about revolution" (214), perhaps even implicates a figure such as Angela Davis, who has indeed existed in both exalted academic environs and radical activist circles throughout her career.

Notably, Davis credits "Stokely's *words*, cutting like a switchblade, accusing the enemy as I had never heard him accused before" (A. Davis 150, emphasis added) with her first attunement to black consciousness and yet later expresses frustration with the UC-San Diego Black Student Council, who "needed an issue around which to struggle" but only "argued [the question] in meetings that never seemed to end" (196). Despite his own critique, Carmichael sought the intellectual's mantle throughout the latter part of his career and relished his role as elder/mentor to student groups black and white. To the Morehouse undergraduates, who likely knew their current events as well as he, he somewhat patronizingly tells them, "I would like . . . to explain how guerrilla warfare really works. You should take notes, because you're students and you have to discuss these lectures" (*Stokely Speaks* 213).

As quoted in this book's introduction, Carmichael's most famous contribution to the civil rights lexicon, the short but to-the-point expression "Black power!" encroached unnervingly in the mid-1960s on the turf still occupied by "Freedom now!" On the Meredith march in June 1966, led by King, CORE's McKissick, and SNCC's Carmichael, "the nightly rallies in Mississippi communities became contests in which the three leaders competed for the support of southern blacks" (Carson 208). "After five hours of debate [at a stopover in Yazoo City], the representatives agreed to avoid competing for the support of black audiences through the use of slogans such as black power and freedom now" (Carson 210). But it is not the case that the expression "Black power!" negated or curtailed the drive for freedom initiated during earlier phases of the movement; as noted earlier, black power suggested the exercising of freedoms beyond any called for thus far. Liberal freedoms (those guaranteed to all in the Constitution) too long denied transmogrified into radical freedoms—the vigorous takeover (with violence if necessary) of urban neighborhoods, media attention, the national agenda, and often the complacent worldview of those targeted by disturbing rhetoric and gestures of communal rage.

Radical SNCC leadership endured arrests, threats, and (in the case of Brown) police gunshots when their speeches were seen to incite rebellion. Carmichael's Waterloo involved statements made in August 1966 in Atlanta's Summerhill neighborhood, where tensions rose in reaction to the wounding of a black resident by police. Carmichael promised the crowd to attend an upcoming rally, at which point, he may have said, they would all "tear this place up" (qtd. in Carson 225). Though he later denied these words, anger escalated, Mayor Ivan Allen was knocked from his perch atop a squad car, and residents sustained tear gas and clubbing (Carson 226). Carson observes that "although Carmichael . . . and other SNCC workers had left Summerhill when the major battles between blacks and police had occurred, white city officials blamed SNCC for the violence" (226). But in the long view, SNCC may seem *more* culpable for having left the scene of impending disaster—that is, for having no permanent attachment to a community that they at least in some way committed to subsequent upheaval. Suggesting an equation between freedom and irresponsibility, Charles J. Stewart compares Carmichael (though this applies to other Black Power spokesmen) to "an old-fashioned tent meeting revivalist [who] came to town, stirred up a great deal of excitement and enthusiasm, made conversions, and then left for the next town. . . . [W]ith no leadership or structure left behind, [except for the occasional riot] the newly energized and converted soon returned to life as usual" (443). Ultimately, "rioting charges were overturned on appeal" (Carson 226), Carmichael spent much of the rest of his career abroad, and ironically, initial public opinion (at least within the pages of *Newsweek*) regarded his successor H. Rap Brown as "far less flammable" (qtd. in Carson 253).

Brown the Fiery Speaker

Peniel Joseph describes H. Rap Brown as "the comet of the Black Power era, a bright burning star whose presence faded after one spectacular streaking ascent" (181). Like Carmichael, Brown would face the repeated challenge of whether his speech was "free"—that is, protected by the First Amendment or guilty of inciting the mayhem that often followed. "Burn it down!" and "Burn it to the ground!" seem to have been Brown's favorite expressions, and an iconic illustration of him holding a lighted match by Black Panther artist Emory Douglas is captioned with his equally famous iteration, "Burn Baby Burn." Joseph aptly describes as a "fiery speech" (188) the most controversial statement Brown ever made, when he seemed to encourage an outburst of politically motivated pyromania in Cambridge, Maryland, in July 1967. Shortly following his departure from the stage, "two square blocks were burned to the ground" (Joseph 188), including a dilapidated school that had been referred to by Brown as the source of long-standing local discontent. Brown's head was grazed by a bullet in the ensuing melee with the police, and days later, Brown was arrested in Virginia for inciting a riot; complicated extradition and legal proceedings more or less ended his career as a movement spokesman, as he joined the ranks of numerous civil rights agitators caught up in the system each year.

In his remarkable memoir from this period, *Die Nigger Die!* (1969), Brown downplays his involvement in the Cambridge incident as well as any violence his words might have inspired. Describing logistical mishaps—a missed flight and an hour's late arrival—he makes no mention of the speech's contents, while afterward, "people were just standing around and talking . . . and everything was cool" (100). When Brown offers to walk a young woman home due to her fear of harassment from white police, the people "were just tagging along behind us, which ain't a cool thing to do"—"ain't cool" being his closest reference to the conflagration that night. Brown's only comment about fire belongs to police "opening fire" on the crowd; later when making his escape (from both danger and arrest), a compatriot attempts to light a cigarette, and Brown is quick to lecture him to "put that match out!" (101). The narrative concludes with a long protest regarding the manhunt and prosecution across several states and general violation of his rights to "Free Speech" (102); when caught, Brown famously accused his captors of "tak[ing] off the black robe and put[ting] on the white sheet" (qtd. in Joseph 188) and flagrantly taunted federal agents with another burning pun: "Did you know that Hoover is a faggot—your boss?" (*Die* 103).

Such fiery, expletive-laced rhetoric characterized Brown's many speeches and comments throughout his autobiography. Starting with its arresting title, Brown hurls epithets and insults at every American institution; not surprisingly, LBJ is even more frequently vilified than Hoover, called "old cracker ass Lightning Bug Johnson" (51) and "Lynch'em Burn Johnson" (136). While an officer with the Nonviolent Action Group (NAG), the early-1960s SNCC branch at Howard where both he and Carmichael got their start, Brown once sat down with civil rights leaders in a meeting with Johnson. Brown is disgusted with the deference shown by NAACP and CORE representatives, who receive only disrespect in return. But Brown gets the last laugh: "And Johnson was a big-eared, ugly, red-necked cracker. I looked at that muthafucka's ears. If he could learn to wiggle them he could fly" (53). He freely admits that on his way out, "I stole some stuff from the White House. I liberated everything I could!" (53). Throughout the text, Brown defends poor people's alternate economies of theft, gambling, drug-pushing, and "living off women" (24); using the term *liberate* whenever describing his own past thefts, he resigns from low-paying jobs in DC and regards free trade as its own con: "White man'll sell you a $20 suit for $50 and call it good business. . . . Profit is a nice word for stealing" (18).

Johnson is a figure of fun not only in Brown's written remarks but in several of the McLuhan-esque collages interspersed in *Die Nigger Die!* Jan Carew called Brown "the bogeyman created by the white dominated media" (A23), and in return, Brown's text is media-saturated and in double-edged dialogue with media's power. In one image, LBJ's scowling face is collaged onto the Statue of Liberty and, near a narrative of Brown dodging the draft, another positions Johnson jabbing his finger next to the famous "I Want You" poster of Uncle Sam (70–71). As in texts written by Marshall McLuhan, Vance Packard, John Berger, and others in the period, media images—here, the role of media in the black community—figure significantly in Brown's analysis; twice he puns on his book's title with the expression "Dye Nigger Dye!" criticizing racist advertising, black media such as *Ebony* and *Jet*, and views in the black community favoring lighter skin and Caucasian features. Using then hip photonegative effects that turn black to white and vice versa (*Die* 5), Brown's paste-up ads for skin-lightening cream and straight-hair wigs critique equations of glamor and success with the white look. Like his advertising-age brethren in the mainstream, Brown regards television as both an essential tool for maximizing his message and an addictive habit enslaving his underresourced community: "Children sit in front of the t.v. set and all they see are fine cars, perfumes, clothes, and everything else they ain't got. They sit there and watch it, telling the rats to sit down and stop blocking the view. . . . They couldn't even get full at supper, but that don't matter. They want an Oldsmobile" (19).

Not surprisingly, Brown, who famously averred that "violence is as american [*sic*] as cherry pie" (144), never went into the rural South without packing heat. Though his SNCC colleagues "have difficulty trying to deal with the fact that I carry a gun" (84), Brown is of the opinion that "violence created a peoplehood," whether this be on the occasion of the American Revolution or more recent incidents in riot-torn cities. Ever the media analyst, Brown notes, "Turn on the t.v. and you go deaf from all the gunfire. Let two fighters get in the ring and let neither one of them hit the other" and the audience will "scream for blood" (38). Confronting a white adversary, Brown's gun is the equalizer that results in fairer fights; when two "honkies picketing the electrical work company" in Greene County, Alabama, yell at him to slow down his driving, Brown backs up and challenges them, gun displayed. Days later, he puts the drop on the sheriff himself, and when the advantage is reversed moments later, he is arrested comically for "fornication" (he was caught in a hotel room with a woman) and his gun being "too short" (88). As will be the case in the early armed confrontations between the Black Panthers and local police (see the next section), Brown seems here to maximize the element of surprise since pistol-packing African Americans in the Deep South had rarely been encountered before.

Cleaver as Pre-Panther Memoirist

Thus far, I have traced a predilection for "talking" over "walking" as a distinguishing feature of leaders in the Black Power and related Black Muslim movements, and shortly I will read the return to organized forms of protest, demonstration, and community service by the Black Panther Party. Eldridge Cleaver is a fittingly transitional figure, as his likely most noted contributions to the Black Power era—publication of his prison writings, *Soul on Ice* (1968), and editing the *Black Panther* newspaper throughout his tenure with the BPP—indicate his role as the sole professional (and arguably most talented) writer in this survey (that is, as someone whose "talk" was its own "walk"—a revolutionary gesture in its own right). Both *Soul on Ice* and the *Black Panther* paper, as well as the iconic photo poster, orchestrated by Cleaver, of Huey Newton seated on a wicker "throne," surrounded by the warrior's accoutrements, performed revolutionary action by financially supporting the Panthers through their epic court battles and mundane house- and office-keeping needs. Before turning professional writer, "jail [for Cleaver], as has been the case for many revolutionaries, was a university of sorts" (Lavelle 57). In her memoir, Anne Moody remarked that at a crisis moment following Medgar Evers's assassination, "I had to get out of all this confusion. The only way I could do it was to go to jail. Jail was the only place I could think in" (249).

Yet attracting with his work the attention of critics and writers such as Maxwell Geismar and Norman Mailer, as well as the editors of *Ramparts* magazine, where many of the essays published later in *Soul on Ice* first appeared, Cleaver did not just school himself in higher thoughts but literally wrote his way to freedom. Per Ashley Lavelle, "While many of his Panther colleagues were fixated on the gun, Cleaver wielded the pen with panache" (57). Cleaver considers paths of escape throughout his prison sojourn, finding both freedom of expression (the writing itself) and freedom of thought to be indispensable precursors to the real thing. Among his fellow inmates, he regards heightened consciousness as "my new freedom. . . . I attacked all forms of piety, loyalty, and sentiment: marriage, love, God, patriotism, the Constitution, the founding fathers" and revels in his role as idol-smasher (*Soul* 6). As much as his own writing, his reading matter is a vital conduit to the free world, since newspapers teach him about the Watts uprising of 1965 and the Free Speech Movement in nearby Berkeley; the legal, political, and philosophical material he gets his hands on further free his mind.

Though critical attention has focused on Cleaver's more political essays, including his critique of James Baldwin ("Notes on a Native Son," 1966), and questionable justifications of his criminal past, Cleaver's skills as both a portraitist and a culture critic are broadly on display throughout *Soul on Ice*. He conveys his regard for a devoted prison instructor, Lovdijeff, thus: "Often he would forego lunch to interview a few students and help them along with their schoolwork or personal problems. He never ceased complaining because officials refused to allow him to eat lunch in the mess hall with the prisoners. Had they given him a cell, he would have taken it. . . . When night school convened at 6 p.m., the Christ [a.k.a. Lovdijeff] would be there beaming, radiating, and he'd teach passionately until 10 p.m. Then, reluctantly, he'd go home to suffer in exile until school opened the next day" (36). Recalling a friendship between himself and a Lenny-Bruce type in the prison yards, Cleaver relates the day they walked toward lunch together and his friend's eyes darted around in search of fellow whites to join in the chow line. Per his trenchant estimation of segregation in America, "The whites want to talk with you standing out in the yard, or at work, standing up, but they shun you when it comes to sitting down" (45). Later, Cleaver enjoys the coming together of both societies under the auspices of irresistible, black-originated popular music: "It was Chubby Checker's mission, bearing the Twist as *good news*, to teach the whites, whom history had taught to forget, how to shake their asses again" (193). Later, "I am convinced that Luci Baines Johnson, dancing the Watusi in public with Killer Joe Piro, won more votes for her old man in 1964 than a whole boxcar of his hog-calling speeches ever did" (200).

Finally, Cleaver was nothing if not a man of "action," since, as Nathaniel Mills points out, Cleaver, like his contemporary James Baldwin, "attend[ed] to the sexual and gendered operations of racial power in the United States" (56) and "espouse[ed] a politics of the body" (57) against the hypertrophied cogitations of white men. His writing makes bold if failed attempts to politicize his early career as a serial rapist, his obsession with white women, and sex in general. But it succeeds remarkably in delineating the psychosexual dynamics of racist American culture as well as sexual expression as a mode of liberation offered, withheld, and eventually regained as a black man in prison. He bridles under the restrictions against any reading material of an explicitly sexual nature—Mailer's *An American Dream*, for instance, and racy novels: "Go down [to the prison library] and try to find Hemingway, Mailer, Camus, Sartre, Baldwin, Henry Miller, Terry Southern, Julian Mayfield . . . J.O. Killens, etc.—no *action*" (*Soul* 48–49, emphasis added). In statements like this, Cleaver equates certain print media with a kind of freedom—sexual release—that he is repeatedly denied throughout his stay in prison, only exacerbating the longing he feels.

A key scene involves a guard destroying a pinup of a white woman in Cleaver's cell on the grounds that such pornographic material is forbidden. Though happy together in their early days—"She, a symbolic representative of the forbidden tribe of women, would sustain me until I was free. Out of the center of *Esquire*, I married a voluptuous bride" (7)—he returns to his cell one day to find that the guard had "ripped my sugar from the wall, torn her into little pieces, and left the pieces floating in the commode: it was like seeing a dead body floating in a lake" (7). Here Cleaver conveys the dense overlap between text and sexuality for a man behind bars; images of women substitute not only for the real women he is denied—he calls at one point for "a system under Civil Service whereby salaried women would minister to the needs of those prisoners who maintained a record of good behavior" (7)—but even for his chance to correspond with any "free" women not his own family members. Exceptions to this rule are women lawyers, and *Soul on Ice* is most famously a series of letters from Cleaver to Beverly Axelrod (and one of her own included collage-style[2]). With Axelrod he formed a passionate attachment through prison visits and said letters while she worked on his parole, and with her he shared a famed affair when he was freed in 1966.

Though bristling against prison restrictions, Cleaver yet recognizes how his imprisoned status heightens the seductive effects of Axelrod's every appearance: "If a man is free . . . and living a normal life with the usual multiplicity of social relations . . . , it may be that he is incapable of experiencing the total impact of another individual upon himself" (23). Gorgeously, he reproduces one of their typical breathless encounters: "He [the imprisoned man] has imperative need . . . to hear a woman's laughter at his words, to answer her questions and be answered by her, to look into her eyes, to sniff her primeval fragrance, to hear—with slaughtered ears—the sensuous rustling of frivolous garments as legs are crossed and uncrossed beneath a table, to feel the shy, delicate weight of her hand in his" (23–24). The sheer joy and intense erotic anticipation described by Cleaver in his devotions to Axelrod constitute his happiest moments in *Soul on Ice*, the material of sexual release, denied at the prison library, that is its own liberation.

To be sure, Cleaver's locating of liberation in white sexuality per se—"the white woman [is] the symbol of freedom. Every time I embrace a black woman I'm embracing slavery, and when I put my arms around a white woman, well, I'm hugging freedom" (160)—is troubling for many readers (see, e.g., M. Wallace 117–118, Joseph 213, and Taylor 90). His admission that as a young man on the outside, "I became a rapist. To refine my technique and *modus operandi* I started out by practicing on black girls in the ghetto . . . and when I considered myself smooth enough I crossed the tracks and sought out white prey" (14), reads as yet another indicator of Cleaver's enslavement to both unbridled physical urges and white standards of beauty that (as Cleaver himself discusses at length) enthrall us all. Yet in Cleaver's own view, "Rape was an insurrectionary act. It delighted me that I was defying and trampling upon the white man's law, . . . that I was defiling his women" (14). In my introduction, I noted that Cleaver regarded theft of property in the midst of a riot as a gesture of liberation (of said goods) that was simultaneously a strike for economic equality. In the same way, here Cleaver regards (or at least rationalizes) his making free with the bodies of white women as a claim upon white men's most valuable possession. Disturbing though much of this may be, Cleaver addresses black women by the end of the narrative as "black bride of my passion" and "my queen," and his marriage to Kathleen Neal in December 1967 was one of the most celebrated and long-lasting (however fraught) in Panther annals. As Kathleen Rout regards the matter, Cleaver's marriage to Kathleen likely "creat[ed] for himself the possibility of a love match that was, at least theoretically, unadulterated by negative psychological motives from the past" (40).

A Return to Action: Newton and the Early Panthers

Cleaver would intersect with the Panthers as their own careers as actors on the public stage—as free persons and arms-bearers per their constitutional rights—made its greatest impact. They thus signaled a shift from rhetorical stances taken by Malcolm X and later SNCC leaders (i.e., talking the talk) back to movement-style concerted action (i.e., walking the walk). Notably, Newton is not on record as an especially gifted speaker; his "high-pitched falsetto" (J. Morgan 147) and tendency toward "abstract" and "dull" arguments (D. Johnson 26; see also Shakur, *Assata* 226) often confused and disappointed his audience. His and co-BPP founder Bobby Seale's original motivation was "increasing frustration with the endless discussions about inequality and oppression that seemed to go nowhere" (J. Morgan 130; see also Avril 17–18) among their fellow students at Oakland's Merritt Junior College. Yet just as King's activist career involved both political gains *and* attempts to address economic inequality (e.g., the Poor People's Campaign and the Memphis garbage workers' strike) that ended in failure if not tragedy, the Panthers' career took a similar course: their early political interventions with Oakland police and the California State Assembly largely succeeded, while their economic "survival programs" were marred by charges of extortion and misappropriation when they were heeded by the wider world at all. As opposed to the nonviolence characterizing all "walks" taken by King and his fellow civil rights protesters in the Southern Christian Leadership Conference and SNCC, the political and economic actions undertaken by the Panthers were underwritten entirely by constitutionally protected arms-bearing and sometimes by illegal gun violence. As noted earlier, even the Party's organ, the *Black Panther*, belongs to the category of "walking" or "action," due to both its politically effective messaging (less its voluminous words than its inspiring images, about which more will follow) and its economic import: selling the *Black Panther* on urban street corners nationwide became a chief source of daily, however poorly compensated employment for Panther rank-and-file, and proceeds were basic to maintenance and operation for Panther offices. Shakur describes her first exhilarating evenings with the newspaper staff: "As we wrapped the papers in bundles, printed addresses, and counted out papers, we sang Panther songs and marching chants. . . . Somebody always gave me a lift home and i [*sic*] would fall into a happy sleep refreshed and renewed" (*Assata* 205).

As in Malcolm's *Autobiography*, Panther leaders sometimes wrote of legal entanglement as a means to attain inner freedom. In *Revolutionary Suicide* (1973), Newton describes his initial bookish route to raised consciousness and social subversion; he studied criminology, police training, and especially local law—its loopholes and inconsistencies, its strong emphasis on defendants' rights—to excuse himself from "petty crimes" of all kinds: burglarizing cars and houses, short-changing store clerks, credit card and payroll check theft, among others. Newton adeptly politicizes every aspect of his crimes and prosecutions: he "never scored on Blacks under any condition, but scoring on whites was a strike against injustice" (82). Following a crime spree, whenever he had "liberated enough cash to give me a stretch of free time" (82), he would read political novels such as Kafka's *The Trial*, Camus's *The Stranger*, and Hugo's *Les Misérables*, wherein he "identified with Valjean" (82). Newton especially enjoyed defending himself in court, where he would dazzle his opponents with his intricate knowledge of the law's exploitable contradictions and in general "show my contempt" for the proceedings (83). He once got away with having won books in a card game that he knew were stolen because "they did not know how to deal with an oppressed Black man who knew their law and had dignity" (86). Eschewing in these early days any bid for economic equality, which the Panthers' Ten-Point Program will stress in its demand for full employment, Newton politicizes his ill-gotten gains: "To take what was mine and what the white criminals called theirs gave me a feeling of freedom" (82–83). The goods and cash stolen are his ticket to "as much leisure time as possible. . . . I wanted most of all to be free from the life of a servant forced to take those low-paying jobs" (83).[3]

Here Newton construes freedom as a monastic disinterest in material wealth: "Though I starved, my time was my own and I could do anything I wanted with it" (83); "I wanted freedom, and possessions meant nonfreedom to me" (71). Thus Newton names the chapter about a massively deprived six months in the Alameda County Jail "Freedom." Sentenced on an attempted murder charge when he stabbed a loudmouth at a party, Newton locates freedom in the self-discipline that deprives his enemy jailers of the satisfaction of wearing him down. He recalls instructions from Mahatma Gandhi, regarding "tak[ing] little sips of nourishment, just enough to keep up one's strength, but never enough to have to defecate until the fifteen days [of solitary confinement] were up" (105). On the bare, filthy floor of "the Hole," he assumes a rigid position "with my back arched and only my shoulders and tight buttocks touching down on the floor" that he later learns is a "Zen Buddhist posture" (106). As Cleaver used *Soul on Ice* as a form of inner focus that allowed him to write his way back into free society, so Newton, though physically confined to an unconstitutional degree, uses the self-imposition of even more severe limitation to create the space between official constraint and his own superior self-control to locate his realm of liberation: "By then [the hole] held no fears for me. I had won my freedom" (107).

Back on the street by 1967, Newton and founding members of the Black Panther Party took up their activist role, facing down a squad of on-edge Oakland police in front of the Party office that had opened a month before. Armed as they always were with a clear understanding of the Constitution, the California penal code, and an array of legally borne weapons, Newton and his comrades observed the statutes barring loaded weapons in a vehicle and thus only "snapp[ed] live rounds into the chambers" (M. Newton 18) of their M-1s once they had stepped from their car. Having completed a relay of stares, threats, and trigger-cocking between Newton and the white officers taking the lead, Newton once brazenly warned the point man, "If you shoot at me, swine, I'm shooting back" (qtd. in Seale 92; see also H. Newton 132–133 and M. Newton 18–19). Panther Party founding member Bobby Seale in his best-selling memoir *Seize the Time* (1970) relates an even more incredible incident occurring shortly thereafter, when a Panther police patrol—in the '54 Chevy that easily rode (and often did) six or seven young black men with guns in full view—drew the attention of "Badge 206." Again Newton at the wheel challenged the officer's (literally) unwarranted opening of his car door and leaning in: "Huey grabbed the pig by the collar, pushed his head back up against the roof of the car, then shifted around and . . . kicked him in the belly, shoving him all the way out of the car. The pig fell backwards about ten feet," and in another moment "Huey's feet hit the ground [and] he was jacking a round off into the chamber" (95). Amazingly, Newton's threat—"go for your gun, and you're a dead pig" (95)—was meekly heeded by the harassing cop, who backed away as Newton lectured him on the Fourteenth Amendment, proscribing confiscation of property (the guns in the car) without due process. As Seale concludes, "This pig was scared" (96).

As often occurred when Newton and company confronted harassing police, a large crowd had gathered for both of the aforementioned incidents. In the earlier one, fellow citizens were ushered inside the protected space of the Party office, where street theater was transformed into street TV; per Seale, "We had a big, wide, clear picture window . . . [and people] were leaning on it, kissing the window just to listen to this shit" (92). Thus in this and other widely witnessed instances, "power to the people" converted into power *from* them—the safety in numbers of vigilant audience members who policed the police's every move (see also Avril 22–24 and J. Morgan). Leigh Raiford observes, "'Spectacular' activities like the Panther police patrols, the sortie into the Sacramento legislature, and the first few in a series of very public trials gained the Panthers increasing visibility and recognition. . . . Their presence on the streets . . . enticed and frightened viewers with new ways of conceiving black politics, black efficacy, and black subjectivity" (144). Newton records on a later occasion, "By now the people were laughing at the cop," and though he had "driven off, steaming mad," he returned to inform Newton that "if it was night [that is, if the audience were home in bed], you wouldn't do this." Newton regards the police to have reduced themselves to the criminal element, "working at night" (131) against inner city victims when no one was watching. Perhaps the most startling chapter from this founding moment in Panther history involves Party members' arrival, once more armed to the teeth, at San Francisco

International Airport in late February 1967 to escort Malcolm X's widow Betty Shabazz to a memorial in her late husband's honor. As popular historian Michael Newton tells it, "At first anxious to disarm the Panthers, [airport security officers] were warned off by Newton's forceful assertion that his men were violating no laws. A hasty check of the criminal statutes proved him correct" (24; see also H. Newton 139–140 and Seale 120–125). In this bygone era of maximum liberty (see also Koerner 7–8), the Panthers walked to the gate, shotguns in plain view, and seated themselves in the waiting area for the hour or more it took Shabazz's plane to arrive.

Of course, it was the Panthers' weapons-bearing that drew both hostility from the establishment and the admiring attention of the Oakland community, many of whom pledged allegiance to the Party in its early days for the express purpose of exercising their own Second Amendment rights under the snout of a harassing pig. In their emerging moment, the Panthers and the police were in mortal struggle over possession of the guns themselves, literally over which Americans did and did not enjoy the freedoms guaranteed in the Bill of Rights: once an officer accused Newton of "just turning the Constitution around" (Seale 90) when he actually expected the cop to respect his right to bear arms. In an equally egregious challenge recorded in Anne Moody's narrative, peaceful protesters are accosted by angry whites who "started snatching the small American flags [they carried], throwing them on the ground, stepping on them, or stamping them. Students who refused to let go of the flags were stabbed with rifle butts" (249–250). At a later demonstration, white police taunt protesters, "Freedom? . . . Y'all wouldn't even know what to do with it" (337–338). In her own memoir, Assata Shakur remarks, "The only time white amerika [*sic*] is in favor of Black people having guns is when we are using them to do amerika's [*sic*] dirty work" (*Assata* 222), as in the Vietnam War. With respect to the Panthers' main allure for the "brothers on the block," Newton remarked that "the weapons were a recruiting device" (113). Seale confirmed that "the gun is where it's at" (92), and Panther movement literature from these early days, as well as a popular chant at demonstrations, informed the black community that "it's time to pick up the gun."

Although the "lumpen" populace most heavily recruited throughout Panther history may have encouraged the Party toward the violent rhetoric and action that led to its undoing (see Booker), it was the action orientation of this vigorous, often desperate underclass that suited it so well to the confrontational stance. Thus the Panthers took their place in a line begun by violent revolutionaries as early as Nat Turner and Denmark Vesey in the nineteenth century, Robert Williams in the decade prior, and recently cut short in the tragic but inspiring assassination of Malcolm X. As early as 1965, Newton countered a white police officer who was about to ticket a black motorist whose car had itself been sideswiped by a white driver: "The people [are] going to get guns of their own and take away the guns of the police. . . . That was the first time I stood a policeman down" (78).

These transformative encounters between armed black men and white police cannot but strike the twenty-first century reader—dealing on an almost weekly basis with national tragedies involving police shooting black citizens whose retaliating "weapon" is a book, a cellphone, or a pair of outstretched hands—as a fanciful tale from the Wild West. At this singular moment in the liberation era, Oakland's Black Panther Party armed themselves per their legal right to do so; the very sight—let alone the self-defensive actions—of "negroes with guns" sent shockwaves through the Oakland police and nearby county sheriff's departments, the California State Assembly, and Governor Ronald Reagan himself in the early months of 1967. In Newton's own trenchant recollections, "At first the patrols were a total success. Frightened and confused, the police did not know how to respond, because . . . never before had guns been an integral part of any patrol program. With weapons in our hands, we were no longer their subjects but their equals" (127). At the dawn of an era eventuating in a tragic tidal wave of gun-bearing (legal and otherwise) throughout inner city neighborhoods nationwide, these African American pioneers who dared take their Second Amendment rights onto the public stage achieved a rare moment of political equality courtesy of the old equalizer.

As Malcolm drew attention to his early speeches by provocatively weaponizing his request for "the ballot" with "the bullet" and as Shakur reacted to the assassination of MLK by contrasting useless news "bulletins" to the more effective response of "bullets" (196), so the Panthers understood that guns on view would create the national audience necessary for their own early statement-making. By early May 1967, a bill sponsored by conservative state assemblyman Don Mulford (and even nicknamed the Panther bill), outlawing the display of guns on public property, had reached the State House floor. The Panthers determined to witness the debate from the visitors' gallery as well as read out Executive Mandate #1—urging oppressed persons of color nationally and internationally to join their cause—to any reporters sufficiently interested to take note. Seale recalls the comedy of errors that constituted the Party's arrival in Sacramento. Assembled before the capitol complex with shotguns pointed skyward, the thirty or so Panthers did not know which building to walk toward when they arrived. Seeing a cluster of reporters, they set off in loose formation and were met with the gamut of reactions from "they must be a gun club" to complete shock. "I remember a brother in the background saying, 'Look at Reagan run.' I thought he was just referring to something symbolic, but . . . Reagan *was* over there with a bunch of kids" (*Seize the Time* 155) and famously interrupted his speech to the group to dash inside the capitol. Once there themselves, the Panthers were greeted with cries of surprise and resistance by security guards, then led not to the visitors' gallery but accidentally onto the assembly floor itself, where lawmakers dove under desks and ran for the exits at the sight of them. Even the Panthers did not mean to cause this much of a stir, and the guards who had sought to prevent their entrance moments earlier now had to "turn them back with sheepish apologies" (M. Newton 30).

And yet their enacting of white America's worst nightmare—armed attack on a state capitol even though absurdly abetted by officials themselves—turned the Panthers' debriefing on the steps outside from mere talk into revealed word. Reporters asked Seale to read the mandate three or four times so that they could get down in its entirety the independence declaration of this newly emerged but deeply disaffected nation. Per Jane Rhodes, "Communications . . . took up a significant portion of the Black Panthers' labors [and] . . . constituted a unique discursive universe" (92). Although national media were ultimately responsible for fear-mongering and distortion in much Panther coverage, Kathleen Cleaver reflected, "We figured being in the news kept us from being killed. . . . As long as the press was there, the police wouldn't go after us" (qtd. in Rhodes 115). The weapons-barring Mulford Bill was voted into law "by a huge majority" (H. Newton 160) six months after the Panthers came into being, but their "armed" protest in Sacramento that day gained them a national spotlight that would follow them steadily over the succeeding tumultuous half-decade. Studying the symbolic, spectacular import of their every political gesture, Amy Abugo Ongiri remarks that the Panthers, despite their reliably negative view of cultural nationalists, would succeed "more in the influence they wielded in popular culture than in military culture" (30).

While at the beginning they exercised Second Amendment rights on an almost daily basis, the Panthers maximized other freedoms guaranteed in the Bill of Rights whenever the occasion required. They insisted upon free speech and free assembly when the police threatened to shut down a rally, once beat a gun charge because of a warrantless search, and stressed to stationhouse personnel the Miranda rights that were breezed over during interrogation and booking. With judges and prosecutors they pleaded the fifth, insisted on self-representation when it suited their aims, and—when during the Chicago 8 trial Judge Julius Hoffman ordered Seale bound and gagged in the courtroom—protested with every available muscle against cruel and unusual punishment. While Martin Luther King Jr. and his early-1960s cohort had ensured the essential physical freedoms (many stemming from Supreme Court rulings) whose long denial to deserving fellow citizens seared the white national conscience, the Panther Party's adoption of both the Declaration of Independence (their ten points conclude with a verbatim restatement of its opening paragraphs) and the Constitution lays claim to citizenship almost two hundred years overdue. As Davi Johnson, reading rhetorical high points of Newton and the BPP, observes, "The jeremiad allows [African American] rhetors to criticize American society while simultaneously expressing faith in its ideals, resulting in a discourse that is at once separatist and integrationist" (18).

If Pantherdom's first chapter began and ended with the revolutionary episode of arms-bearing in the run-down inner cities and expansive legislative spaces of northern California, chapter two—that which in some ways spelled the end of the Party itself—regards the greatly disputed[4] matter of Newton firing one of these outlawed weapons with murderous outcome. During a bogus traffic stop in late October 1967, Newton was taunted by Officer John Frey, whose racist attitudes toward Oakland's African American community were widely known. Newton was threatened with arrest and possible assault and wound up—after what he swore in court was a loss of consciousness—with four bullet wounds to the abdomen. Frey himself was shot and killed and fellow officer Herbert Heanes wounded; Newton and his passenger flagged down a passing motorist (whom they were later accused then exonerated of kidnapping) for a ride to the nearest ER. Following Newton's capture and arrest, an arduous, lengthy, but ultimately exhilarating and identity-forming national action to "Free Huey!" began. Claiming he had been caught in the crossfire of the panicked cops' own gunfire, Newton feared the gas chamber and gained the influential support of Charles Garry, a local white labor lawyer with many wins to his credit. As Garry created a convincing case in the months following Newton's arrest, the Free Huey! campaign in poor urban communities nationwide was spurred by dramatic write-ups in the *Black Panther* and by speaking engagements by Seale, other key Panthers Eldridge Cleaver and David Hilliard, and SNCC luminaries Carmichael and Brown.

Speakers' fees and pass-the-hat collections paid Newton's mounting legal bills, and a huge revenue source was the sought-after campaign paraphernalia: bumper stickers and buttons with *Free Huey!* in large letters and an iconic photo of Newton in a wicker chair, surrounded by the accoutrements of race pride: the spear, the shield, and the shotgun. This image was indeed everywhere in the years during (and the better part of the decade following) Newton's trial, imprisonment, and release in 1970. Though the trial enormously drained the energy, focus, and resources of the Panthers' wider agenda, it provided the Party the urgency, drama, unifying cause, and ultimate reason for being that it otherwise might never have had. Per Ongiri, "The arrest of Huey P. Newton . . . inadvertently provided the symbolic moment around which Panther critique and organizing would focus for the next three years" (45). During the trial, "the Black Panther Party successfully transformed the [steps of the Alameda County] courthouse from its representative role as a vehicle for state power into a theater for the display of . . . spectacular blackness" (48). Yet in the view of journalist Hugh Pearson, Newton's release on a technicality was in fact the beginning of the end for this revolutionary leader and the Party in general: "Newton was released to multitudes who, thanks to the work of Eldridge Cleaver and his friends, viewed him as God. . . . [Recalls a source,] 'He always said he was not that poster on the wall . . . and he couldn't live up to it'" (222; see also J. Morgan 147). Ironically, Newton's newfound freedom led only and immediately to his tragic enslavement to the cocaine addiction and mental instability (including violent paranoia and delusions of grandeur) that would end his life some twenty years later.

The *Black Panther*'s coverage of the Free Huey! saga was also key to the paper's own success; for this and all stories, its heavy reliance on photography to record events lent the figures depicted therein an aura of celebrity and folk-heroism. In Raiford's estimation, the *Panther*'s photo archive did "iconographic rather than simply documentary work. . . . Like the earlier civil rights movement, the Black Panther Party proved itself to be incredibly photogenic" (145). Raiford notes that in *Panther* coverage of notable court cases, mugshots taken from police files were "surrounded by accounts of their cases and what they have endured in police custody. . . . Within this new context, photographs in the *Panther* recast the players in the state's theater: government agencies materialize as perpetrators of excessive violence against innocent community activists" (195–196).

With respect to Newton's own trial, his iconic photo and related images of crowds outside the Alameda courthouse appeared on front pages and in editorial sections, draped with operatically scaled headlines including "World Awaits Verdict" and set amid "wallpapers" of repeated type, such as "Huey must be set free!" and "Free Huey or the Sky's the Limit" (qtd. in C. Austin 184). While the editors declare on a back page in the 23 November 1967 issue that "Huey P. Newton is the victim of a frame-up . . . dragged to jail on phony, made-up charges" (4), this reverses the view on this issue's front page: "A black man, confronted by a bloodthirsty cop . . . has a right to defend himself—even if it means picking up a gun and blowing that cop away" (1). Mid-issue, a telegram from the Progressive Labor Party concurs that "Brother Newton had every right to defend himself" (23 November 1967, 10). In statements like these, Frey's death is read not as a friendly-fire accident void of political significance but as a clearly intentioned reaction on Newton's part to either his own wounding or the prior deaths of thousands in similar confrontations. As Newton himself describes the important propagandistic function of the *Panther* newspaper at this point, "Once we began to give our own interpretation of events, Black people realized how facts had been twisted by the mass media" (169). Rhodes describes the *Black Panther* as "the most important site for the party's efforts at self-representation" and as "the only medium completely under their control" (96).

To the degree that *Black Panther* images found a more receptive audience than the lengthy, hortatory, hypnotically repetitive articles ever did—as Newton himself remarked more than once, "Ours is not a reading people" (see also Brewer 15)—the Panthers' resident artist Emory Douglas (and later the cartoonist J. Tarika Lewis, a.k.a. Mantilaba) presented viewers a starkly satiric, distorted to the point of grotesque, frightfully violent outlook. Erika Doss observes that Douglas's "visually dominant" style with respect to both art and layout "was a 'tremendous factor' in the *Black Panther*'s circulation, which reached over 100,000 weekly by 1969" (179). But this style was starkly opposed "to the 'happy' type and obfuscated styles of psychedelic imagery" (184). Although children were valorized in these pages as the future's shining hope, this framing does not preclude the occasional illustration of a sweet toddler holding a gun almost as long as herself or stacking up blocks to spell out "Death to the Fascist Pigs" (2 January 1971). It is disturbing to consider the effect some of these images might have had on youngsters latching onto issues as paperboys, children of subscribers, or just neighbors in passing: "the pig" in the agonized throes of death, flies about its mouth and eyes, sliced by bullets, hanging by his curly tail from a black hand, or receiving a dose from a can marked *acid* by that same revolutionary hand. Mantilaba depicted scenes of police shootouts, with realistic male figures—black victims or white police in pig masks—spurting blood from bullet holes and toppled against police cars, trash cans, or the garbage-strewn gutter. While Newton once rejected a proposal to distribute a coloring book to the Breakfast for Children clients due to its violent content (Churchill 88), these disturbing *Panther* images did not face the same censorship on the assumption that only adults would see them (88). Per Rychetta Watkins, "Imagery, as much as the articles and commentaries in the paper, reinforces the ultimate goal . . . to revolutionize the black community and develop it into a vanguard" (70–71; see also Davenport). But even Douglas by the late 1970s had gone in search of more affirming images; as he informs Doss, "When the party changed to community action so did my art, from pigs to kids" (186).

Finally, aside from their early confrontations with the police, the Panthers' most vital political gestures were their arrest and imprisonment—the locus of movement-galvanizing (because hugely liberating) "Free Huey," "Free Bobby," "Free Ericka," and related campaigns. Attendance at Panther rallies skyrocketed, as did Panther Party membership, in response to several of these high-profile arrests—all of which indeed resulted in reduced charges, early release, or simple freedom for those on trial. Yet even the Panther movement, whose action-packed early days grabbed headlines and changed many lives, traced downward paths from walking to talking even more tragic than the one followed by SNCC in the early 1960s: wars of vituperation between Panther leaders occupied almost all of the final issues of the *Black Panther* newspaper, reflecting the discord that led to exile for Cleaver and multiple murder and assault charges for Newton. *Panther* paper salesmen and circulation staff were involved in an East Coast / West Coast conflict that resulted in more than one death, and on a lesser but much more widespread level, ordinary Panther members were exploited and disillusioned by endless commands to move more issues. When selling the paper became their main revolutionary activity, many left the movement.

Seale in Chains

As Newton's *Revolutionary Suicide* is minutely concerned with the particulars of his various incarcerations and legal contests, so Seale's memoir *Seize the Time* provides just-as-illuminating perspectives on his own ordeal as a federal prisoner and then defendant in the trial of the Chicago 8. Just as Cleaver espoused in *Soul on Ice* a "politics of the body" (N. Mills 57), so Newton in his memoir exhaustively delineates the indignities and cruelties he suffered due to his uncooperative attitude behind bars. He describes long bouts of darkness, isolation, silence, limited movement, putrid food, and "the Hole's" barbaric toilet system, which was itself a hole in the floor that frequently overflowed. So, too, during the long ride in custody from Northern California to Chicago, does Seale describe physical limitations of every kind; he is heavily chained and handcuffed between two other federal prisoners for the duration of the trip, with whom he must move in lockstep, clumsily settle at picnic tables to eat lunch, and even empty his bladder: "After I opened my pants and urinated, I would step to the side and let the other guy go and then the third guy, and then we'd go on around and one of us would slowly hobble to the face basin and bend real close. . . . You couldn't sit on the toilet if you had to. The only place I could have a bowel movement was inside the jails where we were left overnight" (301). In some ways reminiscent of iconic road narratives from the period—Kerouac's *On the Road* (1957) and Thompson's *Fear and Loathing in Las Vegas* (1972) among other countercultural classics—Seale on his journey through the countryside recalls rejuvenating moments from his youth, including hunting with his father and riding the rails on a lark with a friend. But he also experiences a sense of entrapment intensified by the wide-open spaces around him: "I thought about how this government continues with the private property concept with all that unused land, when there are black people, brown people, and American Indians cooped up on reservations and in ghettoes. . . . Why is it that black people can't have some of this land? We were promised forty acres and two mules when we were freed from slavery" (310).

Despite the several restrictions of the journey, Seale raises the consciousness of his two fellow prisoners and their federal escorts, all of whom are white. Trapped together for the long hours that they are, Seale learns about the impoverished backgrounds of his fellow prisoners and introduces them to the Panthers' interracial, class-based agenda. He "organizes" other prisoners (black and white) in the jails he stays in and remarks upon fair treatment when received from jailers of both races. His work shares with the memoirs of Assata Shakur and Angela Davis an ethnographer's focus on conditions ranging from fair to execrable, including for Seale one in the middle of Missouri that "was the dirtiest, filthiest jail I'd ever been in. . . . The cells had crud in the corners. . . . The bunks were only two feet wide with little mattresses that were ripped and filthy, with bugs crawling all over them" (311). From one such unsanitary jail, Davis contracts a full-body "jail fungus" (302), and at last arriving in Chicago, Seale learns that he has caught a crab lice infestation from his night in Missouri; such cruelties call stark attention to the physical situation of the African American in chains, yet Shakur, Davis, and Seale all use the power of the pen to shame the jails they go through.

Seale's ordeal, famed in the media as the trial of the Chicago 8, was notoriously presided over by Judge Julius Hoffman, whose antipathy to the antiwar movement, led during the 1968 Democratic Convention with tumultuous outcome by the men on trial, was as pronounced as that of his one-time law partner Richard J. Daley, Chicago's mayor. Hoffman also had interest in war munitions manufacture, making his position against the antiwar demonstrators about as biased as it could be. As he did in the police car on his cross-country trek, so Seale stood out from his seven accused coconspirators as the only black man, who in fact had limited to no association with the white radicals charged alongside him: his purpose in Chicago had been literally all talk and no action—speeches on behalf of imprisoned Panther leaders with little if anything to do with the white protest and rioting that characterized the convention overall. In other words, the charges against Seale seem strained at best—yet another attempt by federal and local prosecutors to physically detain, financially exhaust, and falsely impugn the Party's most prominent members.

With leaders of diverse left contingents (including SDS, SANE, and the Yippies) among the defendants, the trial was "an ideological prosecution against dissent itself" (Langum 104), and the "conspiracy" charge that connected them ironically pointed toward the deep schisms characterizing the Left at this point, despite their amorphously threatening interchangeability to the Establishment hauling them into court. Just as ironically, the court may have wished to show its liberal-era "broadmindedness" by purposely integrating its cast of conspirators, again despite Seale's lack of connection to the crimes being tried. Yet Seale like many leaders of the Black Power era understood the huge theatrical impact, in both comic and tragic modes, of criminal trials of the day and in his role here made the greatest political gesture of his career (see also Burris 42–43). Discussing a film character based on Seale, Greg Burris remarks, "Like Seale, Bobby X's behavior in court is markedly different from that of his white codefendants. While they look for ways to defy the law, Bobby X seeks to identify with it [by insisting on counsel of his choice or self-representation and protesting cruel and unusual punishment]. . . . Bobby X asserts an underlying equality by over-identifying with the law" (35).

Judge Hoffman established between himself and Seale an intractable battle of wills when Seale's repeated insistence on his right to self-represent was deemed disruptive, and he was ordered bound and gagged in his courtroom chair. Seale describes the tortuous confinements he endured during this phase of the trial; to prevent Seale from rattling his chains in protest, straps were tightened to the point of stopping circulation—hence the ultimate imposition on his freedom of movement, down to the involuntary movements of blood flow and heartbeat. When an overly tight gag impeded blood to his brain, he nearly passed out. Because Seale maintained a muffled protest behind his mouth tape regarding his Eighth Amendment rights, Judge Hoffman required a literal gag: "When it began to look like I needed breath, [the guard] set the wad of rags right up against my mouth and began to press real hard with the palm of his hand. . . . I could even feel the blood seeping out of my gums" (344). Eventually pitying their captive, even the guards defy "that damn judge" (345) and allow Seale to return to court with only the bandage. Although cameras were not allowed in the courtroom, the press described Seale's bondage in daily detail, and his image was captured by Chicago courtroom artist Franklin McMahon, who eventually drew more than four hundred images from the trial for Chicago and national publications. Chicago 8 attorney William Kunstler declared the courtroom "a medieval torture chamber" (qtd. in Langum 113), and as David J. Langum reports, "A song about the gagging of Bobby Seale rose to the Top 40 chart" (114).

One might contrast the image of Newton spellbinding his courtroom opponents with his command of the law, or the iconic photo of Newton in his own chair—the wicker throne with the spear and shotgun at his side—to the utterly subjugated position of Seale at trial to understand the mounting desperation with which white America greeted the prospect of African Americans asserting their constitutional rights. Though the Newton photo frightened most whites of the period, the image of Seale strapped to his defendant's chair shamed the jury and the public; realizing his strong-arm tactics as a travesty, Judge Hoffman soon declared Seale in contempt of court, sentenced him to an unprecedented four years in jail, and severed his case from that of the remaining seven. From the court records, it is clear that Hoffman had lost control—and lost the respect—of the entire defense team; the Yippies joked their way through the proceedings, Hoffman (Abbie) casting aspersions on Hoffman's (the Judge's) Jewishness (suggesting he should have been working for Hitler), and both Abbie Hoffman and Jerry Rubin draping the defendants' table with a Vietcong flag or coming to court in judge's robes which, when ordered removed by the actual judge, revealed police uniforms underneath. All of the defendants regularly violated Judge Hoffman's proscriptions against standing up and speaking out.

Circus is the word most frequently attached to the trial; Langum quotes the judge reviewing Seale's contempt charges: "On a number of occasions, the trial so completely disintegrated that it could not be said that a judicial proceeding was in progress" (117). Later, Kunstler celebrated the egregious unfairness of Judge Hoffman as a boon to the leftist cause (Langum 109). Yet when not defending themselves in court, Panther chapters across the U.S. were mourning the loss of murdered comrades from Oakland and LA to Chicago to New Haven to New York; the shooting of the first Party rank-and-filer, Lil' Bobby Hutton, in Oakland in April 1968 and leading Chicago Panthers Fred Hampton and Mark Clark at the hands of police in December 1969 were early and late low points in Panther history. The impunity with which Chicago police conducted their raid on Hampton's home, in the middle of the night while the man slept in his bed, with broad smiles as they carried Hampton's body down the stairs, drove many in the Party into a final despair.

Activism and Intra-Party Conflict

Although Panther histories tell the story of the Party's diverse "survival" programs—Breakfast for Children, free clinics, and Liberation Schools—all of the national attention, and much of the national memory, regarding the Black Panther Party involves gun-wielding, gun violence, and repeated demoralizing failures to bring justice to bear; as Davi Johnson notes with respect to the Panther's top figure, "Newton failed to change his popular image as an aggressive demagogue" (27). Regrettably, even much of their community programming resulted from the violent extortion of local businesses or resulted in Newton's embezzlement of private donations and public funds (see Pearson 240–250, chapters 10 and 11). Such strong-arming is even in evidence in coverage in the *Black Panther*. In the 9 August 1971 issue, Bill Boyette, president of the local liquor distributors' association, is vilified as an enemy of the people. The story castigates successful black capitalists like Boyette, who refuse to support the breakfast program for hungry community children, yet the Panthers' insistence that Boyette and fellow businessmen make regular, sustaining donations to Panther programs or face ruinous community boycotts smacks of the protection racket that it somewhat also was. Historian Lauren Araiza reports that following a similarly motivated boycott, "the Safeway store located at 27th and West Streets in Oakland was soon forced to close" (204). Such actions, seemingly necessary and surely well-intended but backfiring in their longer-term detriment to the community, reveal a connection between these hostile campaigns and the more violent and destructive rioting and looting that befell many of the same neighborhoods in this period.

In terms pertinent to this project, Seale commented outside Boyette's store, "We've heard a lot of speeches about freedom must ring out of this land, about freedom this and freedom that. But . . . don't talk no freedom to us until you start talking about giving away something for free to the people" (B). Echoing the Diggers from neighboring San Francisco, whose Free Stores were established in express opposition to the "st. vinny de paul rot" that was the ordinary lot of the poor, Seale insists, "We're talking about giving some brand new clothing away. . . . Brothers and sisters aren't going for any more rummage sale stuff." Not until all of the items promised by the Panthers are "F R E E, [are we] really beginning to deal with freedom" (B). One photo from the Boyette story of a smiling citizen with a box of groceries on his shoulder is captioned "1965, Watts Riot? No, Oakland, 1971," presenting the Panthers' free food program as a sensible alternative to reckless looting. But from the view of beleaguered entrepreneurs like Boyette, there may have been little difference, and the campaign succeeded with little more longevity than did the Diggers' several attempts.

The intensity of the Panther critique of black businessmen indicates the lengths to which the Oakland-based Central Committee would go when crossed in its intentions, and one of the most demoralizing aspects of the *Panther* coverage in the early months of 1971 was its dramatization of the grievous infighting of Newton (who was then billing himself, cult-leader style, as "the Supreme Servant") and his West Coast cohort against Eldridge Cleaver, who led the East Coast faction (from Harlem to Algiers). Shakur, who began her own association with the Panthers on the West Coast, was mainly affiliated with the Harlem branches by this point and was verbally attacked by Newton acolytes when she declared the name "Supreme Servant" to be "ridiculous" (*Assata* 226). A West Coast emissary's "eerie reverence" for Newton "made [her] sick" (229). Although the reasons for the split were many and complex, each group accused the other of insufficient radicalism and failure to pursue Party aims, and Panthers faithful to each faction were caught in the crossfire. Notable is the early-1971 shooting death of Robert Webb, a Cleaver supporter who confronted members of Newton's group selling the *Black Panther* on Harlem's 125th Street. In retaliation, the New York–based Newton supporter and *Panther* distributor Sam Napier was shot to death and then had his body burned in retaliation (see, e.g., C. Austin 313–320).

At this conflict's low point, selling the *Panther* was a badge of partisan visibility—somewhat akin to gang colors in more broadly based conflicts—that sufficiently interested Party members wound up dying for. Once the battle was joined, Newton and company used the *Black Panther* to denounce and purge various "enemies of the people," including Cleaver but also Michael "Cetewayo" Tabor; his wife, Connie Matthews; Richard "Dharuba" Moore; Elmer "Geronimo" Pratt; and the entire New York 21. They embarked on a "free Kathleen [Cleaver]" campaign (6 March 1971), suggesting that she was being held hostage by her husband in North Africa, where the couple had recently emerged following Cleaver's flight from charges related to the police shootout that fatally involved Bobby Hutton. Weeks later, Cleaver's faction began publishing the short-lived *Right On!*, using the black panther logo from the *Panther*'s masthead but countering the denunciations then filling the pages of the *Black Panther*. A story about the death of Webb signs off, "Death to the Supreme Fools, Newton and [David] Hilliard" ("On the Assassination" 3); a later article by cartoonist Brad Brewer calls for "DEATH TO THE REVISIONST" artists such as Emory Douglas, labeled as a "Revisionist Al Capp" (15). In a famous intercontinental phone call recorded for a live television audience (and reproduced in the same *Right On!* issue), Newton and Cleaver took turns ousting each other from the Party. Thus in addition to the many trials, deaths, and related tragedies filling both papers' pages at this point, "the *Black Panther* itself became a tool for defamation" (qtd. in C. Austin 296) and a weapon in an internecine war of shameful and finally deadly proportions (see Pearson 191).

Finally, the story of the Black Panther Party following its early, successful maximization of mid-1960s political freedoms was a series of assaults, arrests, and imprisonments—false, deadly, or otherwise—that both limited the movement of the Panthers themselves (even as they moved the movement itself first nation- then worldwide) and "tied up" whatever funds came the group's way by speaking engagements and donations from white radical sympathizers. Per Langum, "The [government's] plan succeeded beautifully. Black Panthers and other militant groups bled to death" (79). Seale's memoir invaluably accounts for every $25 or $50 scrounged together to bail out "a brother" (an actual Party member or anyone whose plight the Party got wind of) as well as the thousands required to get their fearless leader out of the slammer: "Anytime we can get him out, we're going to free Huey" (108), but "those kinds of bails and enormous ransoms which they put on the brothers were a means they continuously used to deplete our funds" (370). Ward Churchill has documented, via several hundred references to FBI and related official documents, gross actions by local and federal operatives throughout the late 1960s and early 1970s to restrict the physical movement, political reach, and civil or human rights of Party members. The majority of the Panthers' contribution to the late-1960s struggle for civil rights remained a bid for political and then even physical *freedom*, while their several attempts at economic *equality* went underreported, suspected as communist subversion, or reduced in value by their own apparatus of wrongdoing. Both Newton and Cleaver looked back on the Party's early days with fondness and pride; in the original months of its existence, it was just "Panthers, pigs, and guns" (Cleaver, "On the Contradictions" 10; see also Newton 169). As Richard Slotkin observes that America is unique in its assigning of "mythic significance" (13) to the violence it has experienced, so Newton also remarks, regarding the movement as a whole, "Our ten-point program was ignored and our plans for survival overlooked. The Black Panthers were identified with the gun" (357)—as were fellow travelers Assata Shakur and Angela Davis, whose rich lives as activists, daughters, sisters, nieces, and people are overshadowed by histories focused on the gun charges and subsequent trials that brought them each to national attention.

In its final, less lauded era, Elaine Brown famously assumed chairmanship of the Black Panther Power in 1974 by announcing, "I'VE GOT ALL THE GUNS AND ALL THE MONEY" (*Taste of Power* 3) and staring down both pigs and Panthers—male colleagues contemplating a power grab in the vacuum left by Newton's flight to Cuba following more murder charges—as she did. She was intensely identified with the Party's masculinist ethos since her early designation as songstress of the revolution. Her famed ballads were "A Very Black Man"—"I'd cry for the man, I'd die with the man, I'd lie with the man, I'm the woman I am just with a very black man"—and "Poppa's Come Home," a lullaby that frames black male absence in a positive light: "Oh, child, Poppa's come home to take care of you. . . . He went away, long, so long ago . . . not by his choice. . . . Look at him child, look at his handsome black face." In a live performance in 1969 or 1970, Brown plays her piano beneath a collage of male party leader images while a series of men, body guards or stage security, come from behind the curtain to peer over her shoulder toward the audience. Their furtive gestures of concern that simultaneously suggest a threat to Brown's own safety or simply a desire to borrow into her renown by leaning into the shot epitomize the precariousness of Brown's tenure with the BPP. Hailed as the Party's de facto official songwriter, she was even "commanded" (Thomas 85) by David Hilliard to record an album (proceeds from which, like the *Black Panther* newspaper also edited by herself at one point, surely went into Party coffers).

In the aptly named *A Taste of Power*, Brown acknowledges as she justifies the violence she engaged in—"for a black woman in America to know that power is to experience being raised from the dead" (319)—that was also a feint of ruthlessness to fend off incursion from male competitors (see also Deck 369). Reviewer Ellen Dubois discerned the tortured gender politics on display in Brown's memoir, as when Brown "kept [a top staffer] under shaky control by sleeping with him and on whom she depended to beat up opponents" (253). According to Perkins, "Unlike either Davis or Shakur [but reminiscent of Anne Moody], Brown relays . . . moments of uncertainty in her continuing activism, citing the stress, fear, and anxiety of operating under intense police surveillance and repression" and "of enduring gender expectations from within the Black Panther Party itself" (13). Comparing Brown's leadership role to her early stint as a dominatrix (to a man who left before paying for her services), Perkins notes that "her power [within the Party was] rigorously circumscribed by the wishes of another. . . . Newton always retain[ed] the power to usurp control at any time" (123).

Meanwhile, Brown is credited with doing "her best to redirect the party away from deadly confrontations with police and toward establishment of a black militant political machine." In fact, she not only walked the walk but "*ran* for a seat on the Oakland City Council and threw resources into the free-breakfast and Panther educational programs" (Dubois 253, emphasis added). Brown also managed the campaign of Lionel Wilson, Oakland's first black mayor in 1977, and ran voter registration drives in Oakland in a remarkable full-circle return to the older-style programming that inaugurated the freedom movement in the South.

More recently, in 2005, Brown has sought election as mayor of Brunswick, Georgia, on a platform of "full employment for the 16,000 [mainly poor black] residents" (Watson 1) and as the Green Party's presidential nominee in 2008. She has been programming for prison reform (e.g., transportation for families) since 1969, and the most widely known of her several current-day nonprofits is the National Alliance for Radical Prison Reform.

Conclusion: Freedom of Speech and the Right to Bear Arms

Contradictions between constraint and freedom abound in the lives and writings of Black Power leaders from this period; for three of these (Malcolm X, Huey Newton, and Eldridge Cleaver), the confinements of prison provide relief from the endless hustle and directionless drift of their early lives, enabling modes of intellectual and spiritual self-discipline ironically readable as these men's first taste of real freedom. As a boy, Newton was so at liberty in his school environment that his faculty failed to instruct him in basic literacy; prison provided the time, privacy, and relative peace of mind to buckle down to his studies of both the dictionary and the law, and with these tools post-release, he created a movement. Malcolm honed his debating skills, and Cleaver perfected the essay format; all three emerged from their early prison experiences intellectually stronger and—to borrow the phrase from Stokely Carmichael, "ready for revolution." By contrast, Carmichael and H. Rap Brown were college men, while Angela Davis closed in on a terminal degree in philosophy from UCSD, with no need of prison's scholastic atmosphere; these three suffered greatly from the threat of imprisonment, curtailing their freedom to move and speak as the Constitution guaranteed. Just as damaging to their careers perhaps was their having cut themselves loose from the program-based infrastructure that appeared a vestige of a more integrationist age but that the Black Panther Party attempted to resurrect on their own terms to benefit their community.

Early moments of maximal liberation were Malcolm X's early electrifying orations and the Panther Party's remarkably successful, fully armed encounters with the Oakland Police, the San Francisco Airport security apparatus, and the California State House. These groundbreaking occasions of freedom successfully defended garnered terrific media attention, being narratives reminiscent of America's own days of declaring independence, whether the white mainstream hearing the stories and seeing the images recognized the resemblance or not. Immediately after these early successes, the nation's legal apparatus swung into action, hounding SNCC leaders into jail or exile, snatching the Panthers' Second Amendment rights out from under them, and physically confining Panther leaders, East Coast revolutionary Assata Shakur, and West Coast revolutionary Angela Davis—in chains or in death—when the curtailing of political freedoms failed to do the trick.

Throughout this chapter, I have distinguished "talking" (speechmaking) from "walking" (activist attempts to enlarge the sphere of political freedom or to redress economic inequality). As useful as it is to trace the turn within the black rights movement, from action to speech back to action again, it is notable that—per the pattern established in the introduction—most of both the talking and walking discussed in this chapter belong to the category of political freedom sought and enjoyed with phenomenal success: Malcolm's marvelous gifts as a rhetorician and political firebrand will be celebrated forever, and even disarmed, the Panthers' association with "the gun," as well as the skillful inroads they made against police and courts attempting to deny them their rights, are powerful examples of heroic activism with its own lasting legacy. The old-style programming attempted by the Panthers late in their career—the free breakfasts and Liberation Schools—are marked by their rarity in this context, their brevity as successful campaigns, and the extortionist practices that marred their existence. Ann Cook challenged overreliance on cultural nationalism to locate an authentic Black identity when "there is absolutely no substitute for hard organizing. . . . [W]hatever hard cash we need, for psychological reasons, must come from us" (196). Cook may have had in mind not only high-visibility cultural nationalists but even the antinationalist Panthers themselves when she averred that revolution was impossible "when we are spending more time with theatrics than with hard, unglamorous organizing" (201), even as many more recent commentators have noted the great political efficacy of Black Power and Black Panther theatricality per se. Finally, however, nothing should surprise us about the Panthers having to strong-arm black businesses and local grocery stores to fund their programs: breakfast for all and forever would be impossibly expensive for any independent group to provide for long, and the Panthers can probably be credited for inspiring (if not intimidating) the federal government to develop the USDA's School Breakfast Program, begun in 1966 and established nationally in 1975. Ultimately, it is only the system (in Panther parlance, the pigs) that has the economic means by which to realize a revolutionary Breakfast for Children program on a sustained and nationwide basis; this was always the most universally acceptable (however underadvertised) plank in the Panther platform, a single element of social gain that reflects regrettably on many needs yet unmet.

CHAPTER 2

NOTHING LEFT TO LOSE

MAXIMIZING LIBERTIES IN THE LATE 1960S FREE-FOR-ALL

Ben Caldwell's brief, searing satire *Riot Sale; or, Dollar Psych Fake Out* (1966) was one of several written by this Black Arts dramatist, aimed not only at the white power structure but at the hypocrisies of his own black revolutionary context. As with many important plays from this period, *Riot Sale* was "street theater" in more ways than one. Raw, immediate, and hugely relevant to the urbanites of color forming its main audience, it was also set at the iconic corner of 125th Street and Lenox Avenue in Harlem, thus bringing the street into the theater as often as players in this period brought their theater into the streets. Per the canonical Black Arts alumnus Ed Bullins, street theater is "the play or dramatic piece (skit, morality or political farce or black 'commercial' that subliminally communicates blackness) written expressly to be presented upon urban streets or adapted to that purpose" ("A Short Statement" 93). In *Riot Sale*, not only are all of the stores complete with "neon bright" (32) lighting and elderly merchants at the ready, but a riot breaks out—a crisis tragically common to urban streets in late-1960s America. With respect to the inquiry of this project, the play stages a showdown between politics and economics as construed throughout the freedom-era literature: committed revolutionaries with no "property damage [as] their objective" but only "blood. White police blood" (31) versus, in the play's broadly comic reveal, an "anti-poverty cannon" that shoots "millions of dollars!" (32) into the scrambling crowd, causing them to forget their revolutionary aims.

One message might have been sent had the cannon only dribbled out quarters and nickels, appeasing the rioters with the pittance federal administrations have always used to stave off revolt. Caldwell's *The Job* (1968), in which a condescending employment agent is beaten to death by a revolutionary whose "job" it is to destroy the white economic structure, makes such a case. But *Riot Sale*'s "millions" challenge the audience much more radically to reject even major paydays that might have provided a true approach to economic equality. For the committed revolutionary, principled poverty is to be withstood if not embraced on the way to total "freedom!" (32), cried for by the rioters just before the cannon shoots. A Wayne

State student and radicalized witness to the Detroit riots of 1967 shared Caldwell's dismay: "I wanted to see people really rise up in revolt. When I saw the first person coming out of the store with things in his arms, I got really sick to my stomach and wanted to go home. Rebellion against the white suppressors is one thing, but one measly pair of shoes or some food completely ruins the whole concept" (qtd. in Kerner 93). Though the total value of stolen goods looted into each household during urban riots of the late 1960s might have been paltry, the arson that often followed was one way for an oppressed citizenry to take away "millions!" from the powers that be: \$40 million in property damage was recorded for Watts (some \$300 million in today's dollars), \$40 to 45 million for Detroit, and \$10.2 million for Newark. Historian Gerald Horne notes that in Watts, "business—notably big business—did suffer grievously in the fires of August. The harm it endured was a central reason why these events were investigated so assiduously" (108).

As Caldwell and his fellow revolutionaries envisioned, all of the major urban uprisings of the late 1960s originated as a radicalized political response to police brutality, but the galvanizing incident indeed gave way within hours if not minutes to "economic opportunity": the breaking of windows and liberating of necessities and luxuries denied the looting citizens throughout much of their lives. A local reporter described Watts as "a consumer riot, with racial, political, and class overtones" (qtd. in Horne 111), and many studying urban uprisings of the late 1960s point to the underlying rationale for much looting behavior: churches, schools, and libraries spared; credit records destroyed in department stores with the most exploitative terms; liquor stores targeted as often for enslaving their neighborhoods as for their sometimes-coveted goods (see, e.g., Fogelson 129, Kerner 78, Hayden 33). As David T. Courtwright observes, "The 'commodity rioters,' frustrated and tantalized by the seductive [media] images of consumption, helped themselves when the opportunity arose. Television showed them how to do it. (It also showed them—a nice irony—how to steal televisions)" (*Violent Land* 249; see also Lupsha and MacKinnon 6). As a complement to these studies, I focus here on the revolutionary aspects of looting itself, attacking as it did the stark economic inequalities that have always structured American life and using as it did simple theft to reply to the theft of labor, wages, and wealth that had characterized the majority of African Americans' encounters with U.S. capitalism for centuries. Even Langston Hughes's beloved Jesse Semple sagely observed that "when you loot a credit store, you are just taking back some of the interest they have been charging you for years on them high-priced installment things" (qtd. in Horne 188–189).

I do not open this chapter exploring urban-uprising narratives of the late 1960s so as to classify such intensely political actions with the lifestyle liberalisms, enacted most often by a privileged white middle class, to be considered later on. But like acid-dropping, commune-joining, and related acts, decried by the Johnson/Nixon-era establishment (and just as memorably in Barry Goldwater's disavowed 1964 campaign film, *Choice*) as the end of the world as we know it, late-1960s urban rioting was a maximizing of personal liberties that shocked complacent white Americans into whatever raised consciousness they would achieve in this period, even as it inspired others of their ilk to foment the backlash that finally claimed center stage in the Reagan era. Per the position taken throughout this project, I cannot agree with Caldwell's view that attacking riot police (dressed by Caldwell in futuristically impenetrable gear, at any rate) was a larger revolutionary gesture than running off with the government's millions. Certainly, those engaging in urban uprisings throughout the period risked (and, tragically, lost) their lives for much less in numerous looting incidents. The need demonstrated in such desperate acts suggests that the attainment of bourgeois living standards is its own elusive, revolutionary goal.

In each uprising, the vast majority of arrests and an unforgivably high number of police shootings were for theft of stolen property—even an item as minor as a color television—not rock- or Molotov-cocktail-throwing or even sniping from rooftops. To be sure, "snipers . . . were the pretext used by officials to commit thousands of violent acts against the whole Negro community" (Hayden 41) in riot periods, including the inadvertent shooting of apartment dwellers in the midst of firefights and retaliatory attacks on black-owned businesses. But multiple riot histories (e.g., F. Harris 125, Hayden 41) report that few snipers were ever arrested, fewer still were convicted, and "what is certain is that the amount of sniping attributed to the rioters—by law enforcement officials as well as the press—was highly exaggerated" (Kerner 335). Though Horne asks, as we all must, "Why shoot to kill for a box of shoes?" (74), in fact, looters were the easiest targets in the riot moment: hobbled to whatever extent by the booty in their arms; torn as to whether to throw down their stolen goods or hang onto them as they fled; dazzled, however fleetingly, by the prospect of new clothing for their children or sufficient food for the week; looters were easier marks than battle-ready rock-throwers, snipers, and roadblock-rushers encountered elsewhere at the scene. Too, per the terms set down in this project, looters' attempts to redress economic disparity was an irritant so intense to white society that it was deemed as deserving of deadly force as was sniping or vehicular homicide. If anything, looting offended white Americans' naive sense of cheating and fairness *more* intensively than a good old-fashioned shootout between equally armed men. Bracketing now (as it was bracketed then) the toll taken in human lives, the price officialdom paid for shooting snipers was only the cost of ammunition, which postriot ballistics records indicate the police spent with abandon.

Horne quotes a Watts precinct commander who early on "personally made the decision not to shoot looters" (57), and a major general with the National Guard, overseeing riot control in Cambridge, Maryland, in 1967, told the postriot Kerner Commission that "I am not going to order a man killed for stealing a six-pack of beer or a television set" (qtd. in Kerner 329–330), advocating the use of tear gas instead. But an unnamed LAPD officer, who was "not going to make any effort to stop anyone from stealing. They can steal the whole town if they want to," was seemingly mainly motivated to return later to his "wife and two kids" (qtd. in Horne 63)—not out of any humanitarian concern for looters themselves. Horne notes that even such feelings of "alienation," let alone scruples regarding the ethics of deadly force, "soon [were] blown away by with a fusillade of buckshot" (63). In

Newark, when sufficient levels of official frustration were reached, "orders were given for police to use 'all necessary means'. . . . Murdering looters was now possible" (Hayden 34).

From their own standpoint, the Kerner commissioners regarded tear gas technology as a means by which to free law enforcement from the ethical dilemmas involved in deadly force; they compared the effectiveness of CN to CS gases (330) and even hailed the advent of "sticky tapes, adhesive blobs, and liquid foam" (331) technologies, prospects so self-evidently ludicrous that they were satirized by the great Chester Himes in his posthumously published *Plan B*: "Small armed tanks with the latest in anti-riot devices, such as anti-riot glue to immobilize rioters by sticking them together in balls of ten or twelve each, paralyzing gas, sneezing powders to incapacitate rioters with paroxysm of sneezing . . . were all needed by police to patrol the streets" (138). As with the several drug technologies that I will discuss later, freedom-era weapons technologies were considered to provide their users more options, more license, and more liberty in pursuit of immediate goals and gratifications, but each one fomented the anger and frustration that always escalated the conflict between the people and the police along traditional (much more deadly) lines.

As noted in my introduction, urban riots of the late 1960s were a literalization of "Freedom now!" that satisfied longings more disciplined, MLK-style direct actions could not. In Tom Hayden's formulation, in his early review of Newark rebellion, "The riot was more effective against gouging merchants than organized protest had ever been" (30), and moments of unalloyed joy were seemingly their own justification. Harvard urban studies professor Robert M. Fogelson reported that during Watts, residents "left their homes and, with a camaraderie and enthusiasm usually reserved for festive occasions, thronged the streets" (128); Horne describes Watts, a mass inversion of the high and the low, as "a carnival of the oppressed" (239), while in Detroit, "a spirit of carefree nihilism was taking hold. To riot and to destroy appeared more and more to become ends in themselves" (Kerner 91). There, "numerous eyewitnesses [told] . . . of the carefree mood with which people ran in and out of stores, looting and laughing, and joking with the police officers" (Kerner 88). In Newark, New Jersey, Governor Richard Hughes also noted the "'carnival atmosphere' of people looting in daylight. What for Hughes seemed like 'laughing at a funeral' was to many in the community more like a celebration of a new beginning" (Hayden 32). As Hayden observes, "One reason why there was so little quarrel over 'who gets what' is that there was, for a change, enough for all" (33).

In the smoking aftermath of the Watts rebellion, its youthful veterans informed Bayard Rustin, "We won because we made the whole world pay attention to us. The police chief never came here before; the mayor always stayed uptown" (qtd. in Rustin 150). Per Fogelson's findings, "Many believed that the [Watts] riots had improved the position of their race" (122), and sociologist Robert Blauner quotes a Rhodes scholar who, visiting his home in Watts, felt "for the first time . . . pride in being black. . . . Now I can say, 'I'm from Watts'" (Blauner 187; see also Hayden 32).

This young man called the riot a "masterful performance" (Blauner 187), reflecting trenchantly on all of the public confrontations and lifestyle liberalisms to be discussed in this chapter: from the political theater staged in the Attica Prison yard to the spectacle that was anti-Vietnam protest and outlandishly dressed hippiedom to the tragic displays of junkies on the nod, freedom-seekers in this period took to the streets to make their positions plain, and print and electronic media played key roles in creating, magnifying, framing, and ultimately containing revolutionary events in the period. While reading them as "mere theater" delimits the significance of said events, Caldwell and other dramatists show that such stagings also had widespread and lasting political import.

The Riot Narratives

Two controversial reports on late-1960s urban rioting, *Violence in the City* (1965), popularly known as the McCone Report, and *Report of the National Advisory Commission on Civil Disorders* (1968), popularly known as the Kerner Report, indicate the shift in sensibility not only for riot commissioners but likely for much of the American mainstream in the three short but eventful years between them. Writing in *Commentary* in March 1966, Bayard Rustin compared McCone to the equally incendiary Moynihan Report, which Rustin had critiqued in the same magazine eleven months earlier. Both, he notes, pathologize black family life in their diagnoses of ghetto problems; so doing, both "steer . . . clear of confronting the thorny issues of Negro unemployment as such" (qtd. in Fogelson 148). To a certain extent, Watts was indeed a victory for enforcing greater awareness, leading to the more broadminded appointees to the Kerner commission and that report's much more progressive outlook—despite its ultimate failure to induce actual change or even to be acknowledged by the president who commissioned it. Both McCone and Kerner discuss the political aspects of the rioting in question—police brutality, jails, and the courts—as well as its vital economic particulars: not only the valuable looting and expensive arson of the riot event but the joblessness, miseducation, and substandard housing that hugely motivated the rioters in the first place. Thus "freedom" in its most tragic permutation echoes Janis Joplin's plaintive rendition after all: a SNCC officer described the Newark rioters as "young people with nothing to do and nothing to lose" (qtd. in Hayden 17), while a Watts resident explained, "We haven't got anything, our parents didn't have anything, we are not looking to get anything, and we just don't give a damn" (qtd. Horne 100).

Replicating the radical-liberal divide that split many freedom-seeking groups in this era, a young militant in riot-torn Milwaukee told Kerner commissioner Fred Harris, "Don't ask us about little, relatively minor things like housing and jobs; it's your whole system that is bad" (*Alarms and Hopes* 7). Yet earlier that day, another group of men already assuming the yoke of parenthood that might have tamed their radical ways eagerly sought access to that very system: "'We want a job, man. Get us a job, baby. Can't you get us a job? Get us a job. We want a job.' They all spoke at once, almost in unison. . . . 'I want a job, man,' [one] said. 'I've got five kids. I need a job'" (*Alarms and Hopes* 11). Ironically, a final interviewee "lost my job because I was picked up in the riot" (11). In the wake of Watts, as Horne trenchantly observes, black radicalism easily forged an unholy, however accidental, alliance with white capitalism: "The so-called Black Scare as evidenced by the [Nation of Islam] stood for separatism and was ambivalent about dipping into public coffers to fight poverty. . . . Some conservatives felt that the nationalists' emphasis on identity was a welcome respite from the Left's emphasis on income redistribution" (132). Rioting in the long, hot summers of the late 1960s was its own (literal) bridge-burning between the black community and broader society.

John A. McCone was a native of San Francisco and prominent Republican businessman who had just stepped down from four years as head of the CIA under LBJ, whom he felt had insufficiently heeded his pleas to expand the war in Vietnam. He was asked by California's Democratic governor Edmund "Pat" Brown to head the commission investigating the Watts disaster. The commission had access to a dozen full-time staffers, some thirty consultants from California universities, and a witness list preponderant with politicians, police administrators, and civil rights leaders. Only ten of the more than eighty questioned were ordinary residents of Compton or Watts, in addition to a local dentist and a real-estate broker, but Horne reports that "some [local residents] felt the panel would produce a whitewash and did not want to be party to it" (342). McCone's resultant sixteen volumes of research and testimony (Fogelson 129), was digested into a mere 88 pages, a brevity criticized by early reviewers. Seemingly in atonement for this oversight, Kerner's review (of both Detroit and Newark, as well as smaller uprisings) was some 630 pages, with 50 pages of charts alone. The McCone Commission also was chastised for its reductive view of the riot's most active participants as an unstable criminal element. Fogelson critiqued its "riffraff" theory (118–119; see also Horne 343 and Kerner 111), when a much more diverse segment of Watts society participated in and especially encouraged the youthful rioters. Likely McCone and Fogelson came from the same liberal origins in their profiling of the rioting citizens; McCone took care to accord the vast majority of Watts residents its own highly valued status of "law-abiding," while Fogelson would ask the commission to consider the magnitude of the problem when mass numbers of ordinary, and ordinarily law-abiding, citizens yet felt the need to rise up.

To its credit, the McCone Report foregrounded the economic crises afflicting Watts as insistently as would Kerner three years later; it opens diagnosing the rioters as "seeming[ly] caught up in an insensate rage of destruction" (1), but much of the report simply enumerates the many urgent reasons the riot was utterly sensible, not to mention long overdue. First in the commissioners' estimation was "not enough jobs to go around" and second was "not enough schooling to meet the special needs of the disadvantaged Negro child" (2). From the just-brewing Moynihan controversy, the commissioners might have but failed to learn that framing the indeed vital need for better schools in terms of "special needs" and "disadvantage" would be ill-received as a critique of ghetto families. Worse, McCone's reason #3 for the Watts riots is "a resentment, even hatred, for the police, as symbols of authority" (2). Here rioting Los Angelinos appear to reinhabit their zombie-like insensate rage, acting out an inexplicable hatred for the police due to their phobic or superstitious fears of authority symbols. The distance between this formulation and the actual experience of white policing in mid-1960s Watts characterizes the skew of McCone's perspective on police conduct throughout its assessment. Certainly a "symbol" never clubbed a bystander over the head nor shot a man through the chest for stealing a six-pack of beer. Yet McCone relentlessly questions the veracity of citizen complaints against police brutality—in general and throughout the days of the riot—and finds the police to have acquitted themselves with perfect decorum in almost every instance. Though the report will later make "massive, expensive, and frankly experimental" recommendations to improve life in Watts for all concerned, its opening gambit, which would have encumbered zero dollars to state with greater accuracy, is squandered in defense of a law-and-order mentality that would survive as its most shameful element.

Throughout McCone, police conduct before and during the riot is framed entirely in terms of the "impressions" and "attitudes" (28, 29, 32) of Watts residents, against the "facts" (32) delivered to them by the LAPD. In a thesis moment for Blauner, the report "violates its responsibility to truth and impartiality by refusing to examine the factual basis of Negro opinion while stating the beliefs and hearsay of white officers as established truth" (176). The terms *alleged* and *allegations* appear constantly; for instance, "witnesses recited to us instances of alleged brutality and excessive use of force" (28), with the certainty of "witnesses," "recitations" and "instances" well undercut by the commission's view that these are mere allegations after all. In a representative moment, the commission preserves the police from all negative implication: "In each of the 1964 riots, 'police brutality' [quote marks in original] was an issue, as it was here, and indeed as it has been in riots and insurrections elsewhere in the world. The fact that *this charge* is repeatedly made must not go unnoticed, for there is real danger that *persistent criticism* will reduce and perhaps destroy the effectiveness of law enforcement" (29; emphases added). Summing up, the commissioners vow to "correct existing impressions" (29) and not surprisingly reject the prospect of a civilian review board, as it would, with the police once more in the role of beleaguered victim, "endanger the effectiveness of law enforcement" (32).

One of McCone's more worthwhile inquiries regards the shocking aspect of this riot's locale. As pointed out early in the report, a spate of uprisings had occurred the year previously (and in earlier decades) in cities back east, the assumption nationally being that such disorders were specific to rusted-out, tenement-blighted, older cities, not the spread-out, palm tree–lined, ocean-breezed precincts of Tinseltown. The commissioners enlarge the mystery by noting that the homes of LA's Watts district were, as in surrounding white areas, "single-family structures [with] the streets and lawns . . . well kept for a poverty area" (77). As Fogelson observes, for "most Americans, a slum is defined by its deviation from a middle-class residential suburb. And on the surface Watts does not deviate very much—a fact which no doubt helps explain why so many Los Angeles whites found the 1965 riots beyond belief" (138). Yet the commissioners themselves quickly note the deteriorated condition of many of these single-family dwellings as well as the lapses in public services that built resentment within the community. They imply without naming the irony of the spacious, suburban feel of Watts in fact making jobs almost impossible to get to: in "the excellent discussion of [LA's] woefully inadequate transportation system" (Blauner 173), the commissioners show that residents of Watts, with its excessively complicated, expensive bus system, are as "trapped" as those living in concrete jungles back east. Even "the nearest public hospital was two hours away by bus" (Peirce 664). Finally, with respect to housing, it is notable—and noted in McCone—that an egregious economic insult in California's immediate past was as incendiary to the Watts riots as was the political crisis attending the arrest of Marquette Frye, typically cited as Watts's igniting incident: in November the previous year, Proposition 14 repealed the Rumsford Fair Housing Act, its earlier statewide mandate to open neighborhoods to all home-buyers.

However, the commissioners took away with the left hand what they had offered with the right, suggesting once again that the problem lay mainly with oversensitive Watts residents who had "felt or had been encouraged to feel that they had been affronted by passage of Proposition 14" (McCone 4). Rustin wryly critiques the understatement of this admission—"Affronted, indeed!" deploring the "three-to-one majority" (152) by which the proposition had passed. Equally troubling is the all-in-their heads terminology of "feeling" or even simply being encouraged to feel that they had been insulted when, as far as the commissioners were concerned, no actual insult had occurred. McCone audaciously describes the WWII mass migrations into South Central LA as "Negroes pressing ever more densely into the central city and occupying areas from which Caucasians have moved . . . develop[ing] an isolated existence" (2) thereby. In this fanciful rendition of war-era reality (taking place in U.S. cities nationwide), it is Watts residents themselves insistently moving in on top of each other, crowding already-occupied houses and rooms and creating the isolation that breeds alienation, as if redlining, restrictive covenants or Proposition 14 had never occurred.

In the midst of this rampant revisionism, perhaps McCone's truest moment is its realization—despite LBJ's shock and despair that Watts should follow so hard on the heels of major legislative victories and related Great Society measures—that great disillusion prevailed: "Publicity given to the glowing promise of the Federal poverty program was paralleled by reports of bickering over the mechanism to handle the program . . . , and when the projects did arrive, they did not live up to their press notices" (4). To alleviate these disappointments, the commissioners call for "a continuing urban rehabilitation and renewal program for south central Los Angeles" (79)—instead, notably, of either integrating the areas adjoining Watts or connecting existing neighborhoods and residents with opportunities beyond. They propose a "new massive, expensive, and frankly experimental onslaught on the problem of illiteracy" (58), and they support Governor Brown's "California proposal" to the Johnson administration, a $2.5 billion dollar jobs program, $250,000,000 of which would go to California. With more insight than they perhaps realize, the commissioners admit that "especially as Vietnam costs escalate,

. . . one can readily imagine that months, if not a year or two, might pass before approval would be given and money made available, *if it ever is*" (41, emphasis added). While the McCone Report deserves a measure of critique, one could hail its call for jobs, literacy, and better neighborhoods—or lament the fact that such calls, no matter how generous their terms, were never more in the impossibly expensive Vietnam era than howling into the wind.

While the McCone Report seems rightly named for the prominent chair with the conservative views who preeminently shaped its findings, the Kerner Report would have been more correctly named for the two prominently progressive commissioners in the group whose later writings confirm their signature throughout its pages: Senator Fred Harris, a two-term Democrat from Oklahoma, and John Lindsay, the popular liberal Republican mayor of New York. Harris and Lindsay conducted many of the onsite interviews in riot-recovering cities and were famously spat upon by young, disaffected riot veterans who barely stood the presence of their white interviewers. Their joint-authored *State of the Cities: Report of the Commission on Cities in the '70s* (1972) takes up many of the themes detailed in Kerner, including poverty, education, and housing, while Harris's sole-authored *Alarms and Hopes* (1968) also hits these vital themes and reprises notorious incidents reported to the Kerner Commission: Newark buses lined up at city hall and filled with overnight arrestees, Detroit apartment-dwellers killed in a hail of bullets from panicky police. In a 2017 email interview, the then eighty-six-year-old Harris confirmed that he and Lindsay "made every motion" reviewing the staff-generated language constituting the report (see also Cannato 206). They led a six-member majority in the eleven-member commission, which read, discussed, and when necessary voted on every section. Ultimately Harris and Lindsay persuaded the group to their view and to the report's thesis moments: that "our nation is moving toward two societies, one black, one white—separate and unequal" (1) and that "white society is deeply implicated in the ghetto. White institutions created it, white institutions maintain it, and white society condones it" (2). *Implicated* is importantly understood in this project per its Latin origins as *tied to* or *enthralled by*. Kerner's insistence that gross racial inequities do not free one group while enslaving the other but radically curtail the freedoms of all Americans is one of its many enduring legacies.

Its most vital contribution is likely its radical departure from McCone with respect to implicating the police per se; while McCone protected officer conduct by any means necessary, Kerner uses most of its six hundred pages to criticize overreach from local police and federal troops. Especially enlightening is its long view: McCone looked back in fear to a riotous summer of 1964 in eastern cities such as New York, Rochester, and Philadelphia (2), while Kerner looked back in dismay to police going amok in Birmingham and rural Mississippi at the start of the decade. Kerner regarded what I will call southern cops' grievously "liberal" use of fire hoses, attack dogs, and violence against civil rights marchers as directly inspiring to and responsible for urban rioting: such instances of "white terrorism" caused "a general erosion of respect for authority in American society and reduced effectiveness of . . . community restraints on violence and crime" (204, 205), creating a national climate of revolt.

Where McCone complimented the LA courts for "meet[ing] statutory deadlines for processing the cases of those arrested" (25), Kerner lambasted the chaotic and unconstitutional means by which arrestees were booked, arraigned, and tried in the days following each riot: "Regular detention facilities were swamped. Detroit's main city jail, built for 1200 persons, was crammed with over 1700. Precinct lockups built for 50 prisoners received 150 or more. The juvenile detention home built for 120 held over 600 during the riot. . . . 1000 arrestees were held in an underground police garage for several days, many without adequate food or water. Others were held for over 24 hours in city buses" (340). In court, "some judges failed to advise the defendants of their legal rights. After one group-arraignment, a Detroit judge told the next group of defendants, 'you heard what I said to them. The same things apply to you'" (341), and judges regularly set exorbitant bails and imposed harsh sentences by way of sending a message to those on the outside still contemplating the riot option. Newark's chief magistrate, James Del Mauro (who pleaded guilty to tax fraud in 1974), "rejected the attempt by cab-driver [John] Smith's attorney . . . to file criminal complaints against the two police who arrested" him. Gallingly, the judge described Smith, whose brutal beating by police for tailgating ignited the Newark uprising, as "this particular man, if I recall from reading the papers, that originally caused the rioting" (qtd. in Hayden 57). Finally, the issue of late-1960s urban rebellion belongs most pertinently to this chapter on lifestyle liberalism through its focus on police rioting against the urban populace with such excesses of authority that it is readable as liberalism in its worst guise. In this era, even the police as implicated in the violence of the late 1960s were enslaved by (later in this chapter, the term will be *addicted to*) the freedoms they accrued for themselves.

To the degree that urban riots, recalling Caldwell's satire, were street theater at its most riveting, Kerner took incisive aim at the role of media in their coverage of these events. Here the dilemma differentiating a "free" press from a responsible one found numerous manifestations: the use of "'scare' headlines unsupported by the mild stories that followed," "report[ing] rumor that had no basis in fact" (Kerner 364), and à la the McCone Commission, "rely[ing] on police for most their information" (375). Perhaps not at all startling in our current era of reality TV, reporters exhibited a "startling lack of common sense" when they "stag[ed] events, coaxing youth to throw rocks and interrupt traffic" (377). Finally, and also reminiscent of the McCone commissioners, the media "failed to communicate to both their black and white audiences . . . the ills of the ghetto, the difficulties of life there, the Negro's burning sense of grievance" (366). On even an ordinary day, "the press acts and talks about Negroes as if Negroes did not read the newspapers or watch television, give birth, marry, die, and go to PTA meetings" (383). That is, it fails to cover the ordinary and heroic activities of African Americans with anywhere near the frequency of white coverage, let alone include them sufficiently as editors, reporters, anchorpersons, and television personalities. Their omissions "repeatedly—if unconsciously—reflect[ed] the biases, the paternalism, and the indifference of white America" (366). As noted in the preceding chapter, SNCC's H. Rap Brown and the Black Panther Party were acutely aware of the power of the media in the television age as well as their own need to attract media attention to advance their campaigns to the national level. The riot scene is the apotheosis of turning America's white-run media to the needs of a desperate urban underclass too long ignored.

Remarkably, LBJ sent forth the Kerner commissioners with the mandate to "let your search be free, untrammeled by what has been called 'conventional wisdom,'" without need to "put the stamp of approval on what the Administration believed" (qtd. in Kerner 537). Yet per the findings of historian Julian E. Zelizer, Johnson's "rhetoric belied the fact that he had stacked the committee with loyalists so he could contain how radical they could ever be" (xvii–xix). In doing so, Johnson assumed that the commission's findings would in turn free the president himself—that is, exonerate his administration and his Great Society programming—from charges of ineffectuality or, worse, of making matters worse. As Zelizer reports, however, "[chair and Democratic Illinois governor Otto] Kerner lost control. [Vice-Chair] Mayor Lindsay, whom Johnson had never liked much, and who the president believed wanted to use this as a platform for a presidential run, pushed his colleagues to be much more aggressive with their report. . . . Senator Harris, despite his earlier promise [to be a 'Johnson man'] and Johnson's threat [to 'cut his peter off' if he did not behave accordingly], joined the mayor in pushing the commission to be brutally honest" (xxvi). The Kerner Report flew off the shelves—Zelizer remarks upon a rate matched then only by *Valley of the Dolls* and that "millions of viewers watched Marlon Brando read parts of the report [on] . . . *The Joey Bishop Show*" (xxxiv)—but it was soon disavowed by its presidential sponsor. Johnson ignored the commission's many recommendations, refused to officially receive the report on camera, and told an aide, "I can't sign this group of [thank-you] letters [to the commissioners]. I'd be a hypocrite" (qtd. in Zelizer xxxiii). More broadly, "most observers concede that the implementation of Kerner Commission recommendations has been dismal" (Lipsky and Olson 172), while "there is no reason to think that chief executives suffer any penalties if they are faithless to the recommendations" (171). By withholding the stroke of this particular pen, Johnson thus freed himself, his administration, and his nation from having to confront the egregious economic disparities that fomented urban disorders of the period.

The Attica Uprising

Like the urban rioters dancing in the streets of late-1960s urban America, veterans of the Attica Prison riots (9–13 September 1971) fondly remember their early moments of tenure in D Yard as an oasis of freedom within the confines of Attica's heavily secured outer walls, which they never attempted to breach. Per historian Heather Ann Thompson, "Prisoner Carlos Roche very much liked the freedom of movement that the morning's upheaval had netted him" (64). The first evening,

Roche "watched as tears of elation ran down the face of his friend 'Owl,' an old man who had been locked up for decades. 'You know,' Owl said in wonderment, 'I haven't seen the stars in twenty-two years'" (88). As Thompson assesses the scene, "Despite the sense of foreboding, there were moments of levity and even . . . joy as men who hadn't felt the fresh air of night for years reveled in this strange freedom" (88). The only Attica inmate known to have penned a published narrative, Richard X. Clark, thought of entering D Yard as "stepp[ing] into another world. . . . Suddenly the sun was shining and everyone was smiling . . . I felt liberated. I had a sense of freedom" (qtd. in Wicker 18, second ellipsis in original). In the party atmosphere, complete with "drums, a guitar, vibes, flute, [and] sax" (R. Clark 76), another yard leader during the riot, jailhouse lawyer Roger Champen, told *New York Times* columnist Tom Wicker, "It seemed like you were on vacation, you know, a picnic so to speak" (qtd. in Wicker 140). In words close to those of one Watts rioter who construed both freedom and desperation in the act of urban revolt, a supporter of the inmates describes their plight: "When you don't give a damn, you don't have nothing to give up but your life" (qtd. in Wicker 234). Clark concurs, "What [the observers] couldn't understand is that we had nothing to lose. . . . By refusing the few scraps [of settlement] they gave us, which we didn't think they would implement anyway, we lost nothing" (114).

Not surprisingly, Clark's narrative provides a view touching in its detail and simplicity and clearly missing from the official and observer-based accounts. Since cells are opened for only one day a year, the Fourth of July, the men's convergence on D Yard feels like a celebration of patriotic proportions: "Liberation! Liberation!" cries one early arrival, although his theatrics are comically undercut when "shooting a gas pellet gun into the air . . . the wind blew the gas right back at him and he started coughing, and we all burst out laughing" (R. Clark 27). That night, "they served kippered herring and vegetarian beans with tomato sauce. It was hot and it was good, the first hot meal I had eaten in a couple of months" (53). Clark is evidently so elated by the turn of events, and so attuned to how quickly they might end, that "I didn't get much sleep those few lovely nights" (80). Instead, "we walked around, talking softly, just rapping. . . . There were many other brothers walking around that night, in twos and threes, just strolling" (80). The following evening, the men are fascinated by *Friday Night at the Movies* on the yard's TV system, only ever listened to via headsets in their cells before. While I will question later the significance of a hug between a black inmate and white journalist Tom Wicker as Wicker takes final leave of D Yard, Clark's embrace of a fellow inmate departs from the aggression that had characterized their every prior contact: "[A] white dude came up to me and said, 'Brother Richard. . . . I called you a nigger, and I'm white and I know Muslims hate whiteys.' Then he threw his arms around me. . . . Anyway, it was a heavy feeling" (Clark 75). Clark adds, "In prison they always try to make you hide your feelings, and . . . I mean, you dig someone, they make it sound like you're getting in his pants. . . . So what you have to do is set an extra-hard image for yourself" (76), which is allowed to dissolve into simple fellow feeling in the Attica breakout's heady early moments of freedom.

Many of the Attica narratives, however, observe freedom's shift into criminal liberties against fellow inmates shortly into the proceedings: three were murdered for "undermining prisoner solidarity" (Thompson 97; see also M. Bell 10 and McKay Report 283–285) by talking to a reporter, and two nineteen-year-old twin brothers who found themselves at Attica on a parole violation were gang-raped in a bathroom (see Thompson 65) to their lasting trauma. Another prisoner happening past a bathroom "saw a bunch of guys in there, all shooting up" (qtd. in Thompson 65), having "taken advantage of their initial moments of freedom" (Thompson 65) to loot the prison pharmacy. A night under the stars transforms into something more ominous when "the inmates brought a grinding wheel into D Yard. Troopers have seen sparks flying from inmates' weapons in the night" (M. Bell 17). As with many other experiences of freedom gained in this period, this was an instance of personal liberty-taking stretched to a violent and tragic extreme. Though Clark claims, regarding three prisoners later found dead in their cells, "It was the first we had heard of it" (100), he is quick to acknowledge, "With all the excitement there were about fifteen or twenty inmates running around getting high. They'd vandalized the hospital in C-block for drugs. I took the megaphone and asked all the brothers to turn in their hypos. . . . They had everything: pills, Thorazine, reefers, tranquilizers, even some heroin" (54). Later, "there was a problem with the homos. They were going crazy. . . . I told them that this was too serious a time for that" (55).

Like many-another uprising from the period, the Attica riot was a media event played for maximum worth by the inmates themselves as well as by reporters like Wicker, who used his role as an invited observer to pen a major Attica narrative, *A Time to Die* (1975). Special arrangements were made to set up cameras in D Yard, and early in the proceedings an inmate read a "declaration" (qtd. in Wicker 27) with the same political intentions of the Black Panthers' Executive Mandate #1, captured so memorably in TV coverage three years prior. Instead of the Panthers' ten points, however, and indicative of the exhausted excess characterizing such moments by the end of the long 1960s, the inmates make five demands—including amnesty for the uprising and transportation out of the country—followed shortly by "15 practical proposals" (29) that even Wicker the print journalist saves for an appendix, and finally "28 points." These points indeed offer meaningful reform, including religious freedom, a healthier diet, and more recreation time (see Wicker 320–322) but were rejected by the inmates for lacking the key amnesty provisions. Wicker remarks, "To some extent, the inmates' rancor may have been staged, or false. . . . [T]he cameras inevitably turned the moment into 'political theater' as well as political negotiation" (39). The inevitable commission following the disaster, known as the McKay Commission, stated more pointedly, "The televised interviews . . . and speeches . . . undoubtedly contributed to the feeling of power and importance which had been growing among the inmates" (295) and turned the scene into a sort of "national political convention" (296). A McKay witness considered the great potential—and subsequent great disappointment—attending this attempt to televise the revolution: "I think [the inmates] got the idea that they could bring about vast changes for their people on the outside through the impact of the television screen," a misunderstanding that led inevitability to "violence in order to satisfy" (qtd. in McKay Report 296) both the inmates' own dashed hopes and the media's self-fulfilling, never-ending search for dramatic conclusions.

Unlike the takedowns that concluded Watts, Detroit, and Newark, however, the police entering Attica on the last day filmed their own rendition of the events, giving new meaning to the notion of a "media circus," as egregious acts of violence went unpublished or unrecorded. McKay criticized state police cameramen for "still becoming familiar with equipment" as chaos reigned, for failing to provide batteries for cameras once the "prison power supply was cut off," and for lack of advance planning that "could have resulted in a complete and accurate record of the police action, even to the point of . . . identify[ing] individual troopers who acted improperly" (361). A later observer finds it "curious . . . that the cameraman could find his boss on the catwalks, but the tape fails to show troopers during all their shootings down there" (M. Bell 53; see also McKay Report 377). As TV cameras may have fomented inmate bravado during the standoff, so McKay notes that recording equipment would have tempered overreaction during the retaking: "If all troopers had been advised that their actions were being recorded on film, that would have provided some check on police conduct" (361–362). In the instance of Attica, both sides attempted to control the power of electronic media to stage their own story.

The Attica yard setting that at first had enabled such picnic-like conviviality soon became a death trap for the "turkey shoot" that one police commander explicitly warned his troops to avoid. Throughout the morning of September 13, law enforcers again ran amok as had the police in Watts and Newark; in the midst of clouds of disabling tear gas, they shot and killed twenty-six inmates and nine hostages who were brother officers; they wounded multiple other hostages and dozens of other inmates via random shooting as well as a gauntlet of stripping, beating, sodomizing, and barefoot runs over broken glass as prisoners were "rehoused" by force (see also McKay Report 433–435). Not surprisingly, only inmates were ever tried and sentenced for Attica violence—the uprising itself and the beating death of corrections officer William Quinn early on. The McKay Report aptly criticized "inhumane prison conditions" (325) for provoking the takeover in the first place, Governor Nelson Rockefeller for staying away during the negotiations (324), and state police and prison guards for "much unnecessary shooting" during the assault, as well as "exaggerated, embellished, and even fabricated" (335) statements defending their actions later. But such condemnation led to no legal action, and the extensive cover-up that protected these state actors from prosecution churned in the wake of not only the Kerner Commission's damning report and Tom Hayden's Newark exposé but also the Watergate scandal and the findings of the Knapp Commission, regarding cops less inclined to abuse their authority to inflict political violence than to enlarge their wealth at the public's expense (as I will discuss later).

Wicker notes that regrettably, the U.S. prison system by the 1970s had completely abdicated any role it once played as a job-training program for its underskilled inmates (61), but both he and Malcolm Bell, who wrote a later exposé called *The Turkey Shoot* (1985), come to regard (or at least exploit) Attica as their own beneficial career move. Referring to himself in the third person, Wicker conveys in *A Time to Die* his life story as a southerner grappling with inherited, and once firmly embraced, racist tendencies and as a failed novelist with still great longings to leave his literary mark in some way. This lengthy text is as much (if not more) about Wicker's own plight as a wavering liberal and a recently divorced father of two; by virtue of his limited role in D Yard among the rebelling inmates, the narrative mainly describes his interactions with prison officials and fellow professionals in an observers' group, called in by the inmates to aid negotiations however possible as well as bear witness to the deplorable conditions under which they served time. His offhanded reference to "homosexual acts and the use of drugs . . . threatening to get out of hand," not to mention "some stabbings and one multiple rape" (231; also 84, 169), indicates his physical distance from Attica's main action as well as the cultural distance between himself and the inmates that limits his ability to know and narrate these regrettable occurrences.

To be sure, Wicker deftly considers the frustrating ineffectuality of the observers' situation: like the overcrowded prisoners in the decks below, and like the sprawling excess that frequently characterized life itself in this liberal era, there are more than thirty observers crammed like clowns in a Volkswagen into the Stewards' Room where they deliberate. Just as "free speech had come to Attica" (Thompson 70) in the many diatribes issued through a bullhorn by the inmates in the yard, so the observers ramble endlessly on topics meaningful only to each, while valuable time ticks away. Two observers break into a "farcical swing-and-shove affray" (Wicker 198); an evidently uninvited local imam, "incongruous . . . in his robes and rug" (195) joins the group to help as he can; and many grandstanding militants get on each other's nerves with lengthy harangues.

The McKay Report described the observers' many talk sessions as "free-wheeling and highly emotional" (269), and as Wicker helplessly observes, "The group was far too big and diffuse to function effectively" (119); more than once, the session "degenerates into a free-for-all with . . . little aim or control, . . . repetitiousness and posturing" (Wicker 144). In a follow-up comment for the *Chicago-Kent Law Review*, Commissioner McKay even suggested that the lengthy interval devoted to observer discussion worsened the matter, with perhaps less tension and less violence had "prison officials . . . retake[n] the institution, with or without guns, on the first day" (140). Once, in an effort to reduce their numbers, Wicker leads an exodus meant to allow a five-member executive committee to focus its thoughts. Sheepishly, he soon realizes that only a few have joined him, that the majority "simply sat it out and usurped a place in the room" (145), and in fact all of observers seem so committed both to being of use and to leaving their own mark on this vital historical moment that those hoodwinked into leaving are outraged by the door that locks behind them. As all of the negotiations and schemes the observers attempt come to naught and the prison is retaken by deadly force, Wicker admits that his gang of well-meaning but ultimately irrelevant onlookers "had all failed." He correctly suspects that "the observers were no longer a part of things, if they ever really had been" (295; see also McKay Report 261, 289, 320).

Wicker muses on the tragedy of prison as brutalizer to both inmate and guard, asking, "What did it do to those who kept the cages, that their charges were kept in the condition of beasts?" This implication, this enthrallment, goes beyond the prison doors, as "all society was the keeper of the caged; the men with the clubs were only its agents" (59). Later Wicker observes striking demographic similarities between inmate and guard—"emotional shallowness, isolation from social customs and relative inability to profit from social sanctions"—and that both were "'in the joint' together. . . . pitted in a nearly Darwinian struggle for survival" and "spend[ing] their terms in hatred and fear of each other" (87). Despite the ultimately caged condition of inmate, guard, and all of us, Wicker is yet released by (and from) his Attica experience when he enjoys a civil encounter with a black youth in D Yard who thanks him for his work at the *Times* and enjoins him to use his power of the press to tell the world the Attica story: "He [Wicker] felt himself free, for once, of his prideful sense of individuality. He put his arms around the youth and held him fast, held him hard, believing he had overcome the deepest fears his life had given him. . . . The boy smiled and nodded and Wicker walked on, thinking he was *free at last free at last*" (249).

Wicker nicely undercuts such liberal sentiment by noting that only moments later, "He wanted to keep Big Black [another prisoner] between himself and the guns" (251) now taken up by the waiting guards. He concludes his narrative with return to his pessimistic view that "no American would ever be free" (254). But a more enlightened take on the opposition Wicker draws between the "freedom" he experienced during his one-on-one with the youth and his return to racist enthrallment in his objectification of Big Black would regard both of these scenes as variations on the same theme: Wicker is ready to free himself from the threat of violence of the entire Attica crisis by escaping behind the back of a sacrificial inmate, while the friendly black youth is simply another kind of shielded escape. It is a "free" exchange between the two (by which I mean that hugs cost nothing to give or receive) that allows this well-meaning liberal to substitute a brief moment of fellow feeling for the endlessly more complicated and expensive projects of sentencing law revision, prison reform, and employment opportunity without which imprisonment and prison rioting are inevitable. In his own Attica narrative, Malcolm Bell echoes Wicker at his most questionable moment: "Attica changed my life. It brought me freedom, fulfillment, and fun" (397). As I will read in the next chapter the sexual revolution as much more beneficial to men than it ever was to women, so here the lives and deaths of beleaguered black inmates become the ticket out of stagnating middle-class lifestyles for the powerful white men who turn tragic narratives into sensational best sellers.

Cops on the Take

Tom Hayden's *Rebellion in Newark* (1968), the last urban riot narrative of note from the period, is only some twenty pages longer than the infamously brief McCone Report. But the similarities end there, as *Rebellion* is as opposed in tone and intention to the McCone Report as SDS president and renowned radical Tom Hayden was to his opposite number—the ex-CIA, ultraestablishment John McCone. Two-thirds of Hayden's narrative criticizes illegal police activity, with chapters titled "The Occupation" and "The Terror" (again, both referring to police conduct) and with an appendix listing instances of police brutality and malfeasance, including a final vignette of police loading "six portable televisions" (102) into the trunk of a squad car and driving away. Such acts are perfectly coincident with the long tradition of police corruption that came to light following early-1970s testimonies to the *New York Times* by Frank Serpico, investigations by the Knapp Commission, and related memoirs of that era: a decade before Knapp, using operative terms such as "staged a set of public hearings" and a "ritual drama re-enacted" with each new investigation, Daniel Bell reviewed New York police corruption through the ages, back to an 1890s interrogation of "'Clubber' Williams, First Inspector of the Police Department [who accounted] for wealth and property far greater than could have been saved on his salary . . . as land speculation 'in Japan'" (115). By the early 1970s, such corruption was one more instance of lifestyle liberalism in keeping with the traditional sense of this term—a habit of personal liberty-taking that literally bankrolled the lavish lifestyles of erstwhile working-class members of the New York Police Department, causing both a visual and moral blurring between corrupt police and the mafiosi they frequently consorted with and exemplifying liberalism in one of its uglier modes.

As noted at the outset, Caldwell's *Riot Sale* stages a clear opposition between police and citizens, resolved only via exaggerated dark comedy. My readings of riot reports and narratives of actual summer uprisings continued to stage that same stark opposition, a political battle (i.e., power struggle) between an urban populace engaged in both basic survival and riot-specific acts of criminal rebellion and a police force heavily armed and shooting to kill. As the terrain in the context of police corruption shifts from politics to economics—from police seeking to subdue rioting citizens, sometimes with deadly force, to police gaining from citizens' "workaday" criminal activities through a complex system of extortion and graft—the opposition between police and criminal disappears. As biographer Peter Maas phrases the realization of Serpico, late in his ordeal, "His life might be in danger not from crooks but from crooked cops. And then he asked himself . . . was there any difference between them?" (218).

To be sure, what I will term corrupt policing's "street theater of the absurd" in this period of excess and overreach made it impossible to distinguish police from criminal—when it did not outright invert their roles. Maas's narrative describes numerous preposterous scenes from New York cops' protection racket, as when Serpico rejects a bribe from a mafioso and is lectured by his senior partner for "embarrassing the hell out of me" in front of the underworld figure. Serpico is "revolted by the spectacle of a police officer toadying to a racketeer" (158), but in fact criminal actors with money for bribes are regarded by the police not as adversaries but as "clients" (164) to be flattered and maintained. Poorer criminals less able to maintain monthly protection fees are treated as balky employees to be dealt with, if necessary, violently: "If you let them get away with that shit," a partner tells Serpico, "think of what it could start" (167).

Once on the pad (slang for the graft system), criminals are regarded as "cousins" with broad immunity; the police required to make an arrest in response to a citizen complaint, for instance, enact the role of arresting officers, while the criminals play along. Following arrangements to settle one such incident, "promptly at four-thirty, the [policy] collector . . . walked up, smiling, clutching a handful of [betting] slips, although only enough for misdemeanor arrest. The third plainclothesman marched [the collector] up to the desk and booked him. The case was dismissed the next day in court" (165). Robert Leuci, whose corrupt-cop story became the film *Prince of the City* (1981), suggests the equally choreographed nature of the judicial routine; on one occasion, both officers and victims "moved to the bench [when their names were called] with their heads up, knowing the drill, as if they had done this many times before" (5). Later, "here language was everything and winks and smiles were ever-present" (81). When Serpico begins to arrest bookies who protest vigorously that they are "cousins," he violates the fourth wall of the law-and-order charade established for all concerned; in this vertiginously upended scenario, the criminals themselves—simply following the rules laid down for them—are the victims of Serpico's disruptive actions, while his on-the-take brethren are deprived of lucrative clients. In a richly comic exchange, an underworld figure gets tired of the shakedown and threatens to have himself arrested: "I pay all the time, and I get nothing. . . . Lock me up, I say. You want trouble, I give you trouble" (198). He is talked off of this ledge by the unnerved police, not only to keep themselves on this client's payroll but to prevent his ever encountering official police bureaucracy with his lengthy tale to tell.

Serpico's story is unique among police corruption narratives as it features an establishment figure (a police officer) made famous for his hippie dress and countercultural attitudes toward race relations, free love, life in Greenwich Village, and ultimately honest policing. He thus adds layers of irony to the Nixonian law-and-order context in which he served, which sought to crack down on gambling, prostitution, drug use, and related woes of urban life yet rarely if ever acknowledged the aiding and abetting perpetrated by America's finest in cities nationwide. Per the terms of this project, it is average cops with their "clipped sideburns, thick-soled shoes" (Maas 120), and outer-borough addresses, who with "total arrogance" (188) met one day to discuss their pad arrangements in front of the Bronx County Criminal Courthouse, who are the "liberals" in this context. Climbing their "queer ladder of social mobility" (D. Bell 117), they spend, live, and act well beyond the policeman's legitimate salary and the moral pale, and they audaciously conduct their criminal acts within spitting distance of justice's halls. By contrast, law-abiding officers like Serpico and other progressive allies met on his journey are the "conservatives" seeking to honor the original police motto—to protect and serve. The crooked police take liberties with everyone their badge places under their purview, while Serpico, like a medieval saint, feels liberated only by his service to the community. As a young cop on the beat, "Serpico loved walking his post, the feeling of freedom he had when he turned out of the stationhouse onto the street, the sense . . . that he was responsible for the safety and well-being of everyone in the five-and-a-half blocks of the city he would cover during his tour of duty" (Maas 71).

In the throes of his dilemma, Serpico has a dream in which "all the policemen in the city were hippies with beards and long hair and love beads." One "stops a well-dressed businessman driving through a red light," who offers him a bribe, an incident that had recently happened to Serpico. In the dream, the hippie officer tells the businessman, "You straight people are all alike. You think you can buy yourselves out of anything" (102). Meanwhile, the impoverished flower children in his downtown neighborhood must rely on the police for justice, as when Serpico is asked by his neighbors to stop a man—who turns out to be a cop—from stealing cobblestones from a historic street renovation. As was the case with the trigger-happy police who gunned down Fred Hampton and other Black Panther leaders of the period (see chapter 1), the less-empowered are often those adhering to tradition, routine, and the rights guaranteed in the nation's founding documents, while those with sanctioned authority make free however possible.

The Knapp Commission's lead prosecutor Michael Armstrong minimized the contribution of Serpico, since "as an honest cop, [he] therefore didn't have access to real inside stuff that a guy who's dishonest would have" (qtd. in Shecter 28); Armstrong had no such complaint against Knapp's "Patrolman P," later revealed as Officer Bill Phillips, one of the most knowledgeable (i.e., implicated) officers on the force. As Knapp's star witness, Phillips informed stunned audiences throughout televised hearings in October 1971 that every police officer he knew was on the take (see Shecter 270–271). The Harlem riots play a role in "radicalizing"—that is, increasing the extreme racial antipathy—of Patrolman Phillips; identical to the shooting police of Watts, Newark, and Detroit, Phillips in riot mode is "bothered . . . most [by] the crimes being committed against property" (198). In Serpico's story, it is notably the emergency of urban rioting in the recent past that keeps Mayor Lindsay from acting on Serpico's many complaints. Despite Lindsay's commendable role on the postriot Kerner Commission, he informs an aide that "he could not afford upsetting the police because of the prospect of another 'long hot summer' in the ghettos" (Maas 180; see also Cannato 467).

Phillips's biographer Leonard Shecter comments that "homicides, believe it or not, are being sold on the streets of New York" (17), and as a senior partner tells Phillips early in his career, "Collars are dollars" (99). As police were gatekeepers to the city's vast system of jails, courts, convictions, and eventual imprisonment, it was freedom itself that was sold, and dearly paid for, in 1960s New York. The foul-mouthed, philandering Phillips, who expertly sniffed out criminal misconduct, heeded his mentor's advice and became a rich and well-connected man. As Hayden records two police officers stealing a TV at the end of the Newark riots, Phillips early in his already checkered career happens upon an identical scene at a much calmer moment. Having just stolen $186 in cash (and torn up $350 in unwanted checks) from a burgled store, Phillips is shocked (though he should hardly be) to find thieves lining up, like ants at a picnic, when he returns from stashing the money: "Two police officers are there, and they're carrying out the television. One of them says to me, don't worry. Nobody's around. They put it in the trunk of their car and drive away" (91).

Referring to the blue uniform as "the money suit" (80), Phillips and his colleagues "toss" DOAs before medical personnel (even widows) arrive; arrest petty criminals and prostitutes on minor charges, then extort hundreds for their release; and take special pride in harassing the citizens of Harlem, whose streets "if not paved with gold, were at least carpeted by wall-to-wall policy operators" (111; see also English 346). Phillips admits that the Harlem riots, rather late in his career of corruption after all, had little to do with his profiting from Harlem numbers-runners, bar-owners, and even eventually narcotics dealers: "I guess you could say I grew up prejudiced. . . . I am prejudiced against black people" (Shecter 123). Chasing a black burglar through Harlem one day, Phillips freely shoots to kill, since "them guys are hard to kill. Shoot these people in the fucking head and they live" (185). When he in fact succeeds in ending the burglar's life, the man's brother comes to the station to accuse Phillips of having committed murder and is told by the detective in charge to "get the fuck out of here" (185). Phillips's views on the Harlem riots and of blacks in general open a floodgate of opinion from his initially circumspect biographer. Shecter declares "a breakdown to a system which never worked in the first place. In the end police work seems too important to entrust to policemen" (201). He calls for "civilian review boards" (367) and the equally impossible dream of police departments "turned into places where seriously trained and educated men put their training to work with dedication" (365).

Both Serpico and Phillips suffered mightily for the "rat" role they played; Serpico survived a gunshot to the face that, while not inflicted by fellow officers, was very likely received due to his partners' refusal to come to his aid. Phillips, who took such egregious liberties throughout his career, but whose testimony before Knapp came with immunity for his crimes, was tragically denied his freedom for thirty-two years for a murder he did not commit, pinned on him by the NYPD. Notably, Shecter's biography concludes with a rehearsal of the many gaping holes in the prosecution's case and a report of the hung jury that concludes Phillips's first trial: "Presuming Phillips's innocence and acquittal in the second trial, he will then once again become involved in the prosecution of cases he worked up as a Knapp agent" (374). The corrupt police and courts triumphed, however, as Phillips was successfully prosecuted in the next trial and released on parole only in 2007, at the age of seventy-seven. According to a *New York Times* report published just prior to his release, Phillips never stopped suing for freedom; he "studied the law and fought his case, and those of fellow inmates, . . . over three decades" (Lueck; see also Gardner). Phillips's contention, that he was imprisoned simply for testifying against crooked cops, is borne out by the comment from the lone dissenting member of the parole board: although the charge against Phillips involved the murder of a pimp and prostitute, the parole-board member cared only for harm done to fellow police: "Mr. Phillips's crimes 'fly in the face of dedicated police officers who risk their lives on a daily basis to protect society'" (Lueck).

Black Arts Street Theater

As Martin Luther King himself understood, political change in the freedom era always involved the courage of individuals to overcome the stage fright most everyone feels when called upon to take a public stand. In his wording from 1967, "Mass marches transformed the common man into the star performer and engaged him in a total commitment" (17), and sharply dressed members of the Black Panther Party and rioters of all kinds felt free to partake of large-scale events, by way of grabbing the public attention that rarely follows those who stay home. As I suggested at the opening of this chapter, *street theater* was an impactful term in the freedom era; not only were dramatists from Edward Albee to Amiri Baraka to Ben Caldwell writing plays meaningfully set on (and in the case of Baraka's *Dutchman* under) the streets of New York, but television cameras, politicians, and even philosophers like King sought to capitalize on the politically transformative—or simply sensationally marketable—spectacle enacted by that era's civil rights marchers, women's libbers, and war protesters. As social critic Philip E. Slater remarked in 1970, "the media are *inherently* stimulus-hungry. . . . They know a crowd is more interesting than a press conference, a march than a speech. Successful use of television today requires an improvisational looseness and informality that old-culture leaders lack" (145).

As my brief readings of Caldwell's *Riot Sale* and *The Job* suggested earlier, the radical-liberal split was frequently dramatized in Black Arts Theater of the period. Specifically, the revolutionary was shown his duty to embrace freedom and, when necessary, violence and to reject easy payouts and even family ties as the state-sponsored tools of oppression that they were. Liberal elements were roundly rejected, as by Applicant #6 from *The Job*: "We want our freedom, and all you offer is jobs and integration. You've turned us wrongside out. . . . Your ways don't fit me!" (46). Caldwell's widely regarded satire *Prayer Meeting; or, the First Militant Minister* (1969), while not set on the street, enacts the radical-liberal split in the home of a hypocritical preacher. Coming home to his petit bourgeois comforts one night, he is fooled by the thief hiding in his closet into thinking that he hears the voice of God: "Tomorrow you'll lead a protest march to end all protest marches. And I don't want this to be no damned sing-along. . . . You'll demand justice. And if you don't get justice you'll raise hell" (34). Reminiscent of the exhortations of Malcolm X, "many of the burglar's charges against the preacher are intended for the audience. Caldwell . . . tries to shame them into heightened racial consciousness" (C. Fox 80).

Douglas Turner Ward's *Happy Ending* (1966) presents a form of radical liberalism as the revolutionary's best MO: the conservatively dressed Ellie and Vi and their downright fashionable nephew Junie enjoy a well-stocked, modern refrigerator among wall-to-wall creature comforts in their humble Harlem apartment. As domestics to the wealthy Harrison family, Ellie and Vi have been looting stores in the modern way—tripling the orders on steaks and suits for years, even adding in "a scrumptious new collapsible swimming pool" (19) to be sent to Junie's mother down south. Echoing Langston Hughes's defense of looters in his daily column,

Ellie regards their acquisition of goods in Harrison's name as "just gitting back what's owed us" (18). As the play opens, the women fear the Harrisons' impending divorce; at first the militant Junie, who refuses "them jive jobs they try to palm off on ya" (8) down at the employment office, scoffs at his aunts' wails of distress. But when he learns how intensively the books have been cooked in support of his own well-dressed hide, Junie joins his aunts in mourning, and all enjoy a hearty laugh and a champagne toast when Mr. Harrison calls to say the divorce is off. Though the aunts ply their con through an outdated deferential attitude, they are not simply raiding the master's closets for castoffs but walking off with a sizeable share of his wealth—a radical act that Caldwell rejected in *Riot Sale* but that many-another revolutionary might embrace. William Couch Jr. reads *Happy Ending* as "superbly combin[ing] thesis with theater farce, establishing a real, and sometimes half-surreal world in which whites get their comeuppance from black folks whose sardonic cunning is mordant proof that they, like people in general, though less than angels are far more than fools" (xx).

In Jimmy Garrett's *And We Own the Night* (1968), Johnny, a wounded revolutionary, interrupts his battle with police to shoot his own mother in the back. She had moralistically condemned his violence, lack of religion, and refusal to return home, and her son's preparatory declaration is "death to the house niggers!" (68). Quoting Blyden Jackson's praise of "creative violence . . . cleansing violence" in Black Arts drama, William Van Deburg comments that these artists "employed culture as a weapon. . . . [They] showed how folk, literary, and theatrical forms could complement any militant's arsenal" (*New Day* 284). Like many female characters in Black Arts drama, the mother in Garrett's is castigated for sleeping with the enemy and subjected to egregious verbal abuse before physical destruction. The unforgettably tragic Stella of Ed Bullins's *The Corner* (1970) is likewise subjected to violence, although the text deemphasizes a political contest between liberalism and radicalism to foreground the gritty naturalism and family discord of one of Bullins's dramaturgical influences, Eugene O'Neill (see Grant). As O'Neill drew on experience in the Merchant Marine for his earliest work and features conflicting brothers in many of his dramas, so Bullins presents Cliff Dawson and his half brother Steve Benson, both veterans of the Navy, as recurring characters and alter-egos (Scharine 103). *The Corner* epitomizes what Bullins described elsewhere as the purpose of street theater: "Communication with . . . the Black working class, or with special groups (e.g., winos, pool hall brothers, prostitutes, pimps, hypes, etc.), who would not ordinarily come or be drawn into the theater" ("A Short Statement" 93).

Awaiting the arrival of Cliff, whose strength and self-assurance are beacons of hope, however faint, in this blighted community, the other characters obsess over a bottle of wine and trade favors for every swig:

> STELLA (*teases*): Yeah, I know how it is with these youngsters. Don't even have any respect anymore. Pass the bottle, won't cha, hon?
>
> BUMMIE: Sho, baby. (*Hands her the bottle*).

. . . [Stella drinks deeply]

STELLA (*breath*): [Cliff will] come. He knows I'm here.

SLICK: You here? Sheeet . . . woman, he don't care if you're here or on the moon.

STELLA (*drains bottle*): Yes, he does. He's only with that little bitch 'cause she works and gives him money. But he spends it on me.

SLICK (*coldly furious*): Spends it on you? You mean he buys you a bottle of wine to drink with him before he screws you? (81)

For this vicious insult Stella attacks Slick but forsakes even defending her honor when Silly Willie arrives with another bottle to pass.

At Cliff's arrival, Stella feels the only joy her bleak life contains. There is ultimately no way to reconcile Cliff's grievous rebuke of Stella—she is subjected to another loveless tryst in the back seat of a broken-down car, followed by gang rape at Cliff's invitation—and the hero's role he inhabits at play's end:

BUMMIE: You gonna settle down, man?

CLIFF: Yeah, Bummie, yeah. Lou's gonna have a baby. I'm gonna be a father.

. . . .

BUMMIE: Hey . . . man . . . that's great. C'mon up on the avenue. . . . I'll buy you a drink.

CLIFF: Nawh, man. I'm not up to it. I'm goin' in.

Nathan L. Grant remarks that "Bullins never imposes his own view upon the action" (n.p.), and in Samuel L. Hay's rather forgiving assessment, "*The Corner* . . . questions whether facing the plain and painful truth is the only bridge to manhood" (113). For Hay, Cliff's brutalizing of Stella enables "Stella's discovery . . . [her] awakening to the truth" (115) of his total disregard for her, but Don Evans's early reading seems most apt: "The Bullins theater is the theater of confrontation. We are forced to look at ourselves and that part of our community that troubles us in our quiet moments" (16). Per Clayton Riley, Bullins "elevated to the averted eyes of Negro America all the uncool, incorrect, funky Black urban field-hand life style we had always imagined could have no practical serviceability in the design of our new truths, our reconstructed myth-dynamic" (xx). As a Black Arts purveyor of Artaud's Theater of Cruelty, Bullins presents a "form of theater [that is] physically draining, an exhaustive encounter which allows only rare opportunities to relax, to simply be an onlooker" (Riley xx). Surely the hypermasculine context of Black Arts drama may have obscured the contradiction between Cliff's heroic attachment to his pregnant girlfriend and his dreadful treatment of the devoted Stella. Her subjugation is neither condemned by the text nor atoned for by the hero before he is allowed to walk into the light. Richard G. Scharine notes similar abusive pairings in Bullins's *The Duplex* (1971), between Marco and Wanda and between Steven Benson and Velma Best, noting, "There is little nobility in Steve's treatment of Velma" (106).

In the broader "liberation" context in which these works occur, Bullins is one of many authors making free with once-taboo subjects, trampling with liberal abandon an age-old tradition of rescuing the damsel in distress and even the hooker with the heart of gold. Even Sonia Sanchez's *The Bronx Is Next* (1968), the sole woman-authored text included in Bullins's important "Black Theater" issue of the *Drama Review* (1968), includes a character named "Black Bitch." Her strong feminist attitude toward raising her sons—"Smart boys, you hear? They read. They know more than me already, but they still love me" (82)—is derided by one of the protagonists as typical for "another black matriarch on our hands" (82). She is slapped around by the other protagonist for sleeping with a white cop. Larry Neal remarks that in Garrett's *And We Own the Night* Johnny's "vicious attack on his mother" belongs to "a recurrent theme in the sociology of the Black community." As the "economic mainstay of her family . . . the [black] woman's aspirations are closely tied to those of the white power structure and not to those of her man" (38), be this husband or son. Scharine observes that by 1973, when Bullins had completed his transition from "political ideologist to cultural humanist" (108), the Steve Benson of Bullins's novel *The Reluctant Rapist* "assaults women then falls asleep in the same bed, deliberately courting exposure-capture. Bullins, the artist, assaults our consciousness, seeking recognition, and half-expecting, half-demanding condemnation" (108). But even these demands are unmet when "Steve sleeps through the night with his victim, to be greeted in the morning with a request to return" (108).[1] Such details suggest that Bullins along with Garrett and even Sanchez belong in this radically liberal era to the "suck it up, lady" school of women's equality presided over by Norman Mailer, Henry Miller, and related canonical authors. Subjecting female characters to violence once reserved for their male counterparts is a version of "gender equality" embraced for its freedom (cost-freeness) in lieu of the expensive social rearrangement that would actually grant women access to lucrative workplace opportunity, the childcare necessary to access same, and housing options that would free them from the disdain and abuse that constituted many women's—especially poor women's—lives in this era.

The Theatrics of Counterculture

White actors in the cultural vanguard were just as eager to exploit the prospects of street theater as they forged their own (in retrospect, much less urgent) campaign for a free society. But as opposed to the entrenched conflict (motivated by authentic hatreds on both sides) and desperation expressed by rioting urban blacks of the era, and like the white cops with whom they often battled at famous protests of the era, white youth's political conflict with the establishment as well as its economic identification with America's underclasses were ultimately "acts" put on for particular purpose and media attention, concluded at will. Michael Rossman and Dotson Rader wrote two memoirs of New Left protest; notably, both pay minimal attention to the antiwar demonstrating that ostensibly gave their radicalism its reason for being and much more to the personal crises endured when their respective elite universities—UC Berkeley and Columbia—turn against them. Both texts are veritable campus tours, mapping buildings, quads, entrances, and administrative figures onto attempts to liberate higher education from entrenched tradition. In *The Wedding within the War* (1971), Rossman gives due credit to the major episodes of—and his own prominent role in—the Free Speech Movement that inaugurated white counterculture on the West Coast but too much credit to FSM when he repeatedly equates it to the civil rights movement (e.g., 200). Having no need to strive for the equal opportunity enjoyed by privileged classes since they themselves constituted these classes, the white student Left claimed—however falsely—equal oppression as that suffered by racial minorities and the poor.

In particular Rossman's FSM-related sentence to ninety days at a rehabilitation center compares not at all to the imprisoning of nearby Oakland residents Huey Newton or Eldridge Cleaver through much of their youth: both Rossman and Newton credit the isolated hours in prison with creating a campus-like environment, yet Rossman catches up on Joyce and completes writing awaited by "desperate" editors on the outside, while Newton teaches himself to read. Rossman repeatedly compares the "spades" in the rehab center—and throughout the protest landscape of 1960s America—to the "kids" (white college students) running their parallel track; in his own view, "Being in college teaches you . . . how to relate to authority [such as prison guards]—even more than being black does, though the techniques are similar" (191). Regarding limits placed on college life (e.g., women's curfew and traditional syllabi), Rossman repeatedly refers to the campus as a ghetto yet admits that "the spades who are going to jail for the flaming cities are quite a different story. . . . And those brave kids [again, whites] who are choosing quietly, calmly, and without hope, four years in a federal pen rather than [go to Vietnam] . . . are also a different story" (198). Yet another difference between the Berkeley cohort and beleaguered inductees actually on their way to Vietnam is exemplified in a galling moment from Jerry Rubin's memoir *Do It!* (1970). He and a small group stop a troop train moving through Berkeley to the Oakland Army Terminal—"We were victorious warriors. We were ecstatic" (36)—except that the victory is ridiculously short-lived. The protestors get off the track, and the train's passengers (who were poignantly glad to see the hippies at first) proceed to their destinies; Rubin's fellow Berkeley activist Marvin Slobodkin aptly described the event as "the feeblest revolt it was possible to imagine" (102). Despite claims to the revolutionary role, Rossman is most correct when he calls FSM activists "freedom *trippers*, not riders" (198), since for the white counterculture, "freedom, like democracy, is less a political state than a psychological condition" (150)—a state of mind achievable with much less effort and bloodshed.

Ever-attuned to the theatrical possibilities of student protest, Rossman regards it as "a matter of *style*" (147) and refers to his comrades in free speech and education reform as "our troupe" (10). Later, "drama is essential to the organizing of some activities. . . . The sight of seated demonstrators waiting for police to descend is meant to evoke the moral nature of the protest" (83). He, meanwhile, feared the day when protest transformed from an act into actual violence, criticizing Jerry Rubin and the Yippies for luring youth to the 1968 Democratic Convention in Chicago, where indeed his fears were borne out: "Can Yippie's mythy publicity be modified to include an accurate portrayal of the landscape of danger? I doubt it" (265). Just before the convention, Rossman is equally demoralized by the head-busting perpetrated by New York police during attempts to block the Whitehall induction center as well as by the badly scripted meanderings of the protesters themselves. Having "left the protected environment of the West for the first time" (208), "I had never before been in a city with such constant inhuman scales of space and speed . . . nor in a place of such constant random violence" (209). Rossman appreciates the game-like (even childlike) street theater of "Digger Abbie Hoffman and friends dropp[ing] handfuls of dollar bills off the balcony of the Stock Exchange," turning the "avid brokers scrabbl[ing] on the floor below" (293) into unwitting comic relief. "But as a system, jail works better than New York, and I felt safer there" (212), while the Whitehall protest "was the most inept, self-endangering demonstration I've ever seen" (229).

In *I Ain't Marchin' Anymore* (1969), New York's Dotson Rader takes most of the fast pace and even some of the violence in stride; he was at both the Whitehall demonstration (narrating a lot of the confusion Rossman observed) and Vietnam Mobilization Day in April 1967, with its famous march from Central Park to the United Nations. In both these great spectacles with obvious political intent and in the lengthy, seemingly less necessary occupation of Columbia, detailed in the final chapters of the book, protesters meet the boots and nightsticks of New York police as well as the violent response of nearby construction workers, and several of Rader's acquaintances come away bloodied and traumatized. Yet "Running down Seventh Avenue . . . shouting Hell! No! We! Won't! Go!" Rader feels "theatrically revolutionary" even if only "momentarily triumphant" (31). Having himself escaped all blows, his personal victory leaves him only "horny as hell" (37). As in Rossman's narrative, the campus scenes lack in urgency what they make up for in pretension—at Princeton, an endless talkfest hosted by SDS is a waste of participants' (and readers') time; to himself Rader admits "fear for his own safety" (93–94) when attending Columbia, next door to Harlem, yet also "hop[es] the blacks had the guts and stamina to do our [revolutionary] work for us" (94).

Protesting the university's annexation of a park in Morningside Heights, as well as its connections to chemical and military industries, the Columbia students occupy various campus buildings in April 1968. Like the Attica Prison rioters, the students and administration settle into stalemate over the issue of amnesty, yet the similarity ends there when Rader runs out for a drink after a few listless days and comically cannot get back into the locked campus upon return. He winds up on the front line, locked arm and arm with others blocking the door to one sealed building as the police approach, but again departs comically from the rioter's role: "I took out my contact lenses and put them in their case and shoved them in my pocket. I took off my tie to avoid strangulation" (124). The only injury suffered as he at last clambers into a locked building is "my ass being clubbed by a cop as I went inside" (125). At the height of the conflict, "we tried to pull up paving stones from College Walk," but Rader admits that "they were too bulky to carry, and suddenly it seemed absurd. . . . I found myself imagining all these schmaltzy scenes from corny dramas." Now with street theater in its most futile form, "it was a pageant. A show. No real pain or real blood. A spectacle" (141). Moments later, "my courage broke, the fantasy slipped. Reality. . . . I ran. Fast" (142), in the hurry that Rossman found so dehumanizing during his New York sojourn. Todd Gitlin's recollections of various antiwar demonstrations staged by SDS, with whom he played a leadership role, betray his own inflated sense of historical significance even as he investigates the media's damaging, ego-enlarging effects. He takes extensive offense at any coverage in the *New York Times* and other major outlets insufficiently "respectful" (e.g., *Whole World* 69) and refers to minor if not forgotten moments from the SDS narrative—"the Potter speech" (*Whole World* 56), "the Katzenbach Press Conference" (*Whole World* 95), and so on—as if they were Pearl Harbor or D-Day.

If the white middle-class actors of the antiwar Left thus stand guilty of the posturing and speechifying that undermined their claims to historical legitimacy, the Youth International Party (YIP), founded by Abbie Hoffman and Jerry Rubin on New Year's Eve 1967, epitomizes late-1960s lifestyle liberalism as sheer political theater. In fact, *founded* is the incorrect term; although one can found a party with no more than two, as Huey Newton and Bobby Seale did with the Black Panther Party in October 1966, Newton and Seale took their project seriously, and the BPP's ranks eventually grew into the thousands. Hoffman and Rubin never succeeded (nor even tried) to grow the Yippies beyond the original four or five friends who concocted the idea; always it was only an elaborate joke that took off in the popular media and lived a riotous life between January and August 1968 primarily as a media construct. There were no membership drives, dues, or chapters; a lapel button (issued in the thousands) to be worn at Yippie events in New York and Chicago read "Yippie Leader." One was a Yippie—and was even in charge—for as long as one wore the button, an extremely popular medium in its own right in this period. Describing the leadership style of Jerry Rubin even in his pre-Yippie days, Slobodkin shades the free speech context into speech act theory, suggesting admiringly that "the International Days of Protest didn't exist anywhere outside Jerry's head, but the moment he made the announcement, the Day of Protest *did* exist, so it was true" (101).

But Gitlin remarked that during this same Berkeley period, "Rubin acquired a *following* instead of a face-to-face political base. His following was organized precisely as a mass media audience: atomized, far-flung, episodic, not alive politically except when mobilized in behalf of centralized symbols of revolt" (*Whole World* 173). The Panthers' Ten-Point Program, memorized by all Party members, was countered by Hoffman's eight-point manifesto, written anonymously by "A. Yippie," which called for changes as revolutionary as those sought by the Panthers (e.g., "The Abolition of Money"). But it was qualified as "a personal statement" only, since "there are no spokesmen for the Yippies" (*Revolution* 167), and thus each member might have defined revolution his or her own way. Indeed, "We are all our own leaders. We realize this list of demands is inconsistent. They are not [even] really demands" (*Revolution* 167). Written less as a declaration of independence than as a press release, the manifesto advises "all reporters that they ask each and every Yippie in Lincoln Park why they have come to Chicago" (A. Hoffman, *Revolution* 167).

Per Rossman's aforementioned challenge to Rubin, tuned-out hippie culture and the antics of the Yippies in particular "pissed off the straight Left to no end" (A. Hoffman, *Autobiography* 106); as historian David Farber notes, "Movement people tried to steer clear of the Yippies" (89). Between the two wings of white counterculture there seemed a great divide; each regarded itself as the radical alternative to the liberal sellouts of the other faction (see, e.g., Stevens 307). Yet Hoffman and Rubin saw themselves straddling this divide; David Gross remarks that "the Yippies were symbolically important because of their attempt to fuse politics and culture before each became permanently estranged from the other" (111). Epigrammatically, Hoffman "always held my flower in a clenched fist" (*Autobiography* 99; see also Gross 105), and his and Rubin's proto-Yippie attempt to levitate the Pentagon during the March on the Pentagon in October 1967 "would not [have been dismissed] as frivolous" (*Autobiography* 131) by the spiritually attuned, Buddhist Vietnamese on whose behalf they protested. Straddling yet another divide—between peace-loving hippie and violent criminal—was Hoffman's ideological nemesis (and West Coast counterpart as founder of the San Francisco Diggers) Emmett Grogan. In his shamelessly self-aggrandizing autobiography, Grogan declared himself the baddest radical of them all, delivering food to both slumming hippies in Golden Gate Park and hungry families in the housing projects of Oakland, all of it "free" in that it had been "liberated" (Grogan 340) from the backs of delivery trucks hours prior to consumption. Grogan's claim to membership in the underclass is more credible than those by other white radicals quoted in this chapter; as a hood on the mean streets of 1950s Brooklyn, Grogan was evidently an accomplished thief by the time he left high school. Like his fellow New Yorker Claude Brown (who will be discussed later), his childhood was undersupervised and untrammeled; he construed freedom—like the goods he stole constantly from the homes of the wealthy—as "something you have to take" (80) and unlike Brown, failed to avoid the hazards of heroin addiction: he succumbs three times in his memoir *Ringolevio* (1972) and was found dead due to overdose on the F Train to Coney Island in April 1978.

Though here I suggest that the committed Left and the don't-give-a-damn Yips were equally ineffectual in their efforts to end the war and effect social change, Hoffman's career suggests that lifestyle liberals may have had the edge due to their easy relinquishing of all rules of engagement with establishment society. In his *Autobiography*, Hoffman connects joblessness (his own and the general rejection of straight employment) and attendant poverty with the hippie way, resulting in much of life itself lived on the street instead of in the closed spaces legitimized in a capitalist context of property and privacy. Street theater as a way of being was likely hippies' most radical aspect; from another, equally revolutionary corner in that same period, Jane Jacobs celebrated the vitality of street life during all hours for all purposes. She observed, "Lowly, unpurposeful, and random as they may appear, sidewalk contacts are the small change from which a city's wealth of public life may grow" (72).

Ultimately, the random formlessness of the Yippie movement may have been regarded by the establishment as its most fearsome quality. Heads were bloodied at an overcrowded Yip-In at Grand Central Station in March 1968 and later outside Chicago's Conrad-Hilton Hotel during the 1968 Democratic Convention literally for nothing; as Hoffman himself remarked, "YIPPIE! . . . was the biggest put-on of all time. If you believe Yippies existed, you are nothing but a sheep" (*Revolution* 121). Meanwhile, as was the case with SNCC and Panther luminaries Stokely Carmichael and Huey Newton (see chapter 1) and with feminist spokespersons such as Susan Brownmiller and Gloria Steinem (see chapter 3), Gitlin remarks on the media's triangulating, and ruinous, effect on the symbiosis between New Left movement and leader: "What defines a movement as 'good copy' is often flamboyance, often the presence of a media-certified celebrity leader, and usually a certain fit with whatever fame the newsmakers have constructed" (*Whole World* 3–4). Gitlin observes the media's solidifying effects—one message, one spokesperson—on a movement most effective in dynamic, provisional mode (137) as well as its tendency to "present performers who are deviant" (152) where moderation may prevail. Later, those who rose to the top were "personalities who enjoyed performance, who knew how to flaunt some symbolic attribute, who spoke quotably" (153) and who caused resentment among "leaders . . . not chosen" (163) by the mass media. When these vaunted figures failed to deliver—to their own constituents and the broader public—extremism, disillusion, and dissolution followed.

Ever aware of their role as actors in this national drama, all Left groups converging on the 1968 Democratic Convention in Chicago to protest the war—not only the Yippies but SDS and the National Mobilization Committee to End the War in Vietnam (a.k.a. the Mobe)—suffered a crisis of purpose when their epic foil Lyndon Johnson announced in late March 1968 his decision to not seek reelection. Without Johnson's elderly, cracker persona—so clearly responsible for much of the escalation and carnage in Vietnam—to oppose, all groups wrestled with whether to even go to Chicago, a decision made even more fraught when the cozy liberal Eugene McCarthy and the almost countercultural RFK declared their candidacies and did well in early primaries (see Farber 39–45 et passim). Upon the assassination of RFK, Jerry Rubin remarked with his customary scalding humor that "Sirhan Sirhan is a Yippie" (qtd. in Farber 45), since Kennedy's removal from the race and emergence of Hubert Humphrey via old-style party politics blew strong winds into the sails of the radical Left. Yet had they worried whether happy Hubert Humphrey could fill a sufficiently villainous role, Chicago mayor Richard J. Daley, his henchmen in the legal office and police department, and the head-busting ranks of Chicago's finest amply filled their parts: as convention week neared, role-playing police "dressed up as hippie demonstrators complete with long-haired wigs, ponchos, funny hats, picket signs, and other 'hippie' paraphernalia. [An]other group played themselves" (Farber 155), and a staged melee ensued. One of hundreds of federal and local agents provocateurs throughout the period, "Jerry Rubin's bodyguard, who was dressed as a longhaired biker and who pulled down an American flag in Grant Park, was a Chicago policeman" (Gitlin, *Whole World* 189). On CPD's most important night in the spotlight, "the demonstrations and head-beatings that the world watched took place largely because the Daley regime took earlier media reports at face value and rioted against what was actually a small, confused, and intimidated radical presence. . . . The antiwar movement could trigger the paranoia of authorities, causing them to trip over their own feet and to create chaos that would disrupt the war consensus" (169).

Notably, cameras were dark all over Chicago as an electricians' strike wore into its second month when the Democratic Convention began in August 1968. Minimal planning and lots of luck—per Rubin, "Some colossal military fuckup by the pigs" (173)—caused antiwar protesters and police to collide on Michigan Avenue at the Conrad-Hilton, where many conventioneers were housed and "directly in front of the only fixed network cameras set up" (Farber 199) besides those at the convention venue. As Farber documents, "There were also mobile television cameras set up in the intersection" (199), and images of police brutalizing youth in a full-scale riot, made iconic due to the accident of media placement at the right place and time, captured national attention. In the filmography of the late 1960s, these images marked the nadir of Vietnam as a national cause.

As was H. Rap Brown of SNCC fame, both Rubin and Hoffman were staunch McLuhanites who looked upon print and television media with equal measures of cynicism and faith. In their signature writings, as in Brown's, photos and graphics are collaged among the lines of type to make the reading experience as busy, visual, and frequently interrupted as watching TV. Hoffman's autobiography, originally titled *Soon to Be a Major Motion Picture* (1980), is dozens of short chapters, interspersed with photos of friends and family. *Revolution for the Hell of It* is even more diversely designed, with short chapters intercut with rehashed and invented dialogue, type in vertical and diagonal formats, and numerous graphics: photos, floor plans, news clippings, illustrations of the ubiquitous buttons, and—most "communicative" of all—"blank space" (79). Observing that "the most popular word in the English language is 'free,'" (*Autobiography* 117), Hoffman suggests a convergence of mainstream advertising (with giveaways luring customers during every station break) and the "revolutionary politics of free" (*Autobiography* 122) practiced by the Diggers and Yippies of the period. Despite the media's deleterious effects on movement politics, and despite the popularity of funk/spoken-word artist Gil Scott-Heron's lyric, "The revolution will not be televised," Rubin insisted that "you can't be a revolutionary today without a television set—it's as important as a gun!" (108). Gitlin acknowledged the media's ability to "relay news to elites and protesters, the rulers and the ruled, all at once" (*Whole World* 169), but Farber critiques the TV-style antics of the Yippie movement: "The Yippies' style was really just like the TV commercials they dreamed of emulating. . . . They, too, promised what the vast majority of their audience would never have: a kind of never-never land of consumption without limits and freedom without responsibility" (224).

Drug Literature in Black and White

In their police memoirs, Leuci and Serpico each remark upon the policeman's code against taking "dirty money"—graft from the trafficking in illegal drugs, since its victims were so much more badly victimized than those involved with prostitution and gambling. Leuci quotes the "working cop's principle," "no cop in his right mind would take drug money" (107), and Serpico ironically pictures officers "throw[ing] up their hands in horror at the idea of . . . payoffs in heroin traffic" (169), only to observe that "this philosophy of clean money was very flexible indeed" (Maas 169). The slide into dirty money is inevitable because so incredibly profitable; Leuci's cohort makes off with the French Connection evidence (143–146), while a narcotics cop tells Serpico after he is transferred to the division, "We don't fuck around with a lousy eight hundred a month. Last week there was this distributor . . . and each pickup was for forty Gs, and we just waited until he got all the money, and we hit him. You know what that is, four ways?" (274). But to an honest cop like Serpico, heroin is simply a heart-wrenching tragedy; at the climax of his career, he is shot by a drug dealer in a scene that Maas takes pains to dress in urban gothic: "He continued to mount the stairs, and admired the intricate designs on the tile landings, now barely visible through the filth. . . . In a light cast by a naked bulb at the top of the stairs, Serpico saw dozens of glassine bags and, even worse in a way, the flattened tubes of airplane glue that children sniffed before they graduated to mainlining. Here it all was, all the mute horror and degradation of lives made hopeless by heroin" (281–282). As sociologist Erich Goode described the situation in 1972, "The police draw ideological and material sustenance from drugs and drug users. It is not a domain that the police are going to give up easily or willingly. It has profited them too handsomely" (202; see also D. Bell 116).

Drug technologies from the pill to LSD to heroin—many of which reached peak usage in the late 1960s and early 1970s—are readable from numerous angles pertinent to this study: as forms of liberation; as forms of freedom's sharply devalued first cousins escape, release, and abdicated responsibility; and as forms of insidious enslavement in the guises of power, agency, and choice. From its first introduction into the mainstream, the LSD trip was construed as an internal journey of revolutionary proportions. The experience of freeing one's mind into the stratosphere was contrasted by the likes of LSD guru Timothy Leary and Beat visionary Allen Ginsberg to the experience of physical and spiritual conformity that marked the 1950s. Employing terms well worn by this point in the rights era, Leary established the Freedom Center (alternately the Freedom House) in a vacated hotel in Mexico and headed the International Foundation for Internal Freedom (IFIF) throughout the early 1960s. Wrapping himself in the flag whenever the occasion required, Leary strove to guarantee LSD and justice for all in his many confrontations with the straight public and its courts. "A major civil liberties issue of the next decade will be the control and expansion of consciousness" (qtd. in Stevens 190), he wrote with his disciple Richard Alpert; decades after LSD was made illegal, Leary still sang the praises of expanded consciousness as individual Americans' "own Declaration of Independence. My Life, my liberty, my pursuit of happiness" (103). Meanwhile, the Yippies saw much more radical potential in mind-altering substances: "Drugs, above all, seemed to deliver the possibilities of consciousness raising that could provoke revolutionary insight" (Farber 220).

Yet by those who looked askance at the self-indulgent nature of the acid trip, this "ersatz" (qtd. in Lee and Shlain 81) and ephemeral "inner freedom" was regarded as a weak substitute for—and dangerous distraction from—the political, collective freedoms sought after by protesting groups such as civil rights and antiwar advocates. By the late 1960s, observes David Gross, "'personal development' . . . [had] replaced the idea of 'social commitment'" (112) in diverse psychological and pharmacological contexts, and as the acid revolution wore on, the seemingly innocent, questing nature of late-1950s and early-1960s acid trip (undertaken by entertainers as diverse as Aldous Huxley, Cary Grant, and Groucho Marx) devolved into outlandish (sometimes violent) displays of antisocial behavior: from the "program of rock and roll, dope and fucking" (Lee and Shlain 218) advocated by the White Panthers and the Yippies, to the acid-fueled bombing raids undertaken by the Weather Underground (Lee and Shlain 231), to the disorder and violence that ruined the Rolling Stones' free concert at the Altamont Speedway in December 1969, to the horrific excesses of the Manson gang, the personalized, privatized nature of the acid trip manifested in acts of supreme selfishness and gross disrespect for others. Leary's seductive promise in a 1966 *Playboy* interview that "in a carefully prepared, loving LSD session, a woman will inevitably have several hundred orgasms" (qtd. in Lee and Shlain 113) was corrosively recast a fleet two years later as the White Panther mandate to its (evidently all-male) membership that each should "fuck your woman til she can't stand up" (qtd. in Lee and Shlain 218).

By summer 1967, San Francisco's hippie epicenter, the Haight-Ashbury neighborhood, reminded one historian of "old Calcutta" (qtd. in Stevens 339), and "bad trips became the most frequent trips. . . . [F]or the first time the LSD psychotic became something more than a media favorite . . . and the Diggers began carrying guns" (341). Echoing the widow of Robert F. Williams in the early civil rights context (see chapter 1), a prominent publisher of hippie broadsides in the Haight declared, "An Armed Man is a Free Man" (qtd. in Perry 190); the problem, notes historian Charles Perry, is that "peace and love did not return to the battered neighborhood. On the contrary, amphetamine and heroin were bigger problems than ever" (228). As an East Coast / West Coast rift did much to destroy the vitality of the Black Panther Party (see chapter 1) and as cross-purposes blighted the friendship of West Coast Jerry Rubin and New Yorker Abbie Hoffman in the Yippies' later days (see Farber 18–19 et passim), so the falling of LSD's star was abetted by much infighting at Leary's upstate New York compound, Millbrook, and by the divergent styles of the movement's leading lights: "Millbrook's non-welcome strengthened [West Coast Ken Kesey's] Pranksters' sense of their own psychedelic identity, which was both more macho and less intellectual than Leary's. . . . They rejected the reliance on guides and careful programming [essential to Leary's medicalized approach], believing limits of any kind were inimical to the experience" (Stevens 236; and see Perry 33).

As LSD historians Martin A. Lee and Bruce Shlain remark, "Drugs in general and acid in particular nurtured a privatistic tendency within the youth culture, or perhaps . . . the ingrained privatism of American life insinuated itself in such a way as to use the chemical high for its own purposes" (166). But defending users of the period, Erich Goode argued that LSD and marijuana were classified as dangerously addictive by a paranoid antiyouth legal establishment who yet looked the other way when the AMA (richly financed by pharmaceutical companies) classified deadly barbiturates as medically acceptable Schedule III drugs and supported physicians' "tradition of prescribing drugs promiscuously" (128). Notes Goode, "Housewives who use amphetamines . . . are unaware that the substance they are ingesting is labeled a 'drug'; to them, it is just a pill that makes them feel better. A 'drug' is what hippies and junkies take" (133). Goode notes that prescription drug addiction occurs almost always in a "medical or quasi-therapeutic context" and that prescriptions obtained at an affordable rate enable such addicts to "secure their 'fix' without having to steal or prostitute themselves" (155). He thus implies that the factor distinguishing middle-class pill-poppers from "dope fiends" and so memorably rendered in narratives by William S. Burroughs (in *Junky*, 1953) and Claude Brown (in *Manchild in the Promised Land*, 1965) is the gritty urban street.

Thus if LSD, ingested mainly by the disaffected white middle-class youth of the counterculture, was repeatedly construed in terms of mental liberation, such terminology rarely (and only disingenuously) described the experience of heroin addiction, much more frequently affecting American urban underclasses and repeatedly likened to a mental and physical enslavement with deadly repercussions. A riveting scene from *The Autobiography of Malcolm X* describes NOI mentors helping young users turn from heroin with a reviving dose of race consciousness: "'Kick Whitey off your back!' The addict, writhing in pain, is pouring sweat from head to foot. . . . [H]e is vomiting, suffering diarrhea. 'Don't hold nothing back! Let Whitey go!'" (267). As Brown observes in his moving narrative of mid-century Harlem, the NOI was indeed instrumental in giving recovering addicts a new calling: "Now the junkies had a place to go, those who could accept the teachings of the Muslims. It wasn't hard to accept, not for most of the junkies [because] junkies weren't cold criminals at heart" (*Manchild* 331). Regarding the well-attended rallies of the kind where Malcolm X famously got his start, "this was the first time that many of these people had ever seen home boys who had been junkies, pimps, and thieves speak to crowds of people and sound so serious about it. It became a community thing" (336).

In his short, satiric *Junkies Are Full of SHHH* (1970), Amiri Baraka makes the slavery aspect of addiction explicit with white "master" characters, a gang of mafiosi, in prominent roles. The boss Confetti abuses his midlevel seller Bigtime, who abases himself for the drugs that his boss threatens to withhold:

> CONFETTI: You usin' all the stuff yrself?? . . . Get me my money . . . and you betta get that dope out into the community where it belongs. . . .
>
> BIGTIME: Mr. Confetti, please, I never begged nobody before.

CONFETTI: Shit you begged me last week, shine. . . . remember . . . almost the same story?

BIGTIME: But not like this . . . I never cried before, I know that . . . I never cried. (*Weeps.*) Please, please. . . . (12–13; first and third ellipses added)

At the end of the play, militant men of pride shoot to death the gangsters and their accountants; it seems as though they will spare their benighted fellow citizen Bigtime, who makes an impassioned speech to the audience—regarding the urgent need to leave drugs alone—at the heroes' behest. Per the radical tone these texts always take, however, they prepare him an enormous spoon of dope, and his last word is the half-pronounced "Shiiiiiii" (23). Bigtime is hanged from a lamppost alongside Confetti, with the words *slave* and *master* penciled onto signs hung with them, while residents take note and hurry past.

For better or worse, opium-derivative addiction (to both heroin and morphine) radiates the drama and significance essential to multiple vital drug narratives (both black- and white-authored) of the liberation era. The wrenching naturalism of Brown and the dark satire of William S. Burroughs leave their mark in a lasting literary register, while in the scene from *Serpico* just described and in the page-turning potboilers of the best-selling Donald Goines, urban gothic is the mode: per Greg Goode, "To read Goines's description [of a 1970s dope house] is to imagine a bloody, pustulant cross between a pharmacy, an operating room, and a torture chamber, where sick junkies frantically stab at themselves with rusty, clogged needles, trying to hit the track" (44). Cautionary melodramas—including *Dopefiend* (1971), whose subplot about a once-virtuous girl-next-door defines it for Candice Love Jackson as an "anti-heroin tract" (110)—focused on the threat posed by addictive drugs to vulnerable white men and especially women of all races. These include Nelson Algren's Pulitzer Prize–nominated *The Man with the Golden Arm* (1950), Otto Preminger's Oscar-nominated film of the same name (1955), Leonard Bishop's *Down All Your Streets* (1952), and David Hulburd's *H Is for Heroin* (1954). Later, widely read tales from the counterculture such as Helen MacGill Hughes's *The Fantastic Lodge* (1961) and Beatrice Sparks's *Go Ask Alice* (1971) expanded this canon to include other drug hazards. About such texts Taylor Hudson wryly commented, "Middle-class white girls (with mayonnaise-rinsed blond hair) should never even dabble in drugs or booze. One puff, sniff, or swig, and they'll quickly end up in one of two places: the asylum or the grave" (96).

Sparks's text, originally presented as the diary of a fifteen-year-old girl, would be lambasted for (among other reasons) "bizarre symptoms of drugs" with no "believability" (Katsoulis 178); per the unnamed narrator, "Anyone who says pot and LSD are not addicting is a damn, stupid, raving idiot, an unenlightened fool!" (72). In fact, their addictiveness was only in the mind of *Alice*'s middle-aged author—and the parents who sought to ban this book for what Susan Zieger called its "double voicing of pleasure and prohibition" (91). By contrast, as Erich Goode remarks, "heroin addiction . . . has a kind of *crisis quality* to it; more people get hysterical about it than almost any [other drug]" (160), and an early scene from *Dopefiend* depicts one of heroin's more controversial side effects—its integrated community of users: "Here [in the shooting gallery] the color problem didn't really exist. A dopefiend was a dopefiend, whether he was black or not" (Goines 22). Greg Goode remarks that "Goines's eye for interracial social subtleties is acute" (43), and in a preface to Jack Gelber's acclaimed off-Broadway story of heroin addicts, *The Connection* (1957), theater critic Kenneth Tynan comments, "The colour of [the actors'] skin is of negligible importance" (10).

The "crisis" of interracial drug use is underscored throughout the tale narrated to Helen MacGill Hughes, whose white lower-class subject, "Janet Clark," tours the jazz scene and "the Negro 'sporting' world" (Hughes x) on her own road to perdition. One night her boyfriend (currently a white man) is arrested trying to score in the company of a black fellow musician and his white beauty-queen girlfriend. Janet questions why "Bob wanted to go out and cop knowing that the car lights were not working decently and taking a fay along with this spade piano player" (148). Framed thus, interracial ride-sharing is as actionable an offense as is a broken headlight, and throughout the narrative, Clark reports both the establishment's special animosity toward addicts participating in integrated drug culture and the much harsher treatment received by "spades" than "fays" in jail and at court. Due to the tawdry predicaments and rough tones of Hughes's interview subject, her serious sociological study, more accurately classed with those of Fiddle and Larner (which will be discussed later), received the pulp treatment in at least one edition—a 1964 Monarch paperback whose cover featured a shapely white woman in a full slip, one strap off her shoulder, slouched against the wall in a dark room.

While the melodrama of the cautionary texts is received with necessary skepticism today, Burroughs looked on the work of Bishop and Hulburd as competitors to his own pulp narrative and urged his handlers at Ace Paperback to rush it into publication. As in the case of Hughes, Burroughs's own lurid and irrelevant cover art by Ace, of a busty girl dropping her works as the man trying to save (or simply arrest) her grabs her wrist, chased "the phenomenal success of Mickey Spillane" (O. Harris 48). The ruse seems to have worked, as Kenneth C. Davis reports that *Junky*, bundled back-to-back with Maurice Helbrant's *Narcotics Agent*, was "without a doubt the most famous of the Ace Double Novels" (171). The lowbrow origins of *Junky*'s publication history bear upon my reading of drug addiction's politics (i.e., opium addiction as freedom or slavery—a conundrum epitomized by the term *kick* [Burroughs 131]) and economics: for just as the canonical Burroughs started his literary career from the paperback racks of drugstores and train stations, so the criminality that made up long episodes of Burroughs's career as a morphine addict was mostly a lark. At least one critic has credited Burroughs's drug-taking with "help[ing to] account for the hollowness of his voices, which jabber, joke, and rant like ghosts in a cave" (Schjeldahl 74). By contrast, Claude Brown spoke for a community more disadvantaged than almost any other in America; addiction here is enslavement and disability, and Brown seems to have made a success of his life, and written an unforgettable story, only because he managed to steer clear of heroin himself.

Burroughs was the grandson of the inventor of the adding machine and sufficiently wealthy all of his life; although an opium habit ordinarily takes a disastrous toll on an addict's financial circumstances, Burroughs states in the novel's original preface, "My one hundred and fifty dollars a month [some $2200 by modern standards] was always there. . . . It seemed a romantic extravagance to jeopardize my freedom by some token act of crime" (xxxviii). Long before morphine entered his life, Burroughs commits crimes to fill up an underchallenging day: "My criminal acts were gestures, unprofitable and for the most part unpunished. I would break into houses and walk around without taking anything. As a matter of fact, I had no need for money" (xxxvi). During the Depression, when "there were no jobs . . . I couldn't think of any job I wanted in any case" (xxxvii), and thus the morphine habit he develops at the end of World War II is readable as the occupation he takes up for literally lack of anything better to do; twice in *Junky* he describes junk as "a way of life" (xxxix and 127). Thus when Burroughs says that his habit gave him "the real need for money I had never had before" (xxxviii), he suggests less the slide into poverty than simply an appreciation for his trust allowance that escaped him during his early days of listless abundance.

Extravagance though it may be, Burroughs depicts himself engaging in crime throughout *Junky*—rolling drunks, fencing stolen goods, or most often dealing in narcotics himself. Like his wife Joan Vollmer, her daughter by a previous marriage, and their own son, Burroughs's wealth is an underdescribed presence in the text; one moment "I was just barely scraping by" (44) or "I was broke" (66), and per biographer Barry Miles, "His $200 a month from his parents, which in 1946 was plenty to live on, was not enough to feed his habit" (49). Elsewhere in the narrative, "mostly I spent my time painting and working around the house" (62), despite a three-cap-a-day habit, and in Mexico, Burroughs pays for the daily intake of his dealer Ike as well as his own and sends his wife "to Acapulco with the children" (117). Most notably, Burroughs's wealth and privileged background mean that he will never spend inordinate amounts of time in jail; he "drew a four-month suspended sentence" (44) for lush-working and famously talked (and bribed) his way out of punishment for having fatally shot his wife in Mexico, with the aid of an expensive lawyer: "The pillars of the Mexican criminal justice system . . . were bribery and perjury, and in Bernabé Jurado Burroughs had a master in the use of both" (T. Morgan 200). Beyond whatever income street crime afforded him, Burroughs engaged in it because he was fascinated with the hustlers, pimps, queers, and related denizens of the underworld who occupied that terrain. Per biographer Ted Morgan, "Thanks to junk, Burroughs found a place in society which he had been denied repeatedly" (208; see also Miles 43–44).

The Beat classic *On the Road* (1957) is much in dialogue with Burroughs's work (see R. Johnson 21) and includes a stopover with the morphine-shooting Burroughs and his family in New Orleans as one of its many episodes. As in Kerouac's novel, *Junky* comically understates the criminal hijinks that comprise the daily routine of Burroughs's protagonist, the eponymous Bill Lee, and minimizes the interpersonal crises generated by his addiction. *Junky* is also as restless and peripatetic a text as is *On the Road*, with the main characters' frequent movement readable as both flight and freedom: where both Bill Lee and the boys in Kerouac's narrative flee a stultifying parental homestead and stay one step ahead of the law, they also maximize what wealth they have to enjoy freedom of movement. For Sal and Dean this may amount to little more than the borrowed or stolen car they drive, while the considerably wealthier Burroughs sets up domiciles not only in the New Orleans neighborhood of Algiers but in South Texas (where he buys a large tract of land for pot-farming), Mexico, and (in the years subsequent to those narrated in *Junky*) Tangier, Paris, London, and New York. To the degree it can, Burroughs's wealth insulates him from the distractions and desperations that make up the ordinary junkie's life. He never stops traveling and, once begun with this narrative of his addiction, he never stops writing, figuring such economic security as the ultimate freedom. As all great American narratives (and most of the better road trips from the Beat canon) are perhaps destined to end, Burroughs's hero prepares to light out for territory as *Junky* draws to a close: "I am ready to move on south and look for the uncut kick that opens out instead of narrowing down like junk. . . . Kick is momentary freedom from the claims of aging, cautious, nagging, frightened flesh. Yage may be the final fix" (128).

As noted earlier, in important African American writings of the period, heroin addiction is figured rarely as "kicks" but as the enslavement of a community whose long history of bondage in America had taken only its latest turn. In his boyhood, Claude Brown lived a life, for all of its deprivations and violence, of total freedom. Even before school age, "Sonny" and his gang of infant terrorists move through the streets and subways of Manhattan without adult guidance or intrusion; they steal everything within their reach, "ring" cash registers, jostle people for their wallets, and deal each other (and even the hapless girls in their midst) blows to the mouth that result in frequent fistfights. By the second day of first grade, Sonny masters the art of playing hooky under the tutelage of an older boy who teaches him widely in the ways of the street. In and out of reform schools, Sonny meets inspiring counselors but never fails to rise to the top of whatever group he is incarcerated with, so quick are his fists and so wily his methods for pilfering, vandalism, and general mischief-making. Yet of course such freedoms have a broad and hazardous underside, as Brown narrates the desperation of children whose mothers were too busy with their male clients and their own addictions to feed them. One family of preschoolers fights each other for the only egg in the apartment; when this breaks, "Dixie . . . went over to what was left of that old ragged couch they had in the living room, threw herself down on it, and went crying into the cushions" (34). The valiant Sonny, who had impishly ruined the egg in the first place, soon returns having stolen "a dozen eggs and a loaf of bread" (34), and in a few short years, such grievously unparented children turn to selling drugs and their own bodies to survive.

Earlier I suggested that opium addiction was to Burroughs (and to certain of his more privileged associates) an occupation or way of life that had surfaced when there seemed nothing else to do. In the much more underresourced context of 1950s Harlem, drugs occupy a more traditional spectrum of the economy, as a source of income for dealers who will surely realize the best profits when they themselves stay clean. Sonny gets his own financial footing by selling marijuana and then cocaine; this enables him to live independently in his late teens, and he is soon supporting his parents' meager income with drug dealing and fencing stolen goods. By dint of intelligence and some luck, young Claude thrives in this environment and is thus ideally situated to read the "shit plague" (185) that was heroin's onset in Harlem. In his follow-up narrative, *The Children of Ham* (1976), Brown regards addiction as a last-resort vocation: "A lot of people, especially young people, in the Harlem community start using scag just because they don't know what to do with themselves or don't have any specific purpose or goal. Scag was something that would definitely occupy their time, even if it did in the worst way" (53).

To be sure, addiction as occupation is a recurrent theme in sociological studies of the period. An addict talking to sociologist Jeremy Larner in 1964 said that bored teenagers are attracted to heroin as a "game, it's like taking a kid and giving him cowboys-and-Indians. . . . They enjoy it. It gives them something to do" (113). In that same era, sociologist Seymour Fiddle stressed addiction as a vocation or even art form: "Veteran addicts insist there are fewer and fewer good hustlers, especially in the new generation." A hustler who is "'into' something" may be said to have "cornered a market" (56), and sociologist Kenneth Clark observed that "the quality of property stolen by addicts is so high that it has contributed materially to raising the level of goods possessed by people" in underresourced New York neighborhoods (Gottehrer 172). In almost prosaic terms, Fiddle "sketch[es] out a typical day of a man who is a good hustler" (58), relying always on a sharp eye: "The opportunities [for capital acquisition] are as diversified as life itself, and under the pressure of the urge to get straight, the hustler's . . . sensorium will transform reality into a treasure house of possibilities" (59). Finally, "heroin gives a sense of rhythm, rule, norm to life. The morning shot, the afternoon shot, the evening shot. . . . For the man who is not working, is afraid to work, or cannot work, these consumptions points are the equivalent of the workingman's daily schedule" (65).

In a classic essay, Edward Preble and John J. Casey Jr. describe the inflationary effects on the heroin trade after 1957, when syndicate operators left a business that had provided users high-quality product at somewhat low cost for decades, "result[ing] in a relative free market" (7). Release of quality and price controls resulted as well in the liberalizing of junkie behavior; far from the passive, violence-avoidant "mama's boys" they had once been theorized to be, users after 1960 engaged in all manner of profit-oriented crime to support a habit whose costs had increased tenfold in a decade: now, "the heroin user walks with a fast, purposeful stride, as if he is late for an important appointment—indeed he is." Aside from "brief moments of euphoria after each administration of small amounts of heroin," users "aggressively pursu[e] a career that is exacting, challenging, adventurous, and rewarding" (2). An informant describes the alternative of methadone maintenance as the uptown equivalent of the gray flannel suit: "Where you go in a drug-store and get a shot, you get high, but it's the same sort of monotony. You are not getting away with anything." This same interviewee describes using as "a sort of vengeance"

(22) upon an uncaring society, a price extracted to equalize accounts between those who have everything and those with nothing to lose.

Such studies may have flourished in this era because heroin users were such handy specimens—vivid indicators of a city if not a nation in crisis whose dramatic, shamelessly public displays of shooting up and nodding off were street theater at its most frightening and uncanny. In his preface to *The Connection*, Tynan remarks that Gelber's drama "was not like going to the theater, it was like paying a call on old acquaintances" (7). To be sure, Gelber assaults the fourth wall throughout the production, with actors coming up from or addressing members of the audience (including panhandling them during the intermission) and replicating the Beckett-like "waiting" that constitutes the user's existence as drama vérité. Regarding addiction as occupation, Tynan describes junkies as "absentees from the daytime universe" (8) but later asks, "If the aim of life is pleasure, why is it more desirable to achieve it by injecting dollars into a bank account than by injecting dope into the bloodstream?" (9). Brown notes, in accord with the sociologists, "It was practically a twenty-four-hour-a-day job trying to get some money to get some stuff to keep the habit from fucking with you" (180), yet despite the hard work involved, junkies make terrible employees in almost every other respect—no longer suited as numbers-runners or dope-pushers but just leaning against the jukebox in a bar nodding, as Brown finds his younger brother doing at the narrative's low point. The theme of addiction as especially enslaving to underengaged youth is born out in *Manchild*'s last act, when Sonny returns to Harlem after college and observes that "the worst was over for *our generation*" (406, emphasis added). He sees that "most of the junkies around here now are young cats" (407) about to make all of the same fatal mistakes.

Inescapable New York: The Apotheosis of Liberalism in Lindsay's Fun City

In a post-Kerner update, Fred Harris and John Lindsay discuss many quality-of-life crises affecting cities in the early 1970s. For white ethnics in New York, "beer cans" (23, 24) seem to have been a recurring concern and a sign of the cultural liberalism that condoned lax behavior of all kinds—from "the crime wave and the sexual revolution and the drug culture" (21) to the rampant littering that ruined their once-beautiful city. To working-class cultural conservatives, a liberal was lazy, sloppy, and noisy, and they made little distinction between a blaring radio and an antiwar protest with respect to the kind of the "noise" they sought to silence. Both Abbie Hoffman and Todd Gitlin describe "trashing" (*Whole World* 192) as a form of street protest; per Hoffman, on one occasion, "people ran up Second Avenue throwing trash cans into the street. In ten minutes Second Avenue was covered under a sea of garbage" (*Revolution* 54). Jim Carroll's chronicle of the art scene and street life he navigated in the early 1970s, *Forced Entries*, figures both his escape from gritty, grungy New York and his kicking heroin to an abscess on his inner arm, at last successfully lanced: "This was the return of all the bad-cut street-drug garbage I had inserted with such precision all these years. . . . I saw the petty demons marching out. I saw purification, with *new fresh air* being sucked into that cavity. . . . The idol was in ruins" (183).

As Harris suggests in *Alarms and Hopes*, the baby boom was the post-WWII era's first and perhaps most significant example of liberal excess.[2] The disappearance of "elbow room" (F. Harris 29), especially in urban centers, caused interracial tensions, depletion of services such as garbage pickup, and the threat to peace of mind essential to civil traditions. In *State of the Cities*, Harris and Lindsay regard "the ever-increasing physical unpleasantness of the cities—the noise, the smells, the dirt, the jostling and jamming" as an "affliction that every city dweller, young or old, rich or poor, black or white, must bear to a greater or lesser degree" (63). "Sheer noisiness has risen to intolerable levels" (68), and Mayor Lindsay was known for his surprise tours through underserved streets in New York, where he nursed "what amounts almost to an obsession about garbage" (F. Harris 57). Political scientist Andrew Hacker, perceiving "the end of the American era" in 1970, framed the problem not citywide but nationally in the broader terms defining this project: "Americans have endowed themselves with the inalienable right to clutter the national landscape with as many automobiles, children, and tin cans as they see fit" (*End* 128). Due to the nation's origins in revolt against tyranny, "we define as cherished 'freedoms' a whole catalogue of pleasantries and privileges, and we regard official intrusions into them as the onset of autocracy" (217).

Vincent J. Cannato's largely critical view of the Lindsay administration would blame the mayor's liberalism for the city's many woes during his two terms between 1965 and 1973. But Cannato fails to read liberalism in Lindsay's numerous adversaries as well; shortly into his administration, the mayor tried to quell an impending garbage strike with what Cannato terms a "fairly generous offer." Rejecting the package out of hand, garbagemen struck "almost for catharsis"—that is, in "ang[er] at apparent preferences shown the minorities" (Cannato 197). Indulging an impulse to maximize personal freedom, even at the expense of viable economic improvement, the striking garbage workers enacted the liberalism I am focused on in this chapter—what Daniel Bell in a related context describes as "'conspicuous loafing,' . . . the hostile gesture of the tired working class" (233). When Governor Rockefeller is asked to call out the National Guard to alleviate the public health menace threatened by piled-up garbage, the strike figures plainly as the white working-class version of the urban riot, to be matched by labor strikes among teachers, transit workers, and builders throughout the Lindsay years. Ironically, Rockefeller referred to "H. Rap Brown on television" (Cannato 199) as his reason for *not* sending in the guard—suggesting that Brown had taught the governor that bringing in the Guard just makes a tense situation explosive. His equally lame excuse—that the "weekend warrior" National Guard would be "physically incapable of the strenuous labor involved in trash removal" (199)—indicates both the double standard that allowed for white but not black unrest during the period and the politics of liberal low points of the Lindsay era: Rockefeller had already begun to resent Lindsay's success and may have allowed the garbage to sit on city streets simply to tarnish the mayor's honeymoon period, while late in his administration, the state-run MTA purposely acted slowly to clean up the graffiti-covered subways that were another source of despair and defeat for New Yorkers of all classes, not to mention the mayor himself.

Per Cannato, "Lindsay attacked graffiti publically and vigorously" (534). He regarded graffiti as "profoundly depressing—it truly hurt people's moods. The life would go out of everybody when they saw the [subway] cars defaced" (qtd. in Cannato 535), and sociologist Nathan Glazer indicted graffiti as a government failure, as the "inescapable knowledge that the [urban] environment . . . is uncontrolled and uncontrollable, and that anyone can invade it to do whatever damage and mischief the mind suggests" (qtd. in Wilson and Kelling 33). In West Coast hippie communes and related scenes, filth was less class warfare than a badge of countercultural identity. Reporter Rasa Gustaitis observed that the guru of Morningstar Ranch, Lou Gottlieb, is "making freedom from sanitation a matter of civil rights. He thinks we need liberation from our compulsion from cleanliness," which he labels "the Lady Macbeth complex" (139). But the kids at the commune are as hungry and self-interested as are the poor of New York; immediately Gustaitis is relieved of two packs of cigarettes, and everyone's nagging nicotine habit "becomes a rather large preoccupation [which] seems rather wasteful of one's attention" (147). Finally repulsed by the piles of garbage and "those turds along the path," Gustaitis declares, "I still dig my utopia clean" (153). In his memoir of life at Timothy Leary's Millbrook estate, Art Kleps (Chief Boohoo of the Neo-American Church in that period) complained to Leary "about the amount of dog, cat, and goat shit in and around the Big House during the last few months, when the place had disintegrated into a mere comfort station for people and animals" (36). Echoing Gottlieb, Leary, "who was very fastidious personally, replied, 'Art, that's your problem. You have never learned to love shit'" (36).

In Ben Caldwell's ultimately charming *The Wall* (1967), a diverse demographic, including a couple in love, a white hippie and his chick, a church lady, a revolutionary, and a group of teenage boys, all find space on the shared urban turf that is an unmarked wall. An "overflowing garbage can" (91) mars the foreground, and the wall itself is marked with disturbing initial forays—"I HATE NIGGERS" and "KILL ALL NIGGERS" (91)—that on Caldwell's radically liberal stage everyone manages to ignore. But the chance to express oneself "tempts" even the church lady to quickly scrawl "JESUS SAVES" (92); a Nation of Islam follower later writes that "WHITEY IS THE DEVIL" (92), and an irreverent teenage boy amends the black revolutionary's "PRESIDENT NIXON IS A FAGGOT" to "JESUS IS A FAGGOT" (92). The boys comically scrawl remarks about "PUSSY" in every remaining space, and the short work ends on a cartoon gag, with the last boy dragged offstage writing "THE END" (92). With this text, Caldwell invites his urban viewers to regard freshly painted walls as one of "white" society's lesser invitations to declare their love—as when a black man draws "DAVID LOVES MARY" with his girlfriend's lipstick—and make their revolutionary statements. In the words of an inveterate tagger among the youths profiled in Claude Brown's *The Children of Ham*, "I'm just as much as anybody else, and my name is just as important as [white people's names on buildings]. They like to see they names up, and I like to see mine" (13). Brown himself remarks, regarding the abandoned tenement where this family of young teenagers makes its home, "The saving grace of this building might very well be the erratic patterns of the varied and brilliant colors of graffiti that adorn it internally and externally from basement to roof" (7).

Cannato cites another kind of liberal, different from antigraffiti advocates like Lindsay and Glazer, who regarded graffiti as a "chic new art form" (535; see also J. Austin 92–94), while a "sociologist at the Twentieth Century Fund" looked with equanimity on vandalism in public parks throughout the period: "It was a form of recreation. Some people liked to sit on the benches; others like to tear them up" (Cannato 147). Just after the Lindsay era, Andrew Hacker had a similarly broad-minded view of self-interest across the social spectrum: "The upsurge in crime expresses a new sense of freedom on the part of classes which were once kept sternly in their place." Even respectable "people in their forties show much less of the stuffiness other periods praised as maturity"; these establishment New Yorkers "enjoy themselves with much less embarrassment . . . [and] take their cues from the kids who turn in fire alarms" (*New Yorkers* 2–3). Hailing self-interest as a lifestyle revolution long overdue, Hacker argues that "the city gains as a creative center as citizens cut loose from burdens [including laws and children] that dissipate their energies" (3).

Speaking of women's workplace revolution as New York became less factory-based and more corporate, Hacker's comment that "liberation is a post-industrial phenomenon" (5) has broader resonance: as job security in the industrial sector ebbed, the "places" (literally the positions or employments) that all kinds of blue-collar New Yorkers no longer "knew" left only "cutting loose" as an occupation, whose social and economic wages compared poorly if at all. Again it is liberalism that both condones these acts of liberty-taking as rights belonging to all and, per the terms presented throughout this project, foregrounds these liberties to obfuscate the equalities denied at the same time: even Hacker admits that "people will react to their lack of power in various ways. Street crime is one of them; strikes, demonstrations, and vandalism are others" (71). Working-class whites and poor urban minorities ran roughshod over urban infrastructure in the liberation era, in a tradeoff society made freely, because cleaning up, or simply ignoring the problem, costed so much less than the education, jobs, and opportunities that the urban disaffected consistently went without instead.

Conclusion: Crisis in Liberal America

John Carpenter wrote *Escape from New York* in the mid-1970s as a reaction to the Watergate scandal, and by the time it was produced in 1981, the U.S. president in his cast of characters, ultimately humiliated by hero Snake Plisskin, targets Ronald Reagan instead. For most of the story, the president is a passive prisoner, and the Iran hostage crisis of the late 1970s was also in the director's mind during much of the making of the film (Carpenter). Thus Carpenter's repeated reference to his film as "sci-fi" must be weighed against not only these numerous contemporary references but also its broader reflection of national life in the film's original mid-1970s moment. As *Escape* begins, a female robotic-sounding voice announces a catastrophically futuristic increase in crime by 400 percent, necessitating the drastic step of turning the island of Manhattan into a walled prison. Recall, however, that in my introduction, I quoted statistics regarding an increase in robbery of 825 percent, in burglary of 480 percent, and murder doubling in New York between 1960 and 1968 (Schneider 117). Regrettably, there was nothing speculative about such spiking crime; to its original New York (and national) audience, it was literally yesterday's news, and the film's sets strewn with garbage, wrecked furniture, open fires, and junk cars, as well as the inner walls of abandoned buildings covered with graffiti, would have been depressingly familiar. Two pundits from the era proposed turning New York into "a 'sandbox' to contain undesirables because 'I don't want these people climbing up over the [suburban?] walls" (J. Austin 97; insert in original). True to the liberalism of '60s-era indifferent policing, what is most frightening about New York in Carpenter's film is the freedom with which the criminals run the streets in total anarchy. Food is dropped via helicopter once a month, and the free-for-all that otherwise makes up existence is sharply reminiscent of the violence that overtook the inmates of Attica's D Yard when power struggles and maximized liberties resulted in rapes and murder. Although the cynical police and politicians hovering at the margins of the main action are framed as murderous hypocrites, the radical hijacker who crashes Air Force One into Battery Park fares no better. She is a send-up of Weather Underground leader Bernadine Dohrn (resembling the actress in the part), Patty Hearst, Valerie Solanas, Angela Davis, and other "extreme" females of the period. Her ineffectual attempt to change the world by hijacking the president's plane causes the trouble that endangers the hero, Snake.

As perhaps a precursor to action films' compulsion for black actors in the role of U.S. president, it is not the president here (played by the Carpenter mainstay Donald Pleasance) but the Duke of New York who is brought to life by soul icon Isaac Hayes. With a nod to Blaxploitation hits once more from the recent past, the Duke rides around New York in a tricked-out limousine, complete with chandeliers mounted over the headlights and a disco ball twirling from the rearview mirror. His lavish expenditure of both gasoline and electricity in one of the few working cars on the island critiques the excesses of the late 1970s, when the gas shortage that hobbled Carter's presidency was as much a tolling of the bell as was Watergate. But Carpenter seems oblivious to the broader racial allegory promised then dashed by his plotline: although the villain's part is a coveted role, played skillfully by Hayes with his imposing presence and booming voice, the Duke presides over a gladiatorial battle between Snake and an evil giant, telling his audience that tomorrow "we will roll down that 69th Street Bridge, on our way to freedom."

It is impossible to miss here echoes of King (the name Duke even suggesting a connection) in his role at the head of freedom marches throughout the civil rights era, using these exact terms. Hayes increases the poignancy of this otherwise violent scene by employing King's trademark vibrato over his major syllables. When the Duke is gunned down—by the U.S. president no less—just as he reaches the end of the bridge, King's failed first march to Selma and his own tragic assassination come unavoidably to mind. Pertinent to the context of the film itself, the Duke represents the thousands of urban blacks who simply did not make it out of dangerous cities in this period; the white president and the white hero escape, and a violent allegory of white flight and residential segregation is enacted to the subconscious satisfaction of Carpenter's mainly white audience.

Dick Gregory comically chided his 1970 audience at Bronx Community College for having "done give us *all* the major cities—without a fight! . . . Y'all drive two hours every evening to get to the cave. We sure want to thank you. And dig the capital, your capital, Washington, DC—that's *all* us! I mean, can you believe your insanity?" Here Gregory skewers the panic mentality of white flight that indeed ceded many miles of urban turf to ethnic and racial minorities in a headlong dash to the postwar suburbs—a nationwide social expenditure or wealth transfer that, though radically politically conservative, was just as economically liberal in Gregory's ironic rendering. Except for the Attica massacre occurring in rural upstate New York—and the killing fields of Vietnam, never far from the minds of the antiwar Left—all of the ground contested, burned, bloodied, and transformed in the social protests discussed in this chapter was city ground. Gregory's witticisms remind us that many of the contests—the riots, police shakedowns in Harlem, and ruinous influx of heroin in black neighborhoods nationwide—were harshly racially inflected. And perhaps the parallel tracks down which whites and African Americans ran in these contexts—the many differences between dropping acid and shooting horse, hip and antiwar activists appropriating black suffering for their own aims—only reemphasizes that racial divide, even as participants in diverse campaigns regarded themselves as all coming from a shared left-wing perspective. The layers of complexity that I have applied to the term *liberal* are to indicate how difficult traditional Left/Right distinctions can be. In the liberation era, urban Americans across the social spectrum spent with abandon the words, actions, bullets, tear gas, garbage, and graffiti that advanced the goals of "the people" or "the pigs" and turned against each other in extortion and violence when the money to maintain a policeman's extravagant lifestyle or a junkie's expensive heroin habit ran out. Per the views of Lindsay-era sociologists, filmmaker John Carpenter, and comedian Dick Gregory, it was deemed throughout the liberation era so much better—because so much less expensive—for the white middle class to turn out the city lights and lock the door as it left; whoever tried to scale the wall was violently turned back, and the urban shambles that was left behind ironically paved the way for the Disneyfications and gentrifications of the Reagan era.

CHAPTER 3

TOOLS OF THE TRADE

WORKING WOMEN AND RADICAL WOMEN IN THE LIBERATION ERA

The Miss America Pageant debuted in Atlantic City on 8 September 1921, as a gimmick by local businessmen to extend the summer tourist season beyond its traditional Labor Day demise. In addition to the commercial interests that motivated the event, coincident history may also in part explain the pageant's origins—or at least its initial tremendous popularity: a year earlier, the nation had ratified the Nineteenth Amendment, guaranteeing women the right to vote, and a decade of relaxed sartorial and sexual rules had begun. At this moment, a group of male business leaders and, to be sure, a large contingent of mixed audience members (not to mention the enthused contestants themselves) seemed to seek reassurance in traditional femininity displayed for general consumption. In other words, no sooner had women staked out for themselves a measure of political, personal, and sexual freedom than they found it recouped to their detriment by those exploiting female sexuality for public and private gains.

Just as ironically, the 1968 Miss America Pageant provided the stage whereupon second-wave feminism impressed itself on the national consciousness for the first time. Influenced by the street theatrics of Abbie Hoffman's East Coast Digger collective (Bradley 63), the New York Radical Women (NYRW) marched on the boardwalk, carrying signs that read "Let's Judge Ourselves as People" and "Cattle Parades are Degrading to Human Beings"; in keeping with their "meat" theme, they crowned a live sheep Miss America. Not surprisingly, they also filled up a Freedom Trash Can with "instruments of female torture" (R. Morgan 584), including false eyelashes, copies of *Playboy* and *Ladies' Home Journal*, high heels, make-up, and the "pneumatic" (Greer, *Female* 39) bras of mid-century repute. Although they were denied the necessary permits to ignite the toxic, plasticky load into a stinky blaze, so expected was the conflagration that would conclude the trash can stunt that the appellation "bra-burner" was born soon after and attached pejoratively to the second-wave women's movement from then on.

The Thursday following the event, Art Buchwald's column "The Bra-Burners" lamented the protesters' decision to give up the accoutrements that drew men's attention; without them, he comically averred, they would soon resemble the eccentric musical performer of the era, Tiny Tim. Buchwald's column thus fanned the flames, so to speak, regarding the second wave's pyromania for female foundations; as Ruth Rosen has observed, "Bras seemed to mean a great deal to those journalists who couldn't tell the difference between the sexual revolution and women's liberation" (160). Later, "'bra-burning' became a symbolic way of sexualizing—and thereby trivializing—the women's struggle for emancipation" (161). With respect for the basic truths of Rosen's assessment, radical women's liberation and potentially recuperative, exploitative sexual freedom were as intertwined and interdependent for some (see, e.g., Ehrenreich et al. 40) as they were mutually exclusive for others. The ultimate payout was complex indeed: the Radical Women's legitimate complaint, for instance, against painful, denaturalizing bras, corsets, and girdles—and myriad cultural confinements keyed to their presence on the public stage—could not but pale in comparison, as an overdramatized bra-burning, in the crisis-ridden landscape of money-burning (by the Diggers of New York and San Francisco), draft card–burning, and cross-burning in that era. Inverting the terms of chapter 1, where Black Power leaders' incendiary speech was blamed for the urban violence (including arson) that sometimes followed, Patricia Bradley remarks that the promise of bra-burning "might have done more to bring reporters to that boardwalk for the event than the fiery rhetoric of [its] press release" (60).

This release, titled "No More Miss America!" and written by NYRW founder Robin Morgan, closed with the ten-point manifesto that no self-respecting rights movement broached the public scene without at this time. Critiqued there were the pageant's overt racism (there had never been an African American finalist), its tours of Vietnam (mocked as "the living bra and the dead soldier"), and contestants as walking advertisements for the hair products, clothing, and cosmetics manufactured by the pageant's many sponsors. The Radical Women challenged Miss America's ideological import, causing all women to be divided into winners and losers based on appearance, and as each Miss America subsides into obscurity at the end of a year's reign, so women in general were made to feel obsolete as soon as they reached a certain age, weight, education level, and so on. They contrasted the real power wielded by the U.S. president (which any American boy can grow up to be) to the fake crown and scepter and spurious political power bestowed on Miss America (girls' only role model) the night her dreams come true. Finally, the protesters critiqued the "Degrading Mindless-Boob-Girlie Symbol," whose specter of unachievable perfection shadowed ordinary women throughout their lives and emphasized the victimization of Miss America contestants themselves, forced by the "Madonna-Whore Combination" to walk the invisible line between sweetness and sexual readiness as precariously as they stepped in high heels across the stage of the swimsuit competition.

As the New York *Radical* Women, this group, many similar others, and many prominent spokeswomen of the liberation era directly opposed the *liberal* feminism promoted by equally prominent leaders of the day, most famously Betty

Friedan and her National Organization for Women (NOW), less pronouncedly Gloria Steinem and her widely read feminist magazine *Ms.*, and a host of like-minded middle-class aspiring professionals. These women turned to Friedan's ideas—especially her emphasis on women's work and women's modes of entrée into the male-dominated professions—for information and inspiration, for tools of the high-skilled trades they sought to enter. By contrast, radical feminists rejected the capitalist rat race—even the bid for economic equality—under any circumstances. At the Miss America protest, the only "professional women" the demonstrators saw were the prostituted Miss America candidates themselves, and this chapter will return throughout to the prospect of women achieving legitimate careers in the shadow of women's oldest profession. Per the spectacular, street-based, male-dominated contexts established in chapters 1 and 2, radical feminists published raucous best sellers and took their message to the streets (or large indoor public events such as the pageant itself, which the NYRW did infiltrate), while liberal feminists sought to integrate the halls of political power and the interior spaces of corporate success (an exception being the historic August 1970 Women's March down New York's Fifth Avenue, headed by Friedan and NOW leadership). Both groups, meanwhile, were forced, as the male actors in the freedom era never were, to fend off the designation as "streetwalkers" simply for going public with their demands. In other words, in the freedom era, women novelists, women thinkers, and female characters (some of these penned by popular male authors of the period) wrestled endlessly with the issue of whether the professional woman would ever successfully free herself from the demands for sexual attractiveness that enabled her success or—when she was simply too pretty to let out of the house—led to her professional or personal demise.

The sexual revolution, and the contraceptive technologies hugely enabling it, presented modern women the dilemma of sexual freedom: How could they make it truly their own, and when should they use modern medicine to limit or curtail their fertility so as to succeed in the modern workplace? While reproductive and related technologies thus will be read in this chapter as additional tools of the trade, the NYRW worried that their beleaguered sisters parading around at the convention center were simply the latest in an endless parade of "tools" more traditionally construed: pawns in the trade relations between powerful men or, as noted at the outset, tools in a capitalist scheme to keep the Atlantic City Boardwalk—and later, the pageant's many sponsors—commercially viable. In the broader context, beautiful women have "traded" their sexuality for legal marriage by which to protect their children and secure for themselves a domestic life. Women have almost always preferred such safe and sanctioned trades to the illegitimate bargains struck by the paid sex worker, though radical feminism emphasized the similarity between the two; this chapter will thus conclude by considering a few of the era's happier hookers and the radical liberalism, thus the radical threat, they posed to feminists and establishment alike.

Meanwhile, as correct as Morgan and the NYRW were in their published critiques and in their attention-getting street theater, the hated Madonna-whore complex emerged in the midst of the movement itself. If the sexual revolution meant everything from liberal feminist demands for equal pay for equal work (a workplace revolution for the female sex) to some radical feminists' demand to enjoy sex outside marital bonds (a revolution in women's sexual roles), second-wave feminists claimed only qualified success in either sector: they fell far short of equal professional opportunity and remuneration and faced the nearly impossible task of building a self-determined, self-serving sexual identity that did not immediately redound to the benefits of men. The pill, for instance, did as much if not more to release men from their own burdens of monogamy, marriage, and parenthood than it ever did for women, and save for the singular example of lesbianism political and otherwise, the freer women felt to be dynamic, nontraditional, sexual persons, the happier men were to enjoy the favor without having to pay it back.

Barbara Leon of the radical Redstocking group wrote ironically in 1971, "Our brothers are offering us freedom . . . freedom from love; freedom from emotional support; freedom from sharing the material privileges they have enjoyed for so long" (qtd. in Gerhard, *Desiring* 110). Women of the Black Power movement critiqued male emphasis on women as bearers of revolutionaries: "What plans do you have for the care of me and my child? Am I to persist in the role of Amazon workhorse and house slave?" (205), asked Toni Cade Bambara in an influential 1970 collection edited by herself. Elsewhere, "and when's the last time you fed one of them brats you've been breeding all over the city, you jive-ass so-and-so?" (qtd. in Cade Bambara 205). Another Redstocking, Patricia Mainardi, distinguished "liberated women" from "women's liberation." The former, says Mainardi, "warm[ed] the hearts (not to mention other parts) of the most radical men" (94), while the latter named a campaign for rights and equality that had little to do with warming men's parts, radical or otherwise (see also Densmore, Dunbar, and Segal 31). Yet Mainardi's simple inversion suggests how slender the distinction between these terms remained throughout the period.

The conundrum is exemplified once more in a famous photo from the Atlantic City protest (see figure 3.1). Despite the militancy of the demonstrating women, it is doubtful that the beefy, scornful viewer of this display has women's equality in mind. To be sure, their poster of an attractive, nude, alluringly posed model, with her flirtatious cowboy hat and sultry, over-the-shoulder glance, helps matters not at all, and one might ponder forever the motivation that led the protesters to make their statement with this particular image: surely it exploits the very "sexual sell"

Figure 3.1. Members of the National Women's Liberation Party hold protest signs in front of Convention Hall, where the Miss America Pageant will be held in Atlantic City, New Jersey, on September 7, 1968. The picketers, also seen behind, are protesting the annual pageant as degrading to women (AP Photo).

that the Radical Women critique in their ten points, and yet mid-century feminists clearly sought to recoup such images for their own purposes. In their hands, they might insist, this image was not a sexual come-on but a disturbing irony meant to get attention and change minds. Yet they risked worsening the very problem they sought to alleviate whenever they dared to publicize and politicize women's sexuality.

This chapter will consider an array of liberation-era writing, thinking, and literary or cinematic characters; each text contributes meaningfully to the question of women at work, the tools of their trades (from pharmaceutical technologies employed in Jacqueline Susann's *Valley of the Dolls* to the aviation technologies in texts as diverse as Erica Jong's *Fear of Flying*, Donald Bain's *Coffee, Tea, or Me?*, and Louis Sher's soft-porn blockbuster *The Stewardesses*), and their radical moments of escape from both traditional marriage and "selling out" in the capitalist workplace. In these works from many genres, diverse renditions of and responses to women's personal, sexual freedom appear, although even in some feminist classics, "sexual freedom" is rendered a contradiction in terms by the end of the narrative, where punishment has lain awaiting the erring heroine throughout literary history. In these works, I will gauge freedom itself in diverse ways: How free is female sexuality from the bonds of matrimony, legal or physical coercion, or wider social sanction? Is it free from the mandate to pledge oneself to one true love or even from love feelings of any kind? Is it engaged in freely—frequently and "on demand," without the usual frustrations and subterfuges of traditional courtship? Do the adult characters discuss sexual needs freely—as unencumbered free agents with full rights to privacy and self-determination? How do these texts position sexual activity in contexts that are simultaneously "free" (engaged in consensually and without social constraint) and yet also freely participating in the prostitution economy wherein the sex in question must be paid for and is often quite expensive?

Though qualifying a text as authentically feminist—liberal, radical, or otherwise—may be endlessly open to debate, I instead examine in these works the more concretely identifiable phenomenon of women's break from traditional sexual mores that had controlled their behavior for decades prior: maintenance of virginity until marriage or at least engagement, marriage for life, sexual fidelity, and a host of truly tragic outcomes related to these constraints, including marriage due to unplanned pregnancy instead of love or compatibility; lifelong entrapment in abusive, deceptive, or otherwise loveless relationships; lesbians (and gay men) all but forced to marry members of the opposite sex, and so on. Despite sexual freedom's indeed questionable elements, it is a premise of the argument commencing here that said freedom constitutes its own revolutionary gesture, which indeed greatly impacted women's (and men's) lives in not only sexual but political, professional, and economic spheres. As Barbara Ehrenreich et al. argue, regarding *Valley of the Dolls* as a harbinger of the sexual revolution, "women's sexual revolution grew out of the same frustrations and opportunities that inspired the feminist movement and, like it, initially represented the aspirations of the 'New Woman'" (40). Per Clare Knowles, in novels such as Susann's, "the making visible of the previously hidden [e.g., intercourse and other taboo sexual subjects] is a powerfully feminist action, regardless of authorial intent" (65; see also Lauret 93–94). But because I have also argued that this freedom could never be other than its own double-edged sword, I will study the political gains as well as losses depicted in these texts, with special emphasis on liberation-era technologies that freed or hindered women and on the mix of sex with financial gain, as this reinscribed or revised the "whore" image so vigorously denounced by second-wave feminists. Perhaps not surprisingly, these texts present occasions of violence—successfully avoided, cynically exploited, or tragically manifested—as an enduring response to radical expressions of women's sexuality.

Sexual Freedom in the Postwar Intellectual Context

The late-twentieth-century transformation of sexual mores, enabled mainly by the birth control pill but also by relaxing attitudes toward established cultural traditions across the board, found its philosophical underpinnings in an influential generation of post-Freudian thinkers who regarded an honest approach to human sexuality as the sine qua non of modern life. As the title *Eros and Civilization* (1955, 1966) indicates, Herbert Marcuse wrote in direct response to Freud's *Civilization and its Discontents* (1929), challenging Freud's thesis that the repression of sexual instincts was key to social stability. Where Freud trumpeted the powers of sublimation, the rechanneling of sexual energy into the work humans did to build society, Marcuse argued that such suppressions made people susceptible to fascist authority. Both he and his fellow German Jewish émigré Wilhelm Reich politicized sexual relations and family structure and linked conservative forms of both to the rise of Hitler and other twentieth-century dictators. As Marcuse observed, "Intensified progress [the building of society through sublimation] seems to be bound up with intensified unfreedom" (4), and in *The Sexual Revolution* (1945, 1962), Reich attacked sexual prudery, marriage, and family, insisting that all three were moralistic social constructs that made men and women frustrated, miserable, and once again susceptible to "submission to authority and Führers" (xxiv). He advocated total sexual freedom for teenagers and adults and is credited with coining the term *the sexual revolution*. In *The Function of the Orgasm* (1942, 1961, 1968), Reich promoted a theory of mental and physical health based on regular exercise of the sexual function, and such theories influenced sex-positive intellectuals of 1960s, including William Burroughs and Norman Mailer, both of whom owned Reich's "orgone accumulator" (a phone-booth-sized box that was said to contain sexual energies and have healthful effects on whoever sat in one).

In *Life against Death* (1959) the American-born social philosopher Norman O. Brown echoed Marcuse's critique of the relentless human tendency to sublimate. Where Marcuse and Reich saw repression leading to Hitler worship, Brown targets the hydrogen bomb and argues for "a little more Eros and less strife" (312) to counter modern manifestations of the death principle: repression, sublimation, capitalist hoarding tendencies, related work fixations, and the arms race itself.

He advocates play and even "polymorphous perversity" (308, 313) as essential to a secular "resurrection of the body"—a reinstatement of bodily, sensuous, and sexual enjoyments into modern life. In *Love and Will* (1969), the American psychotherapist Rollo May agrees that Eros is missing from modern life, yet he distinguishes passionate interpersonal regard from depersonalized acts of sex. May thus questions the sexual salvifics promoted by Reich and others, regarding "the preoccupation with achieving a simultaneous orgasm as another form of alienation." He is especially concerned with the pressure his female patients feel to perform: although feminists of his era would supplant the mythical vaginal orgasm with clitoral satisfaction, May reverts to Freudian tradition by averring that "the technical preoccupation robs the woman of exactly what she wants most of all, namely the man's spontaneous abandon at the moment of climax. This abandon gives her whatever thrill or ecstasy she . . . [is] capable of" (44).

The feminist theorists influential to this discussion argue less often for sexuality as a weapon against political repression than as a weapon of oppression used against themselves. Like Marcuse and his left-leaning brethren, they are as conversant with Marx's tenets as they are with Freud's; Germaine Greer, for instance, reads women as the "true proletariat" (25), and the title of her famed *The Female Eunuch* (1970) describes the ideological construct that all women, to liberate themselves, must revolt against. The eunuch for Greer is drained of her sexual and personal "energy," which she associates with the concepts of power, agility, movement, and health. Though the eunuch may be as sexy as a Barbie doll, she is just as sexless as the stiff-moving, pubic-hairless, nipple-less, odorless Barbie as well, displaying no sexual characteristics or urges of her own. In response, or in revolt, Greer is therefore glad about women's discard of overpadded brassieres: "Women [should] refuse to wear undergarments which perpetuate the fantasy of pneumatic boobs, so that men must come to terms with the varieties of the real thing. . . . Recent emphasis on the nipple . . . is in woman's favor, for the nipple is expressive and responsive" (*Female Eunuch* 39). Greer deplores the phobic response to women's natural smells, menstruation, fertility, genitality, and all failures to conform to the ideal physical type. She concludes her remarkable chapter titled "Loathing and Disgust" thus: "She will continue to apologize and disguise herself, while accepting her male's pot-belly, wattles, bad breath, farting, stubble, baldness and other ugliness without complaint. . . . Women are reputed to never be disgusted. The sad fact is that they often are, but not with men; following the lead of men, they are most often disgusted with themselves" (293).

Greer, like many mid-century writers on the subject, distrusted the early versions of the pill, which did indeed arrive on the market overloaded with hormones conducive to dangerous side effects. She challenges other contraceptive methods as ineffective, "painful," "oddly disquieting" (315), and in general, "taking a toll on female sexuality" (314). Greer yet enjoins her reader that she "must not marry" (359) or must be ready to leave a marriage that does not serve her well, even à la Ibsen's Nora Helmer leaving children with their father if he is better situated. In standard radical-feminist terms, Greer advises that women choose living and child-rearing with other women in "household cooperatives" (364) and urges that they turn to liberated sisters for support when escaping their "enemies, the doctors, psychiatrists, health visitors, priests, marriage counsellors, policemen, magistrates, and genteel reformers" (23) that surround them otherwise. Greer refers to sex separatism as a joyful "struggle" (23), suggesting that women without marriage will enter reduced financial circumstances, whose solution she describes vaguely if at all. As she freely acknowledges, "Liberty is terrifying" even if it is "also exhilarating" (22); she later asks women to recognize "insecurity as freedom" (274). Though she remarks somewhat irresponsibly in the preface to the twenty-first-anniversary edition, "*The Female Eunuch* does not deal with poor women (for when I wrote it I did not know them)" (11), in fact Greer is on the way to creating them when she recommends the joyful embrace of poverty by revolutionary women as a preferred alternative to the limits of life as a kept housewife or cog in the capitalist machine.

Barbara Seaman was a women's health advocate and medical editor for women's magazines (see Bradley 136) whose *Free and Female* (1972) defines "the liberated orgasm" as "any orgasm *you* like under any circumstances *you* find comfortable" (73). In reference to New York feminist Anne Koedt in her influential "The Myth of the Vaginal Orgasm" (1970), Seaman concedes that both clitoral and vaginal versions may exist but attacks damaging ideologies of frigidity and maladjustment (see also Gerhard, "Revisiting" 450). But regarding the liberated breast and nipple, celebrated by Greer as a natural, diversely made organ, one of Seaman's female interviewees worries, "The way some of the girls in New York City are revealing their cute little tits now, I don't know how the men can stand it. I'm surprised there isn't more rape" (qtd. in Seaman, *Free* 150). Though Seaman advocates "the economic liberation of women[, which] will probably make for better sex, for all" (211), her emphasis on job-sharing and "a great increase in part-time jobs" (287) so that women can have a career and motherhood echoes the utopianism of Greer's call for women's joyful embrace of reduced living standards.

Like Greer, Seaman considers birth control as a sword that cuts far more against women than it cuts away. She critiques "doctors [who] continue to prescribe the pill as if it were sugar candy" (*Free* 178) and urges readers to liberate themselves from naive faith in a wonder drug that "hasn't been invented yet, and what's more, there is little reason to believe that it is about to come down the pike" (239). Between publication of this text and her earlier, landmark *The Doctor's Case Against the Pill* (1969), Seaman played an important role in congressional hearings regarding the pill's side effects and medical disclosure (see Marks 150–151 and Seaman, *Free* 253–255 n. 28, 29). Notably, years after improvements to the pill's hormonal content has allowed for safe use, the pill has economically liberated employers as much if not more so than female employees: now, women's ability to plan (or forgo altogether) pregnancies, and even alleviate the menstrual cramps and heaviness of flow that might have disqualified them from daily labor in the pre-pill era, have made them more reliable (i.e., man-like) workers with improved career prospects but at perhaps significant personal cost. In an article for *Esquire*, Gloria Steinem remarked that the pill was even good for business when "stock values of its distributors . . . jumped amazingly. Each day, about five hundred more women begin using the pill" ("Moral" 154).

In the Black Power context, the pill was viewed by both men and women as no sort of liberator but instead as a bullet "targeting poor blacks" (Critchlow 83). In a dystopian drama by Black Arts dramatist Ben Caldwell, *Top Secret* (1968), a federal program named Operation Pre-Kill develops a birth control pill with genocidal intentions: "Within twenty years . . . there would be a severe—and most welcome—shortage of black people" (Van Deburg, *Hoodlums* 102). In an early reading of this play, Charles D. Peavy reports on a black Pittsburgh physician interviewed by the black Muslim journal *Muhammad Speaks*: "Using Pittsburgh as an example, the doctor says that nine birth control centers have been placed in only four black districts in Pittsburgh, where there are not even that many schools. These clinics have been placed in mobile units, public housing projects, and even flophouses" (45). Finally, CORE director Floyd McKissick wrote a noted short story, "Diary of a Black Man," in which a white-run America of the future develops a "Pill Bomb" the size of an aspirin and targeting inner-city neighborhoods "without danger of fallout in the surrounding areas" (*3/5* 162). Robin D. G. Kelley reports that "members of the Nation of Islam invaded birth control clinics and published articles . . . [depicting] bottles of birth control pills marked with skull and crossbones" (146).

As Donald T. Critchlow demonstrates, the Johnson- and Nixon-era rhetoric of "family planning" and even "Planned Parenthood" had nothing to do with the abortion rights these terms call to mind today[1] but with the Moynihan-style social engineering that would abet the War on Poverty by reducing welfare rolls through contraceptive technology. In Van Deburg's concise summation, "Zero Population Growth was devil-speak for 'no more black babies'" (*Hoodlums* 104; see also Critchlow 113, 139–141). As Critchlow observes, the *Black Panther* newspaper and other militant publications warned black women away from contraceptives on a regular basis (61, 109–110, 143–144), and family planners in Washington had only limited success confronting the "cultural and religious reasons" (Critchlow 159) why motherhood was regarded as key to women's identities in high-fertility black and Hispanic communities. In this period, Angela Davis remarked that abortions among black women and Latinas were "not so much about the desire to be free from their pregnancy [as in the white women's campaign for reproductive rights] but rather about the miserable social conditions which dissuade them from bringing new lives into the world" (*Women* 204). Marshalling copious evidence of then rampant sterilization programs in poor communities, Davis observes that "while women of color are urged, at every turn, to become permanently infertile, white women . . . are urged [via barriers such as waiting periods and informed consent] to reproduce themselves" (*Women* 221).

Studying a low-income St. Louis community from the period, Joyce A. Ladner reported that "90 percent of the males and 94 percent of the females disapproved of abortion as an alternative to a hypothetical teenage premarital pregnancy" (257). She wryly remarked that "the protective shelters which society has imposed on white women have never been problematic for Black women, because society has refused to offer them the same protectiveness. . . . As a result, Black women have always been 'liberated'" (277). Per Toni Morrison in 1971, "In some way, black women have known something of the freedom white women are now beginning to crave. But oddly, freedom is only sweet when it is won. When it is forced, it is called responsibility" (64).

Yet Per Ladner, "Black women of the era indeed accessed contraceptive technologies and, after 1973, legal abortions. . . . [I]t is ludicrous to assume that Black women who have had all the children they care to have and can afford should be denied information on ways to cease giving birth" (256). The Black Women's Liberation Movement also rejected "black women . . . being asked by militant black brothers not to practice birth control because it's a form of whitey's committing genocide on black people." Instead, this group considered the pill as "the freedom to *fight* genocide of black women and children" (405; see also Critchlow, citing Cade, 144). In Cade Bambara's trenchant summation, "The pill gives [the black woman] a choice, gives her control over at least some of the major events in her life. And it gives her time to fight for liberation in these [social and economic] areas" (208). In her archly comic review of raising two children when a man skips out on his obligations, Joanna Clark anticipates the vitriol of Marilyn French's children-hating mothers: "My first words after coming out from under the ether after I had my son were 'I think I made a mistake'" (75). Later, "Black Ladies, the last thing we have to worry about is genocide. In fact, we could use a little" (85).

Despite this context of concern raised by Black Power spokespersons, Seaman, and the "Pill Hearings" (Firestone 224) in Congress, NYRW and Redstocking cofounder Shulamith Firestone nevertheless places chemical contraceptives and all manner of cutting-edge technologies at the center of her own case for the imminent feminist revolution. Like Greer, she calls in *The Dialectic of Sex* for communal living arrangements to disrupt traditional hierarchies. While Greer advocated communities made of women and children, Firestone specifies ten-person households of "adults of various ages [who] could apply for a license as a group in much the same way as a young couple today applies for a marriage license" (262) for seven to ten years, renewable. Just as specifically, "a regulated percentage of each household—say one-third—would be children" (263), and adult members would shift in and out, as compatibility required. In each household, the group-raising of children would mean "that no one person would ever be involuntarily stuck with [them]" (264). Firestone regards as a goal children's complete ignorance of their biological mothers (271–272) and even more radically, "relations with children would include as much genital sex as the child was capable of—probably considerably more than we now believe" (272).

In addition to contraceptives freeing all women from unwanted pregnancy, Firestone envisions a technology of reproduction that would spare women (and men) who desire children from the "barbarism" (226) of pregnancy, labor, and delivery. In sum, "as long as we use natural childbirth methods, the 'household' could never be a totally liberating social form" (263). Hailing from a similarly radical worldview, Davis also argues for housework "redistribute[d] equally to men and women alike" (*Women* 223) and later that "childcare should be socialized, meal preparation should be socialized, housework should be industrialized" (*Women* 232). Says Firestone, ceding all aspects of reproduction to "test tube" and other artificial means will also solve the population crisis worldwide (258), and the advent of the fully automated workplace will release workers (both men and women) from the drudgery of manual labor. In contrast to the nightmare of robotic takeover described in Ira Levin's *The Stepford Wives* (which will be discussed later), Firestone's term for all of this is *cybernetic socialism*, and in her view, machines will soon release humanity from its need to survive, flourish, and reproduce through oppressive labors or possessive relations.

All these feminist texts vigorously challenge the sexual status quo, including vaginal heterosexuality, standard styles of intercourse, and the centuries-old tradition of reducing women to their reproductive function. Shifting emphasis from the vagina and the womb, the typical battleground states on the women's body, to the breast and nipple, the underappreciated clitoris, and a generalized, polymorphous, multiorgasmic sexuality, radical feminist thinkers defined a sexual practice freed from perceived dependence on the male provider and the male member per se. Others considered sexual freedom as freedom *from* sexuality in all of its oppressive cultural permutations, with women "dubious about the revolutionary potential of sexual pleasure" (Gerhard, *Desiring* 110) opting for nonsexual intimacy without the pressure to "put out," to go without a bra or even panties (Greer, "Down" 8) without assault from men, or to wear miniskirts if these were deemed liberating without critique from feminist sisters. Yet surely, radical writers and the women they represented found it easier to revise sexual practice as constituted in the mid-twentieth century than to extricate themselves from the sexual rat race altogether.

Just as surely, those radical feminists so freely criticizing the aims of economic equality sought by liberal feminists never embraced the radical alternative to productive employability as they preached all should. Greer was a successfully employed academic throughout her career, and like her liberal counterpart Gloria Steinem, who made a lucrative place for herself in print journalism, she surely enjoyed some measure of professional success due to her marked sexual attractiveness. Per biographer Christine Wallace, Greer's view on the actual poor "dripped with an embarrassing romanticism that only someone who did not know real poverty could display" (194). Meanwhile, Kate Millett authored the hugely influential *Sexual Politics* (1969) but worked on the undercompensated fringes of academe, and both she and Firestone dealt with mental illness, which reduced Firestone to final decades of public assistance and mysterious death in her Lower East Side apartment (see Faludi). With regard to the progressive enclaves promoted by some radical thinkers, the most famous commune of its era, regrettably, was the Manson clan, where women and men indeed enjoyed perfect economic equality—they were all equally destitute. Within feminism, the collectives founded by Firestone and other early activists soon dissolved into vitriolic infighting (see Faludi, and see Cohen and Echols), and numerous members of such groups were ousted for reasons key to this argument: their desire to succeed as teachers, writers, media professionals, or simply spokespersons—to be successfully employed at all—was regarded as "male-identified" and as grounds for ouster. Notably, all of the major feminist criticism from this period, save Friedan's landmark *Feminine Mystique*, belongs to this radical tradition, while the full complement of best-selling novels and feature films discussed henceforth grapple with the crises of sexual freedom, professional success, and the technologies that helped or hindered both that mark them as mainly indebted to the liberal-feminist mode.

Women at Work in the Early and Late Feminist Era

From either side of the dynamic and eventful interval that marked the second wave come Jacqueline Susann's *Valley of the Dolls* (1966) and Marilyn French's *The Women's Room* (1977), two lengthy, exhaustive, and exhausting feminist melodramas of the sprawling-epic variety. Though the publication date of Susann's novel lies well within the era of pill-sponsored sexual liberation, the story itself—labeled "protofeminism" by reviewer Mim Udovitch on the back cover of the Grove Press edition—evinces a mid-century landscape hooked tightly to Susann's own story as an aspiring Broadway actress in the years immediately following the Second World War. That Susann's campy, schlocky soap opera and French's densely realist, excessively talkative diatribe were each international best sellers, bringing fortunes sufficient to each author to liberate her from financial concern, indicates the tremendous shift undergone by women's fiction and female readers in the eleven transformative years separating their publications. A key difference—for both the heroines in each story and their original readerships—regards the shift in women's professional roles: Susann's working women employ all manner of pharmaceutical technologies to maintain toeholds in both the cut-throat entertainment business and a series of regrettable marriages, while French's heroine achieves an exalted professional situation—a PhD from Harvard and tenured academic employment—which yet leaves her disappointed and lonely.

Valley of the Dolls begins at a moment flush with Rosie-the-Riveter optimism regarding women's ability to join the national economy and dead-ends in the thoroughly domesticated mid-1960s as Susann's three heroines seek, find, and tragically lose romantic fulfillment. French's narrative starts in these same confined and repressed mid-1960s; spirals through a golden period of feminist intellectualism, friendship, and love; and makes its own crash-dive into the morning-after of principled but embittered, solitary survival. In both stories, the heroines and their peers wrestle with and succumb to the bogey of lonely abandonment, concluding with vivid portraits of main characters miserable without a man's love. Though focused on straight female heroines, Susann sensationalizes and French romanticizes the man-free alternative of lesbian orientation, and Susann's narrative is sensational at all turns—including scenes of drug addiction, abortion, and oral sex. By contrast, French's pronouncements—including most infamously, in the words of her charismatic radical feminist character, that "all men are rapists" (630)—might have struck original readers as visionary even as they strike more skeptical twenty-first-century audiences as oversimplified and overwrought. Notably as well, the depressing endings of both stories point clearly to their respective take on the collision between sexuality and freedom: instead of seeking the divorce she so well deserves, Susann's Anne Welles escapes into drug addiction as her faithless husband bags a conquest in the next room, and French's Mira Ward ends up unfulfilled at a community college in coastal Maine. As French dismally sums up, "She saw her choice clearly as being between sex and independence. . . . If Mira wanted an independent life, she would have to give up being sexual" (44).

The Second World War (again, the initiating context of Susann's novel) catalyzed a boom in medical and material technologies disseminated to the mass market as soon as war's end made it feasible to do so. Yet while DuPont and its industrial brethren preached the gospel of "better living through chemistry," many such war-era interventions conferred upon their beneficiaries new freedoms that came with their own burdensome, traumatizing responsibilities: if improved cleaning fluids, frozen foods, and small-appliance technology freed the 1950s housewife from drudgeries of housework, the crushing boredom of those now empty hours simply loomed more formidably. As Martin Halliwell has observed, "The clean, healthy home could offer protection from germs and disease, but it could also be a breeding ground for neuroses and mental health problems" (275). And as discussed earlier, if the birth control pill liberated American women into a swinging sexual revolution, it all the more liberated their male partners from the responsibilities of marriage and child-rearing, specifically from the traditions of marrying early and staying married, that had guided mores for decades. Women, especially those wanting children and marital sanction of same, became burdened with the responsibility to stay "marriageable" for longer than ever: slim, youthful, lively, and eternally suggesting the delicate blend of innocence and experience that would land the perfect husband.

Throughout the 1950s and 1960s, one war-era technology thought to liberate both bored housewives and swinging single girls was the prescription drug assortment prescribed for sleep, anxiety, or weight control. Seconal and Nembutal were two popular sedatives administered to thousands of postwar women, Miltown was a widely sought-after tranquilizer that kept its user awake but calm (see Tone 161–166 and Healy 5), and Dexedrine was an early weight-loss wonder drug whose other "speed" properties (alertness, focus, sense of well-being) were equally desirable. As it enthralled a generation of ordinary American women, so Seconal was infamously responsible for a number of celebrity deaths, including actress Lupe Vélez (d. 1944), actress Carol Landis (d. 1948), singer Dinah Washington (d. 1963), and legend Judy Garland (d. 1969). Per the indispensable biography of Susann, *Lovely Me* (1987, 1996), penned by none other than the antipill advocate Barbara Seaman, both Landis (whom Susann knew and formed a passionate attachment to) and Garland (whom Susann seems to have never met) figure prominently in *Valley of the Dolls*. By the time Susann's post-WWII autobiographical novel reached its 1960s youthful readership, the amphetamines and barbiturates that enabled her heroines to their various professional gains transformed into the bennies and goofballs of a recreational drug culture promising little if any professional benefit but enduring as points of identification between the generations.

The story traces the fortunes of three close friends, diversely enmeshed in the world of show business and alternately seeking and fleeing traditional fulfillment in marriage and child-bearing. Notably reflective of Susann's own ricochet through the lower echelons of Broadway; the powerful men she loved, bedded, or simply married; and the female stars (both the ephemeral Landis and the iconic Ethel Merman) who were idols and lovers, the novel's show-business theme accords perfectly with its underlying ambivalence regarding roles for women: the success of Anne, Neely, and Jennifer within this high-powered *business* figures them as liberated professionals inspiring to their youthful, feminist, mid-1960s readership. Yet the significant aspects of this business as only *show*—a charade of accomplishment based more on appearance than talent and a platform from which to marry well then quit the business—undermine the women's merit-based achievements. Indeed, the heroine Anne Welles is read by her boss as guilty of this very ploy: she begs to be kept on at his office, even as marriage to a millionaire looms, only to stay close to the man she really loves, dashing but commitment-phobic Lyon Burke, who eventually loves, leaves, and destroys her.

Due to the novel's situation in the immediate postwar period, one pill missing from its pharmaceutical landscape is the pill itself, yet its three main protagonists—Anne, her plucky and talented roommate Neely O'Hara (closely modeled on Judy Garland), and her sexy, glamorous friend Jennifer North (the Landis figure)—manage a fully liberated lifestyle, in keeping with the "swinging" context into which this novel was born. While each at some point employs "birth control" in the most traditional manner possible—that is, becomes pregnant in order to prop up a failing marriage—each also employs some form of mid-century contraception, per her respective location on the morality spectrum: the reserved and elegant Anne successfully manages the "rhythm system" once she achieves sexual relations with Burke; the low-borne Neely inserts a diaphragm when necessary but insists often upon oral sex (which she prefers anyway) to prevent pregnancy; and the sex goddess Jennifer has had seven abortions by the time of her early demise. In seeming cosmic retribution for this extreme departure from social norms, Jennifer is diagnosed with breast cancer (as Susann herself was in the months before she wrote this book) just as she finds the man of her dreams and decides to give up her career in the French porn industry to be his wife and raise his children. Though curable with mastectomy, Jennifer rejects this disfiguring impingement on her role as a nursing mother and coveted sex object to her doting fiancé. Well aware of his fetishistic obsession with her breasts (which both he and Jennifer refer to as *his* "babies"), she chooses early, gorgeous death with a handful of Seconals, the little red "dolls" of the novel's title and infamous reputation.

We may read the Seconals, Nembutals, and Dexedrines variously ingested by the three protagonists as once-removed technologies of birth control in their own right. Seconal and Nembutal, specifically, are sleep aids; they keep the women snoozing instead of screwing, and in all cases, they enshadow or invert the technologies of birth control traditionally construed that would indicate fulfilling sexual relationships: each of the women takes sleeping pills in search of "release" or "escape" from her loneliness and sexual abandonment—in other words, the crushing burden of her hard-won, now boundless freedom. As birth control pills are not only pregnancy-preventers but body-shapers, sparing their users the "fat" and sexual unattractiveness of visible pregnancy, so the Dexedrine compulsively taken by Neely and the plastic surgery to which an aging Jennifer later subjects herself are forms of technological control seemingly "chosen" by the women accessing them but in fact insisted upon by the men managing their careers. Per the stories surrounding Garland's (and Susann's) own lifelong predicament, Neely struggles to keep off the weight; the Dexedrine limits her appetite and speeds metabolism, and even the heavy dosing of sleeping medicine can be construed as a diet aid: at one point, Neely is offered a modern-day rest cure, not constituted by bed-bound overfeeding in the nineteenth-century mode but by drug-induced coma of several days' duration, from which she would emerge a thinner woman. Meanwhile, the alcohol and the caviar that Neely also consumes in excess add calories, and the full range of substance abuse, meteoric professional success, and emotional instability following therefrom leave her unwanted and unloved—in no danger, in other words, of unwanted pregnancy in the midst of numerous other personal and professional crises.

As struggling girls in a boarding house early in the story, Anne argues that it is too early to marry, that she has had only "two months of freedom" (Susann 42) in New York. But Neely shouts back, "Freedom! You call this freedom? . . . Living in a hall bedroom, getting up at seven and rushing to the office, . . . tagging along with Bellamy and some client and freezing in that black silk coat?" (43). While Anne presents the liberated women's perspective, Neely reminds her that marriage can liberate a woman from want and ignominy, as it has for ages and still does in 1945, in 1966, and beyond. When her boss warns Anne at novel's end that unveiling Burke's affairs will harm only herself—"If he [knew that you knew] you'd *have* to ask for your freedom" (387)—Susann perfectly indicates the double-edged sword that "freedom" presents. Anne's crisis at novel's end—on New Year's Eve, she slides into pill dependence, trying not just one "beautiful [red] doll" (442) but two for the first time—suggests how easily pill-assisted agency turns into enslaving addiction. As her protagonists wrestle with the dilemmas of "freedom from" and "freedom to," exhilarating liberation and desperate escape, their personal and professional gains, and the men's uncanny ability to always capitalize on these, Susann's protagonists and the young female generation whose story they live turned to physician-prescribed, personalized technologies of diverse kinds to enlarge the size and force of their liberatory gestures—but with less than total success.

While Susann points to the glaring shift in mores by the mid-1960s, leaving old-fashioned Anne Welles struggling to survive in a modern world, French in *The Women's Room* suggests that her heroine Mira Ward is lucky to survive into the late 1960s, at which point her love of learning and female companionship can reap its just reward. Ironically, the bored, frustrated housewives of the early chapters—barely tolerating their children, boozing up throughout the day, half-heartedly attempting suicide, and seducing each other's husbands with abandon—are far better drawn than the frowsy, longwinded feminists of Mira's grad-school cohort met in the novel's second half. As Kim A. Loudermilk observes, "*The Women's Room* is very good at detailing the oppression of women's lives during the 1950s . . . and at arousing anger in response to these details" (51). By contrast, she and others find fault with the all-talk-no-action feminists of the Harvard clique and especially the portrayal of Val, who is regarded as extreme if not insane by the other characters when she undertakes a fatal act of insurrection: "Activist politics in this novel, then, are always fanatical and always punished" (Loudermilk 56; see also Behrent 272–273). Thus despite the lengthy tour through second-wave academic feminism, French's novel is at its most liberating (i.e., anger-inducing) when it explores the frustrations of domesticity in the vein of Friedan's nonfiction and chronicles each character's slide into promiscuity and addiction à la Susann. Deeply autobiographical, it compares structurally with *The Autobiography of Malcolm X*, where the protagonist moved through danger and intrigue in his misdirected youth, while the dawn of political enlightenment coincides with action slowing to a crawl (see chapter 1).

Although Mira remains moderate in her views, the novel emanates a radical/separatist (Friedan would say "man-hating") feminist perspective in its unrelenting portrayal of men as swine: brutish and insensitive or overly passive, possessive, boorish, self-centered, and compulsively philandering. Mira's husband Norm criticizes his wife for not managing the housework and children so that he can study for medical school (where a clear lack of acumen manifests itself) in a peaceful, orderly household. Eventually he spends more and more nights away and leaves his wife for his secretary; ironically, then, Mira would never have found liberated selfhood at Harvard had her husband not forced her to do so. French holds up for special contempt the lot of the story's Catholic housewives, who are ground into early middle age by an exhausting succession of births, while their still-youthful husbands enjoy professional success and the attention of the other wives. Even in the liberal-feminist context of a professional, progressive environment—her graduate program at Harvard—the men are needy and grasping or blustery and pedantic, and the love of Mira's life, Ben, falls from his pedestal when he reverts to unbending traditionalism: she must forfeit her own career, following him to Africa to bear his children, or lose him forever. Per Jean-Thomas Tremblay, "French narrates an institutional disillusionment so pervasive that it extends beyond Harvard to encompass everything and anything that might count as an institution," including marriage to a soulmate like Ben. Many of this book's original reviews took issue with the widespread demonizing of male characters: to Libby Purves, they were "malevolent stick figures, at best appallingly dull and at worst monsters" (qtd. in Woo), and in the *New York Times*, Anne Tyler first described French's novel as "fine writing" but later calls it a "very long and very narrow" tunnel in which everything that happens to the women "seems almost purely negative." She adds that "compared to the women . . . the men tend to blur together. They're all villains and cardboard villains at that" (7). "Men can't be that bad" (73), Christopher Lehmann-Haupt maintained in another *Times* review; as Lisa Maria Hogeland notes, both the mainstream press and even feminist publications like *Ms.* criticized French's slanted portrayals of men as un-literary and as antithetical to the project of big-tent feminism (see Van Gelder 42–43 and see Hogeland 82–86), despite the enormous popularity the novel enjoyed.

Portrayals of sexual activity are equally pessimistic in Mira's pre-feminist and feminist (graduate school) contexts. Mira marries a man she does not love mainly to avoid the threat of rape—and committing the social offense of being a woman alone—and none of the subpar suburban husbands and their victimized wives seem to enjoy a satisfying sex life. Mira's once passionate attachment to Ben results in bitter disappointment, and the rape of Val's daughter Chris is exponentially worsened by the callous response of the police and courts. It epitomizes the novel's dismal view of heterosexual relations and leads to Val's pronouncement that "all men are rapists. They rape us with their eyes, their laws, their codes" (630). In other words, Mira, Chris, and French's entire female cohort live out Susan Brownmiller's influential thesis from this period that rape is "nothing more or less than a conscious process of intimidation by which *all* men keep *all* women in a state of fear" (15). In Pamela Barnett's view, French "represents women aspiring to and enjoying sexual freedom in both heterosexual and homosexual relationship" (xiv), but in my own estimation, French's portrayals of lesbian sexuality are little more satisfying—or liberating—than the straight ones are. Barnett is correct that the novel's "portrayal of lesbianism is its utopian aspect" (119), but the utopian (fantastical, nonexistent) qualities of its lesbian sexuality are its most problematic feature.

While French employs graphic (however bathetic) terms to describe Mira's desire for Ben—"Her vagina felt wet and open just looking at him" (434)—Iso and her lover Kyla share some gentle hugs, a kiss on the top of the head, and a restful sleep in each other's arms. When later this is referred to as "the relation" (553) and "an affair" (556), its "utopian" (Terry Castle's term is "apparitional") aspects are all too obvious. Iso's other lover Clarissa "felt a close rapport with her friend; she felt utter trust in her" (639) and little if any frank sexual desire. Iso is the soul of generosity and consideration—"more than anyone, it was Iso who taught us this kind of love" (502)—and her door (and refrigerator) are always open, no matter how pressed she is to complete her own graduate work. Her saintly bearing not only sets her apart from the rest of the group but deemphasizes whatever is desirous and self-asserting about her own sexuality. That both of her lovers approach her under duress—fleeing abusive marriages (that they periodically return to) and thus mainly in search of a safe harbor, even a break from the pressures of sexual engagement—isolates Iso (hence the name?) further as the only actual (not simply "political") lesbian in the group. Barnett is correct that Iso's desire to keep both Kyla and Clarissa as lovers when each of them demands her exclusivity is a bid for a nonnormative sexual arrangement: "Iso compellingly argues that fidelity and long-term commitment are not natural responses" to the desire she feels for each of them and that unfortunately "Iso's lovers are not ready for her vision" (120). Yet this triangular arrangement, to the degree that its (literal mathematical) oddness underscores Iso's own imputed identity as a sexual irregular, forecloses any instance of a lesbian who is as happy to pair-bond with only one other individual as most heterosexuals are.

Thus if Susann's heroines are done in by the pressures of show business and the crisis-ridden romances befalling them, one might be surprised to find that in French's novel, enlightened feminism—and the best professional training offered in the United States—causes as much misery for her female characters as bored domesticity ever did. In the words of Brigitte Weekes, the story presents "a lonely chaos repellent to most readers" (qtd. in Woo), and to be sure, almost none of Mira's fellow students complete their degrees. One nonstudent in the group fails as a dancer and becomes "a wife who did not love" the man she married (French 681); Val is killed attempting to free a minor character from jail; her daughter Chris, the rape victim, is returned to her overbearing father's control following her mother's funeral; and Mira winds up overeducated and unfulfilled on a backwater faculty in Maine, where she is invited to only "one or two parties a year" (15). As above, her abjection originates from the fact that she did not even come into her own until her insufferable husband kicked her out of the marriage, and though we might hope that "the women's room" of the title is the sex-segregated setting where committed feminists plot insurrection together, in fact it is the locale of the opening scene, where Mira crouches in a toilet stall waiting for classes to resume, so fearful is she of the younger students' questioning gaze. As Susann's heroine, using pills to free herself from the burdens of her loveless marriage, describes a woman's liberation with darkest irony, so French's Mira, a solitary figure on a cold gray beach—"I have opened all the doors in my head. I have opened all the pores in my body. But only the tide rolls in" (687)—is so utterly, disastrously free from human entanglements that she could walk into those waves and never be missed. Notably, film versions of both these novels insisted on a positive ending: Anne dumps Lyon and returns to the loving women of her homestead, and Mira teaches in a lively and well-populated college classroom, surrounded by adulating students. Although the broadcast television industry that adapted French's novel underestimates its material and audience given any chance, in this case the happy ending imposed on *The Women's Room* created a better "commercial" for liberal feminism—professional independence *and* personal happiness—than French's downcast novel managed to do.

Sex, Work, and the Happy Ending

Helen Gurley Brown's landmark *Sex and the Single Girl* (1962) and Erica Jong's *Fear of Flying* (1973) read as the comic obverse of the melodramas written by Susann and French. The same "proto" and "post" interval separating the novels of Susann and French also separates the work of Brown and Jong; the same feminist-saturated, other-side-of-midnight candor informs Jong's work as it does French's. Susann and Brown were good friends, having met through mutual publisher Bernard Geis, for whom each made a small fortune with her runaway best seller. Where circles of women surrounded the heroines of the melodramas, the "girls" in Brown and Jong are singular "picaro" (Butler 308) figures, adventuring in a world of lunging, loving, or otherwise "eligible" men. Like Susann's, Brown's text is protofeminist at best, and *Cosmopolitan* magazine, which Brown revolutionized in 1965, was picketed by Kate Millett and other feminists in 1970 for its seemingly retrograde views on women's sexuality (see Scanlon 179–180). For all its scandalous reputation, a full 70 percent of *Sex and the Single Girl* covers topics typical to the women's magazine that *Cosmopolitan* was before Brown "did not so much revamp . . . as vamp" it (M. Fox): party and decorating tips, fashion, hair, make-up, living on a budget—even recipes for the likes of Pepper Steak España and Spiced Cherries.

Sex's truly revolutionary statements come from its first and last chapters, where Brown invites the single female to consider a wide range of males, including coworkers, service providers, clients, blood relatives, and "the husbands of your friends" (18), as "the men in your life." Within this list, there are "eligibles" who are bona fide marital prospects and a much wider spectrum—all but the relatives, one must assume—who are there for the single girl's potential sexual enjoyment. And if her advice regarding premarital indulgence were not shocking enough in 1962, Brown's bold suggestion that the single girl indulge *within* the bond of matrimony—someone else's—truly crossed the line of acceptable subject matter, let alone humorous treatment of same. Brown deepens the scandal by attaching the expectation of expensive gifts to most if not all sexual forays; especially married men are "generous with gifts and money," and the "visiting married man on an expense account is the greatest date since Diamond Jim Brady" (20). Brown's suggestion that a single woman exploit a man's (especially a married man's) guilt over winning her sexual favors—or later, that he bring "presents" to offset the power imbalance between the socially powerful married man and the socially vulnerable single woman (220)—departs clearly from the decorous however hypocritical views of courtship in traditional romance advice-writing. How, finally, would an early-1960s feminist rule on Brown's irreverent injunction to "tak[e] married men but not tak[e] them seriously. . . . Use them in a perfectly nice way just as they use you" (23)? Certainly better credentialed feminists have discussed these matters just as forthrightly; Brown recasts the single woman's scene of seduction as a two-way street, as the exploitable commercial transaction it in so many respects already is. As biographer Jennifer Scanlon remarked, "[Brown] saw no reason for women to refrain from playing the system by exploiting the inequities of the dating game. . . . [Her] particular version of equity troubled many feminists but spoke to longstanding realities of life for working-class women" (xii), though one could easily refer to middle-class single women's equally underresourced plights as well.

Brown's chapter "What Is Sexy?" begins with much in common with the radical writings of Greer, Seaman, and other feminist-identified authors of the ensuing decade. Though the clitoris never rears its tiny head, and though Brown avoids too deep a questioning of women's failure to achieve sexual fulfillment via vaginal channels, her source *is* Kinsey (not Freud), and a sexy woman is not the one who is especially beautiful, curvaceous, or best-dressed but, in the self-interested terms Greer and Seaman would applaud, the one "who enjoys sex" (58) and "occasionally . . . an orgasm from the roots of her hair to the tips of her toes" (61). In her study of second-wave feminism, Jane Gerhard remarks that Brown "brought a 'singles' identity to a national audience." She pairs Brown's *Cosmopolitan* with Hugh Hefner's *Playboy*, arguing that they "replaced the traditional husband-wife dyad with a new pairing: the bachelor and the single woman. Both Hefner and Brown . . . became beacons of sexual expressiveness and symbols of the joys of singlehood" (*Desiring* 85).

In several respects, *Fear of Flying*'s scandalous reputation is equally undeserved. Though its sexual content is detailed and ubiquitous, its broadly comic, often farcical situation douses an authentically erotic charge of any kind. Jong's hugely autobiographical heroine Isadora Wing was read as a female Portnoy by the *Cleveland Plain Dealer* and by John Updike in his favorable review for the *New York Times*, which largely enabled the book's success. In an Afterword to *Fear*'s thirtieth-anniversary edition, Jong refers to the "arty cover" (436) given the first paperback edition and quotes a man she met at a dinner party: "Whenever I saw that book on a woman's nightstand I knew I was gonna get lucky" (438). The cover Jong refers to is indeed lit like a stag movie, and the nude body peeking out from behind the infamous zipper looks nothing like Isadora's, which is described on several occasions as having medium-sized breasts and a "big ass" (see figure 3.2). But while certainly the cover might have promised the young man from Jong's dinner party an easy lay, the rollicking sexual misadventures inside bode nothing more than a ribald night at the comedy club downstairs. In other words, it is remarkable how well the book's cover misrepresents—in classic misogynist fashion—the story within for the purposes of marketing it most effectively to young woman readers and the men who visit their bedrooms: not only does Isadora never experience good sex with the "zipless fuck" who picks her up at a conference with her husband in Europe, but she never gets over her fear of flying either—moving, as Jong herself notes, always "away from one man's tyranny just to fall into the tyranny of another" (428).

Updike and Henry Miller wrote two noted reviews that hailed the protagonist's irreverent descriptions of one lover's limp penis and another's failure to wipe himself properly after defecating, among much other sexual candor. Miller in his review wondered "when or if Germaine Greer is going to give us a book of this order" (441), and Updike was glad that Isadora's "saga [is] so uncranky" (448). Updike

Figure 3.2. Paperback cover of *Fear of Flying*, 1973 (Penguin Random House).

compares *Fear of Flying* to Norman Mailer's short story "The Time of Her Time" and "other seriously sexy male fiction" (448), and both writers seem relieved that at last a woman writer has made a good dirty joke of men's sexuality, as this would renew their own license as literary misogynists in future works. But again, though Isadora expresses frank sexual desire for Adrian Goodlove—"My underpants were wet enough to mop the streets of Vienna" (39)—almost all of their sexual encounters are failed. Once she and Adrian take off on their mad tour of Europe, Isadora is so depressed she can only enjoy herself when blind drunk; although these episodes are comically rendered, they are sadly reminiscent of the pill-popping and daytime-drinking women of Susann's and French's novels.

"Flying" is variously construed as the ultimate sexual encounter with an anonymous stranger, the ability to survive as a single woman, or the heroine's dashing with mad hilarity between husband and lover in the hallways of the stuffy academic conference. Just as French's heroine Mira Ward rushes into marriage when she is threatened with gang rape during a night on her own, Isadora has a dark epiphany when dumped by Adrian on a roadside in France and is hobbled by a heavy suitcase: "I had forgotten how awful it was to be a woman alone—the leering glances, the catcalls, the offers of help which you dared not accept for fear of incurring sexual debt. The awful sense of vulnerability" (378). Just as Mira is only able to find her professional calling—and a better love with her fellow student Ben—after she is pushed out of marriage by her boorish husband, so Isadora only comes to ask, "How could I have left [husband] Bennett?" (378) after she is pushed out of the car by Adrian. As romantic-comic luck would have it, Bennett is still just across the channel; she is in the bathroom of his London hotel room, scrubbing off several days of road dirt and menstrual blood when he enters the room. Worried earlier in the story (like Susann's quaintly pre-pill heroines) that she is pregnant from either her lover or husband, the resumption of her period is an experience of purifying filth that returns her to her sanctified marital state under conditions traditional, however dramatically inverted.

At the story's thesis moment, standing alone on the side of the road, Isadora realizes, "I was nobody's baby now. Liberated. Utterly free. It was the most terrifying sensation I'd ever known in my life. Like teetering on the edge of the Grand Canyon and hoping you'd learn to fly before you hit bottom" (372). Indeed, she has a dark night of the soul in a seedy Paris hotel room, where her several neuroses overcome her until she plucks up the courage to go behind the curtain shielding the sink and bidet. She has a long-needed pee, gives herself a half-successful sponge bath, and sits on the bed among her old journals to locate the inspiration she needs to write the novel now in the reader's hands. Although she comes into her professional calling at that moment, she is yet back in her husband's bedroom before the next sun sets, such that singlehood is figured as singleness of purpose or an independent professional identity but not actual manlessness for any notable length of time. Tremblay compares this novel to French's, seeing the "firetrap" that is Isadora's Paris hotel room as resembling the toilet stall that sets the opening scene in *The Women's Room*: "Jong's novel leads nowhere beyond the firetrap . . . [but]

offers a crash course in livening up the tone of liberal disillusionment." Notably, writing (like prostitution) is one of the only professions women can do without leaving home, with Isadora's professional breakthrough occurring on a bed to underscore the point.

Isadora fantasizes about the erotic setting of a European railway car, yet the airplane itself with its mythical Mile High Club was a modern sexual technology widely reputed as a scene of liberation-era seduction. The novel's title and "arty cover" indicate that the heroine will find sexual fulfillment beneath a scratchy airline blanket in the closely packed seating of coach class. In fact, Isadora's fears of flying are comically literalized as she neurotically sweats her way through the transatlantic flight to the conference, then brags about sex "in the bathroom of a 707" (251), only to admit that the story is a lie. "Flying" for Isadora is the leap to personal independence that she never risks, while for Susann's heroines, flying high on their various prescriptions, flight is an escape from the pressures of modern womanhood—in other words, the defeat of revolutionary feminist potential by suffocating tradition.

Just as problematically, the sexiest aspect of flying in the decades following World War II was the presence of the stewardess herself, an iconically "liberated" career girl whose inherent glamor, necessary transience, and association with sleek, modern technology distinguished her from the nurses and teachers of the traditional women's career spectrum. Firestone singled out the stewardess as a modern professional identity "based on the sex appeal of the young woman, and thus can be only [a] limited way station on the way to a better job or marriage" (258). As she was so plainly a creature of the modern age, the stewardess was cast in the part for her marked physical charms, her willingness to do whatever it took to satisfy a largely male clientele, and her literal positioning above and beyond the sexual rules governing ordinary grounded experience. The airplane's close quarters and especially the airline flight's status as a temporary escape from the rules of work and marriage made the sexually attractive, seemingly sexually available stewardess a key marketing tool in modern airlines' original growth and success. National Airlines' early-1970s "I'm Cheryl [or Jo or Laura]. Fly Me" campaign pictured attractive young women in two-page, full-color ads, and all airline stewardess uniforms of this period, verging on exotic costuming, emphasized breasts, hips, and legs. "Coffee, tea, or me?" was the set-up of a crude joke, whose punchline, "whatever is easiest to make" (Bain xi), was a favorite among pilots of the period.

In airline executive Donald Bain's glowing recollection, air travel of the 1960s and 1970s was a "glamorous and alluring" affair. "You dressed up before boarding a plane" and enjoyed "caviar, smoked salmon, Chateaubriand carved to order at seatside, and chocolate mousse" during a typical on-board meal. "Back then," Bain adds, "everyone was a jet-setter. Sinatra's 'Come Fly with Me' was written for and sung especially to you" (xi), and "the early 747 jumbo jets had a pianist and a singer in the upstairs lounge. . . . And oh, those stewardesses," his reverie continues, praising their confidence and physical perfection and recalling "the admiring eyes [that] were on them every minute [as they] basked in the adoration." Bain notes that "dating a stewardess!" was a badge of honor for liberated playboys of the

1960s and 1970s, as prestigious as being with a "Hollywood starlet" (xii) or runway model. The excited exclamation of the stewardess's boyfriend, however, rings in the modern ear less like a claim to honor than a bawdy appreciation for the sexual bonanza the fortunate swain had happened into—similar to the recognition that the date of the *Fear of Flying* reader was "gonna get lucky" almost courtesy of the book itself.

In his introduction to the thirty-fifth anniversary edition of *Coffee, Tea, or Me?* (1967), Bain narrates the origins of the multimillion-selling, multinational cultural phenomenon that this text became. As a successful ghostwriter for a previous title at Pocket Books, Bain was offered the chance to turn some "funny stories" from two former Eastern Airlines stewardesses into a full-length memoir. Because the women's own narrative seemed (at least to their male ghostwriter) too paltry for a full-length work, Bain "used his own airline experience—and imagination—to get the job done" (xiii). He even gave the women their largely unearned "pen names"—Rachel Jones and Trudy Baker—and these otherwise anonymous former airline workers, masquerading as the authors of their own story, hit the airwaves on a nationwide promotional tour. Like all of the books discussed in this chapter, Bain's made the *New York Times* best-seller list, and like Susann and French's narratives was made into a "bad" (Bain xiv) film—this one very loosely adapted for TV.

As in Jong's text, the rollicking comic situations—assisted by Bill Wenzel's illustrations of preposterously curvaceous "stews" serving obnoxious passengers with confused, irritated, or cynical looks on their faces—undermine to a large degree the sexual sell of the book's subtitle, *The Uninhibited Memoirs of Two Airline Stewardess*. Reading sexploitation film posters from the same era, Eric Schaefer observes that many also used cartoon illustrations to "displace direct erotic appeal with humor," thus perhaps "avoiding censorship" (23). Bain's primary storyteller, Trudy, has a conventional true love, a pilot named Chuck, who "might be interested in marrying [her] someday" (282) but who postpones the date not out of duplicitous self-interest, in the manner of Susann's cad Lyon Burke, but in order to extend Trudy and Rachel's working-girl adventures for the duration of the story and into several sequels during the late 1960s and early 1970s. This is also the extent of the plot, since chapters are loosely connected vignettes with a few recurring characters and many changes of scene and circumstance. Thus, while Trudy is pledged to the all-American Chuck, she has a fling with a celebrity, interrupted only when his wife appears and joins the sexual fray. When even the piano player hired for the evening starts doffing his pants, Trudy is out the door with a toss of her head, and all manner of sexual harassment, near-rape, drunken pilots, and even plane malfunction resulting in death are skated along in sprightly fashion.

Finally, Bain's male perspective and the genre in which he writes preclude any further comparison to Jong's just-as-bawdy but exponentially more substantial text. Much closer in tone, theme, and perspective to *Coffee, Tea, or Me?* is its softcore realization, Louis K. Sher's *The Stewardesses* (1969–1971). The film is unique for its technical achievement (i.e., camera and projector innovation that enabled a low-budget, high-quality X-rated feature in 3D), its continued revision throughout ten months of screening (as the film gained popularity nationwide, characters and plot were added), and the overall quality of its production and marketing campaigns. *The Stewardesses* left its mark in the era when pornographic films found wide acceptance by male and female filmgoers across age and class demographics; as Gerhard observes, "Liberalization of obscenity laws [via Supreme Court rulings between 1957 and 1967] had immediate effects on the status of pornography in terms of its mainstream acceptance. . . . [By the early 1970s] pornographic films like *The Devil and Mrs. Jones* [*sic*] and *Deep Throat* became enormously popular and were viewed widely" (*Desiring* 86; see also Schaefer 35).

Like these better remembered films, *The Stewardesses* was a box-office smash, earning back its original production costs many times over. Like Bain's text, Sher's film—described by several crew members as a comedy with many "absurd" scenes and much "charm"—is a series of vignettes featuring stewardesses making announcements over an airplane's intercom in a sexy voice, flirting in outlandish Hawaiian smocks with passengers by propping themselves on their armrests, and unwinding after hours by all manner of sexual unorthodoxy: hanging around in various states of undress in a multigirl living arrangement (Bain called these "stew zoos"), dropping acid and humping a lamp base shaped like the head of Greek statue, and enjoying masturbation, lesbian sex, or sex in a bar. One stewardess treats a soldier going off to Vietnam to a night of physical release, and a good-looking pilot has sex with a new stewardess while "fantasizing about" (i.e., actually) having sex with half a dozen other women.

Referring to a 1967 Supreme Court ruling, writer/director Allan Silliman recalls in an interview attached to the fortieth-anniversary DVD that the film avoided obscenity laws by its "secondary subplot," a line of action with "some socially redeeming significance." This is the ill-fated love story between the stewardess Samantha and Colin Winthrop, a handsome ad executive who reveals in a late scene that he was the victim of his boss's homosexual predations in his youth. Although they plan to escape Colin's trauma by taking a two-year cruise on his yacht, Samantha must first submit to a night of brutal sex to earn a lucrative contract as a lipstick model, also in Colin's hands. In a final shocking twist, Samantha wakes up before Colin, deeply scarred by the previous night's assault. She madly takes revenge by bludgeoning Colin to death with an erotic marble sculpture then leaps, naked of course, to her own death; Elena Gorfinkel describes such cautionary conclusions as "moralist punctuation that provided narrative buffer for the [sexploitation] mode's indulgence in sexual excess" (10), while Jeffrey Sconce observes that "the reassertion of the 'moral center' remained a fixture in the most explicit wings of the sexploitation industry" (248) so as to preserve "the moral agency, social legitimacy, and personal responsibility of the spectator" (247). Bain's narrative takes the same tragic turn when a "dumped" plane kills Trudy and Rachel's friend Sally Lu, depressing a crew already done in by a Christmas Eve spent at a tawdry, smoke-filled, hotel-room party in Buffalo. Yet together the heroines decide to "give [their jobs] one more year," anticipating that each will be married by then and can quit while they have a few shreds of dignity left. The upbeat ending of *Coffee, Tea, or Me?* parallels the recovery sequence from Sher's film: the surviving lovelies get back on their luxury airliner following the tragedy of Samantha as if it had never happened.

Laura Frost, Lisa Maria Hogeland, and Jay Hood have each argued for the role of "erotically charged fantasy" (Frost 40), however politically incorrect this may be, in feminist texts like Jong's *Fear of Flying*, with Hood reading the novel as "a compromise between desired fantasies and achievable realities" (150). Timothy Aubry renames the politically incorrect confusion, contradiction, even hypocrisy discerned by some readers as a meaningful "ambivalence" for Isadora, since ambivalence well characterized the plight of Jong's original readership. Per Aubry, women in that era "found it necessary, if difficult, to reconcile themselves to an economic system they continued to see as antagonistic . . . but which suddenly offered them unprecedented possibilities for success and social mobility" (435). Isadora is an aspiring writer, French's Mira Ward becomes a college professor, and the career girls of Susann's and Bain's narratives also face the same ambivalence—if not the prospect of mutual exclusivity—between work and married lives. Notably, this dilemma is represented most trenchantly in Bain's text, where airline policy of treating male customers like pampered kings—even if they were staggering drunk, criminally hostile, or sexually assaultive—epitomized the gauntlet women breaking into professions all over corporate America were expected to run. The stewardesses put up with no end of humiliating behaviors, and Bain presents their forbearance as indicative of their excellent training and top professionalism: what is most pointedly defined as workplace achievement is the women's unending toleration for outright sexual abuse. Boxed in on all sides by the catch-22's of the sexual revolution, Rachel submits to one pilot's sexual harassment, lest she be thought of as a "square" (91), and an entire chapter is devoted to whether "the girls" should supplement their income by turning tricks in layover hotel rooms. Paula Kane, who wrote the mid-1970s exposé *Sex Objects in the Sky*, described the psychological damage incurred in the stewardess role (e.g., 85–86), likening the women who quit the job at soaring rates in the early 1970s to Vietnam vets dealing with PTSD. Like the prostitute characters that will be discussed later, these grievously harassed workers in this legitimated wing of the sex industry indicate the original and perennial "tools" of women's trade—the penises they have had to handle with care in their centuries-long climb toward economic independence.

The dilemmas presented in these narratives would have most resonated with liberal feminists of the era, whom Aubry argues were in the ascendency by 1973, when "the radicalism of the feminist movement had lost momentum as career possibilities became available to middle class women" (435). Yet these liberal-feminist texts reflect the movement's broader difficulties disengaging itself from the gender-based assumptions of the mid-century; they suggest an inability during the sexual revolution (and even to the present day) to enter desirable long-term relationships without enormous sacrifice—or to even pen a narrative in which this is possible.[2] Ironically, the least literary and least feminist text considered thus far—*Coffee, Tea, or Me?*—presents the reader with both the harshest realities regarding women in the '70s-era workplace and the happiest outcomes for its minimally realist heroines, reinforcing the equation ventured by the more literary texts: that women's professional and personal fulfillment is a fantasy—and one dictated by men at that.

Violence and Death in Liberation-Era Thrillers

Major authors and directors with diverse famous texts to their credit and/or no specified allegiance to the feminist cause present the works discussed in this last section; Ira Levin's *Rosemary's Baby* (1969) and *The Stepford Wives* (1972) were made into major motion pictures by male directors (esp. Roman Polanski, directing Mia Farrow, John Cassavetes, and Ruth Gordon in *Rosemary's Baby*) who hardly enjoyed high ratings in feminist circles. Betty Friedan famously denounced *The Stepford Wives* as a "rip-off of the women's movement" (qtd. in Klemesrud 28), but in it, Levin archly satirizes the tranquilized zombies of Susann and French and stands out here as the single author to equate traditional marriage with out-and-out horror. As Sharon Marcus observes, *Rosemary's Baby* (although the situation is identical in *The Stepford Wives*) ultimately "contains female 'paranoia' by making it impossible for Rosemary to convince anyone that her theories are not delusions" (132). The "monstrously" sexual women depicted in Judith Rossner's *Looking for Mr. Goodbar* and director Alan J. Pakula's *Klute* are threatened—and in the case of *Goodbar* done in—by violent death due to their unsanctioned ways. Levin's novels sharply outline the fatal hypocrisies of the sexual double standard, as his good girls suffer fates similar to those of the bad girls from *Goodbar* and *Klute*. Only *Klute*'s Bree Daniels is rescued from mortal danger by the heroic actions of the male detective for whom, notably, the film is named.

Both of Levin's gothic tales draw deeply from the genre's conventions: bizarre settings of suffocating entrapment and innocent young women whose pluck and intelligence cannot save them. They thus present the very opposite of liberation-era physical and sexual freedom sought and achieved in examples throughout this chapter, although in a notably feminist gesture, Levin disguises gothic's monster as rescuing hero: Rosemary (of *Rosemary's Baby*) and Joanna (of *The Stepford Wives*) are surrounded by seemingly benign but ultimately dastardly men (neighbors, doctors, father-figures, and prospective lovers) and married to the biggest creeps of all. The unrelentingly evil male characters in French's melodrama caused cries of disbelief from critics, but their preponderance in Levin's stories only adds to the horror effect. As Greer cautioned women to trust only feminist sisters for comfort and advice, so Levin positions Rosemary and Joanna in supportive feminine circles, only to have their efficacy drained away by the supervening forces of vicious men. Marcus compares young, urbane Rosemary Woodhouse to the heroines of *Valley of the Dolls* and *Sex and the Single Girl*, but for no-longer-single Rosemary, "horrific . . . marriage and maternity could overpower the liberating effects of the urban location" (129; see also Scahill 197). As Anne Williams observes, both of Levin's works "abandon the female Gothic for the equally old and conventional Gothic mode in which heroines are most interesting as bodies suffering at the behest of the powers that be. . . . The Stepford husbands are basically high-tech Bluebeards" (88).

Violating every law of propriety that has justified the marital bond since inception, the husband in each story sells out his wife's sexual personhood to the perverted interests of local men to improve personal standing. For Guy Woodhouse, the despicable pimp married to Rosemary, this is success as a Broadway actor following his wife's drugged submission to the Devil himself for the purpose of bearing his next manifestation into the world. For Walter Eberhart, the mean-spirited wimp married to Joanna, this is entrance into the Stepford Men's Association, whose members all subject their wives to violent takeover by brainless sex-bots. Jo Agnew McManis regards Guy as even "more despicable" than the Faust figure he descends from "because he bargains with the body, eyesight, and life of other human beings, whereas his predecessors had bargained only with their own souls" (34). Per Antoinette F. Winstead, "The exchange [between Guy and his diabolical neighbors] resembles the deal made between Satan and God over Job" (39) as well as a reenactment of Adam blaming Eve for his own weakness. Guy's aspirations to the stage—and his role as a "*marvelous* liar" (Levin, *Rosemary's Baby* 8) when he extricates the couple from a lease in order to move into the mysterious Bramford—underscore the implication that men are only ever "acting" when they claim to love and respect their wives (see also Langan 56 and Fife 51).

Were we to evaluate Rosemary's own feminism in terms of her departure from the traditional role of faithful wife, supportive of her husband's career and eager for motherhood, we would read her sex with the Devil—witnessed by all of the Woodhouses' elderly naked neighbors and during which she enjoys a tremendous orgasm (see also Wexman 38)—as her only nonnormative sexual moment. Regarding Rosemary as "the New Eve, charged with Original Sin," Lucy Fischer points out that "it is *she* who has arranged to live in the Bramford (despite its chilling reputation). It is *she* who pushed association with the Castavets" (9), despite Guy's initial demurral. And yet, since the adventurous sexual activity is conducted utterly without Rosemary's consent and with only her wooziest understanding of what transpires, it comprises instead a woman's worst nightmare and confirmation of second-wave feminists' bitterest condemnation of gang-raping male behavior.

If the average horror heroine makes an almost culpably stupid fatal mistake, Rosemary's misstep is motherhood itself (see also Wexman 37) in a medical context of patronizing doctors who regularly lied to their female patients and who drastically limited a woman's options with respect to terminating a dangerous pregnancy. Though the last thing Rosemary wants is the abortive technology available to medically compromised middle-class women in the pre-*Roe* era, the withholding of this liberating rescue by the men in charge of her fate critiques both Rosemary's old-fashioned devotion to motherhood and the age-old sorceries that relegate Rosemary to terrifying birth-giving at home instead of in a modern hospital. The film's theme of "reproductive freedom" (Valerius 119; see also see Hoffman; Marcus; and Scahill 203–205) critiques Rosemary's final, entranced acquiescence to mothering the little devil she brings into the world; as Fischer observes, "Even in the hands of the devil, the dominant (Christian) ideology of mothering obtains" (13).

In *The Stepford Wives*, motherhood is again the heroine's Achilles heel, with Joanna giving up her career in New York to move her school-age children to the suburbs of Connecticut at the behest of her overbearing husband.[3] As Bryan Forbes's film version opens, a man crosses their busy street in Midtown with a naked store mannequin; Joanna, an aspiring photographer played by the soft-sexy '70s icon Katharine Ross, begins snapping photos, while her husband ironically regards the scene as evidence of the sexual perversion they are leaving New York to avoid. (It is doubly ironic that Walter will soon come to mirror this man with the mannequin when he causes his wife to be transformed into a live dummy; see also A. Williams 90.) In the film, the vulnerable-mother theme is emphasized in the climactic scene, when a voice recording of Joanna's children, seemingly in distress, is used to lure her through the dark hallways of the Men's Association, where her transformation will take place.

The film is also able to indicate Joanna's allegiance to feminism via her appearance without a bra in several scenes. Per the conventions of the period, Joanna and her friend Bobby dress in youthful, swinging styles and make fun of the Stepford women for their heavy padding and frilly dresses. Yet as suggested by Seaman earlier, bralessness is a double-edged sword: Joanna's obvious nipple definition beneath clingy fabrics is a form of nudity on view only at this brief moment in Hollywood history, after the demise of the studio-era Production Code and before the MPAA rating system, though launched in 1968, rose to full juridical authority as the Reagan presidency hove into view. David Cook describes in this period an "embrace [of] exploitation as mainstream practice, elevating such B genres as . . . horror to A-film status" (qtd. in Milliken 40), and Christie Milliken sums up, "The 'excess' of many of these genres was frequently bound up in issues surrounding sexuality and its representation" (40). Joanna's going braless may have indicated confident feminist identification to original female viewers, yet it only suggests overexposed vulnerability to modern audiences, who add the film's own pandering leer to the host of other sexual threats besetting the heroine throughout the story.

The film is as explicitly focused on Joanna's eyes as it is surreptitiously upon her exposed nipples. So enamored must Forbes have been with Ross's own lovely eyes that Joanna even keeps both eyes open when shooting photos, causing the binocular vision that would screw up any shot. Though Ross had many onscreen talents, acting did not top the list, and her half-baked handling of the tools of Joanna's putative trade undermines the film's feminist credibility on that score. Notably, "photographer" was a less frequent career for women at mid-century, a behind-the-camera role conversant with contemporary feminist film theorists' search for representational moments "when the woman looks." Yet while the photographer's "eye" is even more important than the camera as a tool of critical and aesthetic discernment, women's eyes are often the focal point of filmgoers' enthrallment and a special locus of vulnerability in the gothic/horror context, further explaining what seems to be the director's command to his lead actress to never close either one of them. Just as keeping both eyes open behind a camera guarantees loss of vision in both, so Joanna's decision to *see* a psychiatrist late in the film opens her eyes to horrid truths but cannot prevent her blind foray through the forbidding mansion of the Men's Association, whence she never returns. And as will be noted later, the eyes and nipples form coordinate pairs in the film's climax, echoing Freud's famous equation in "The Uncanny" between the boy's fear of eye-attack by the Sandman and the castration complex.

In two key scenes, Joanna's bra-free exposure is most evident—while serving coffee to her husband's associates the night Walter is initiated into the group, and while presenting her photographs to an effete gallery owner back in the city. Preparing coffee in the kitchen, she is accosted by the dashing but villainous Dale Coba, and a mutual seduction is simultaneously a shifting power struggle. Notably, Coba is a Disney executive, and Disney Corporation's mid-century forays into entertainment-based robotics take on a sinister sheen in this narrative—yet another liberation-era technology that might have freed women from the housewifely drudgery but is turned against them here. In Elyce Rae Helford's view, "with Joanna boxed into a small room and Dale looking at her through the doorframe . . . castration anxiety is both acknowledged and assuaged by turning the active Joanna into a passive object for male pleasure" (150; see also Silver 116). To be sure, Joanna returns Coba's advances with a mix of confident feminist posturing—straight back, level gaze, sardonic remarks—and the wispy, come-hither femininity that Ross trademarked across a short string of hugely successful films in this period. Her erect nipples "stare back" at her suave seducer with the same steadiness as her actual eyes, curtailing his impulse to focus on her breasts since he would be caught in the act by their own policing gaze. As Helford adds, noting the temporal coincidence of this film with Laura Mulvey's feminist classic "Visual Pleasure and Narrative Cinema" (also 1975), "the film can even be argued to address gaps in Mulvey's theory in suggesting the possibility of a female gaze" (152).

With Coba contained thus, it is nevertheless the film's own prerogative to focus on Joanna's exposed breasts for long takes, drinking in their desirability despite their small size. Coba's final chivalric bearing of the coffee tray out from Joanna's grasp removes the last prospect of shielding her underdressed torso from the view of the audience and her fellow actors in the next scene. In the living room, Joanna receives thirsty male gazes from every direction, adopting the sexualized servant's role to gain admittance to a men's club meeting with an inscrutably vague agenda. As is suggested by the sketch artist in the club, who works intently to capture Joanna's eyes throughout the scene, the most important and yet most difficult body part to replicate is the human eye—our most humanizing, individuating element and the window to Joanna's soul that meets its demise in the final scene.

In the professional context of the photography gallery, Joanna's breasts are again center stage. Here the quality of her work should be the issue, yet the peeking nipples are as distracting, implausible, and unprofessional as is her both-eyes-open technique behind the camera. Worse yet, she cajoles the stuffy Mr. Atkinson with trivial banter and shameless appeals to her maternal role. Yet any impulse Mr. Atkinson might feel to stare at Joanna's breasts is again curtailed by their own unblinking gaze, and her work meets with his approval in an important professional breakthrough. Joanna's free-and-easy attire is starkly contrasted to the lifted, padded specter of Bobby, now irrevocably damned to robot eternity when Joanna returns from her successful trip to the city. The scene in Bobby's kitchen is the film's most overt indictment of oppressive foundation garments, as Bobby's newly confining brassiere and confinement to sex-slavery are clear contrasts to Joanna's freely extruding nipples and her own last hours of personal freedom.

In the film's climax, Joanna becomes trapped by her robotic double, naked except for a flimsy negligee and approaching menacingly with the same mix of saccharine sweetness and sexual invitation she will provide real Joanna's husband from then on. It is a toss-up as to whether robot Joanna's oily eye sockets or her radically enlarged breasts are the uncannier horror at this crisis moment. Fittingly, the weapon by which real Joanna will be mysteriously subsumed is a women's foundation garment; the robot twists a pair of pantyhose, once more equated with women's physical constriction and symbolic death, as she approaches her hapless victim (see also Silver 121). As mentioned earlier, Freud's analogy of the boy's eyes to his testicles in "The Uncanny" is translated here into an equation between Joanna's eyes and breasts. As the boy in Freud's essay feared loss of both his eyes and private parts, so real Joanna's final vision is of her eyeless double modeling a castration of its own—her diminutive breasts destroyed and replaced by monstrous false ones. Modern medical technologies are denied to the desperate Rosemary, but the robotics of the Stepford men hark back to the excessive—and eventually fatal—enthrallment to plastic surgery, body-shaping, and the refusal of disfiguring mastectomy suffered by Susann's Jennifer North.

Just as many Muslim women feel undressed and undignified in public without the traditional head-covering of the hijab, so Western women have tended throughout their own sartorial history to feel a similar sense of self-defeating exposure without a bra or clothing equivalent. Though a woman—perhaps especially a small-breasted one like Stepford's Joanna Eberhart—may still make the case that if men do not have to deal with confining brassieres then neither will she, most women today, some of them ardent feminists, are as loath to do without that protective support as are most men to underdress their own sexual appendages in a Speedo bathing suit. As artifacts such as the film version of *The Stepford Wives* make clear, it was only at this singular second-wave moment that women deployed the shock value of their sexuality as a bold declaration of their arrival on the public scene. Though male-authored Hollywood films ultimately profited from these dilemmas, Joanna, Bobby, and their many real-life counterparts risked a predatory response to achieve their goal of living comfortably with their own sexual bodies. The film stages a tragic struggle between Joanna's freely expressed body and the forces of containment that finally do her in; it is both a trenchant comment on the realities of that era and an enactment of the irresolvable dilemma that helped bring that era to a close.

The heroines of these final two texts live lives of maximum sexual freedom. Not only are both Theresa Dunn of *Looking for Mr. Goodbar* and Bree Daniels of *Klute* resolutely unmarried for the duration of their narratives; both take on a series of sexual partners for whom they have little if any affection, if they are other than total strangers. As an elegant call girl (living nevertheless in a shabby, bohemian apartment) Bree plies the world's oldest trade, her situation constituting a nadir of oppression per some feminists of her day. But Bree is neither an enslaved wife nor an impoverished member of a radical commune; instead she gains forthrightly from the sex economy entrapping all women, if nothing else living free from the hypocrisy that characterizes the bought-and-paid-for situation of respectable women entering socially sanctioned marriages. In other words, she is the wealthiest, most entrepreneurial female character in this survey, making gains in the "professional" sphere that any liberal feminist might applaud. Theresa Dunn is not as financially well-situated, occupying the traditional woman's job of underpaid teacher to young children. Thus her approach to female sexuality is more "radical" for being experienced "freely"—again, with any male partner she feels inclined to invite home and *without* the monetary compensation that said partners, and American society as a whole, assume into play so as to categorize and ultimately contain sexual activity such as Theresa's. Because Theresa's habit of engaging in anonymous sex not for money but for sheer self-interested pleasure is the more aggravating departure from social convention for attractive white middle-class women such as herself, so the price she pays is much higher: though both she and Bree are mortally threatened, only Theresa has these threats actually visited upon her; she is brutally slain for her transgressions, while Bree is rescued from harm by a representative of the state in the figure of Detective John Klute.

A useful context is Gail Sheehy's 1971 exposé of New York's prostitution boom, archly titled "Wide Open City." The city's early-1970s takeover by the prostitution industry (including not only the women themselves and their nefarious pimps but the hotel operators, convention planners, XXX theater operators, look-the-other-way doormen, and ever more jaded police and court ministers) is surely notable. But Sheehy actually writes to report an epidemic of violence breaking out in scenes of paid seduction all over town—not by the johns against the hookers (as such assaults are tragically too typical to mention) but by the hookers against the johns. Sheehy describes prostitutes alone or in pairs escorting unwitting Iowa salesmen up to rooms in seedy hotels, insisting on the men's showering beforehand, then stealing their wallets, tossing their clothes, and beating a hasty retreat (see also Coleman 27). In the shoes (or at least the feet) of those naked, humiliated salesmen, Sheehy's readers might have felt most indignant about these women absconding with wallets without ever actually putting out. If anything is more scandalous than a hooker resorting to cons, deceptions, and even the classic New York mugging, it is her refusal to complete the capitalist relay of the bargain fairly struck. Sheehy elaborates, "Today's liberated woman, forgetting that she is dealing with an ignorant, often initiates sex and expects her partner to perform. The man . . . risks ridicule and humiliation" (*Hustling* 2–3).

In addition to Sheehy's exposé, Rossner's novel must be received in the true-crime context in which it actually originated—the 1973 New Year's night murder of Roseann Quinn at the hands of John Wayne Wilson, a drifter she had picked up in a singles bar and brought back to her apartment for a one-night stand. As traumatizing as Quinn's murder was, to all New Yorkers and all American women who heard the story, it was only the latest in a series of equally shocking, sexually inflected homicides stretching back more than a decade, most notoriously Nancy Clutter's 1959 near-rape and slaughter in her bedroom, as depicted in Truman Capote's unforgettable *In Cold Blood* (1964); Kitty Genovese's rape and murder outside her Queens apartment in 1964; the now largely anonymous nursing students who succumbed to the deadly machinations of Richard Speck in their Chicago apartment in 1966; and perhaps most heinously, the beautiful, famous, and obviously pregnant Sharon Tate done in by the hand of the Manson clan in 1969. Each of these cases achieved its legendary status due to some shocking feature that turned the event from simply tragic into truly sensational; this term, in addition to my own classification of these texts as "thrillers" in the heading of this section, suggest both the horrifying aspects of these stories and the shameful satisfaction we experience when women who go public with their sexuality—or even, in the case of a Nancy Clutter, are simply too pretty to ignore—meet bad ends. As Susan Brownmiller incisively construed the matter, "By putting great store in the murder of a beauty, beauty acquires the seeds of its own destruction" (341). "The rape story that a big-city 'picture newspaper,' is apt to feature," she adds, "is a *selected* rape, enhanced by certain elements of glamour. . . . It is often the only news of women that can be found in the important first few pages of a paper on a given day" (337). Later, "the occupation of a female victim is buried deep within the story . . . unless the occupation has a glamorous connotation, however tenuous. Model, actress, stewardess, show-girl, go-go dancer, career girl, heiress, and divorcee are the words to conjure with" (340).

New York Times reporter Lacey Fosburgh, in her book-length treatment of the Quinn case, demonstrates that it would not have been solved had it never received front-page treatment from the dailies. When it finally sifted up from police records into the "Unusuals" file (Fosburgh 240), the press jumped on the story, and the incessant coverage frightened her slayer Wilson's one-time boyfriend into approaching his lawyer with information. Although the press had sympathy for Quinn, the shocking circumstances of her death—found naked and blood-soaked in her messy apartment with a large red Christmas candle inserted in her vagina—had all the titillating features that would encourage the public to condemn as it sympathized: Roseanne Quinn would not even wash her own dishes, and she was thus a failed woman in every respect. As Brownmiller adds, "Women who went drinking with the offender prior to the act, . . . and women whose past sexual history was alleged to be 'promiscuous' were assessed by juries in [a] national study as having taken an undue risk and morally not worth a conviction for rape" (374).

As Rossner's Theresa frames her own diagnosis, "There was a Miss Dunn who taught a bunch of children who adored her . . . and there was someone named Terry who whored around in bars when she couldn't sleep at night" (121). David Willbern even suggests that Theresa has a "multiple personality disorder" (60), while Richard Brooks, who directed the film, echoes Ruth Rosen—quoted at the start of this chapter—when he declares that Theresa's "problem is that she mistakes sexual freedom for women's liberation" (qtd. in Daniel 204). And though the term might be excused as just an expression, Theresa does not actually "whore around"; instead of her behavior understood as, for instance, a necessary however shameful attempt to augment her meager teacher's income, Theresa's only concession to the "whore" profile is her rather catty tendency to head to the local bar with only "her keys" and no wallet, knowing that the drinks will be purchased by whichever guy she brings home. Instead, she repeatedly rejects these men's attempt to leave her money and denies the term *prostitute* that she imagines her square boyfriend James using if he ever found out. As Theresa asks, "What was the right word for someone who did it just for fun, not money?" (221), and her secret is exposed in a scene making repeated use of a loaded term: James "confess[es] to feeling jealous of anyone who feels *free* to call you at this hour," and when he asks whether Theresa has been sleeping with other men during their own courtship, her insouciant response is, "I feel *free* to" (225, emphases added).

Though Fosburgh's account depicts Quinn as a drifter as desperately down-and-out as her murderer, both novelist Rossner and filmmaker Brooks translate such drifting into swinging, and their Theresa Dunn insists upon the need to "make the point of her freedom" (Rossner 225). Quinn's two real-life brothers are revised in Rossner/Brooks into two sisters—one a multiparous stay-at-home and the other a stewardess with a boyfriend on each coast and a penchant for orgies who initiates Theresa into a sexually unorthodox lifestyle. To a large extent, the fact that Theresa has sex for free frees her to do so much more readily than a paid worker would—free from prosecution by the law, free from the need to recoup or retrench when a john will not pay, and free from the sidewalk display that all but the highest-class prostitutes must make of themselves in order to attract customers. In a revision of the prostitutes in Sheehy's article, who take money but refuse to give sex, Theresa is a woman who "whores around" but has financial compensation nowhere among her motivations for doing so. As she herself frames the problem, "To admit the need when there was no man [i.e., husband] to fill it seemed to be telling the world that you did forbidden things to yourself to gratify that need" (77).

Theresa's casting of her sexual encounters as things done "to herself" underscores her tendency to engage in sex for her own pleasure, with little if any interest in her partner's needs. She only pines after the boorish Tony Lapanto for the great sex he gives and is repeatedly cruel to the loving James for his attempt to curb her "restlessness." This term is deployed throughout the novel and perhaps names Theresa's greatest offense: her radical attempt to conduct her sex life as irresponsibly as a man might.[4] In the film, she fights with her father about her refusal to bear children, while in the novel, Theresa completes her usurpation of the man's role by not even bothering with contraceptives; she simply states that "she would never get pregnant" (205), and, quite freakishly if not monstrously, she never does (see also Zita 34–35). She mocks the inability of the man who eventually kills her to maintain an erection, like Sheehy's "liberated woman" making humiliating demands upon a sexual "ignorant." Her taunts regarding his failure to "like girls" and her final insistence that he "not fall asleep" (i.e., that he leave her apartment) after the failed sex attempt ignite the confrontation that results in Theresa's death by bludgeoning with a heavy lamp base. Elaine Showalter, who pondered at the end of the 1970s whether a spate of violent women's novels did not indicate "a projection of female violence, an extreme form of [their own] anger" (159), reads Theresa Dunn as wanting "the illusion of control that comes from her own destruction" (164); she and her killer "fatally converge because they're both looking for Mr. Goodbar, the escape through sexuality, but also escape through a violent, omnipotent force" (165; see also Wolff 110–111).

Though Rossner does not excuse the killer's violent action, she creates sympathy by emphasizing his status as an impoverished drifter, a Vietnam veteran with a friend in New York who had promised help but then disappeared. (In fact, the sympathetic veteran angle is Rossner's own, since the real-life Wilson did no military service.) In the real and fictional versions of this story, the killer is pathologized as a closet-queer, sexually exploited by the gay man keeping him but who in Rossner's rendition could no longer stand to perform as sexual slave; when he happens into Theresa's apartment that New Year's night, he has nowhere else to go. While this story's mid-1970s context frames Wilson's tortured sexuality as its own brand of monstrosity, the twenty-first-century reader cannot but lament the social constraints that made such a man a stranger to himself and might account for any number of pathological behaviors. To humanize him to the degree Rossner does unavoidably condemns restless, callous Theresa to the same degree. In Showalter's reading, Theresa's killer "confuses the reader's sympathies, especially since this murderer . . . 'had a very clear sense of himself as the victim'" (164; see also Fishbein 181). E. Ann Kaplan reads him as a scapegoat as well, a gay character who "permits . . . the dominant class of men to avoid identification with the final, most brutal act" (81; see also Nystrom 137). In Fosburgh's account, one of the cops remarks, "He was caught up in something bigger than he was, and he just didn't have any place to go" (277). Ultimately the role Rossner's Theresa plays as the respectable schoolteacher who enforces her hegemonic class status against this homeless, destitute gay veteran feeds the sensationalism of Quinn's own story—that of the middle-class professional who had other options, or other socially sanctioned obligations to perform, and perversely turned her back on these.

If this reading closes with the equally controversial statement that Roseanne Quinn, and especially Rossner's heroine Theresa Dunn, got what she had coming to her, it does so not to join in the chorus of blame that countless female rape and murder victims have suffered since Quinn's time and throughout history. Instead "what was coming" is the tragic inevitability of deadly violence, sooner or later, for women of this period who attempted to conduct their sexual affairs as subjects instead of objects and on the most radical terms. As with the catch-22 confronting the heroines of *The Stepford Wives*, and the millions of young, would-be liberated women whom they represented in this period, the Quinn/Dunn story again forced upon women the collective realization that what was most revolutionary in their actions was also that which made them most vulnerable to attack by predatory men and, in the cold light of morning, a shaming and self-righteous public.

It is remarkable that in the same year that Sheehy reported the epidemic of prostitution and related crimes, 1971, Mayor John Lindsay's Knapp Commission approached its peak of publicity and power (see chapter 2). Named for Whitman Knapp, a prominent New York attorney later appointed a federal judge, the panel was charged with cracking down on the rampant police corruption that aided and abetted such crimes as prostitution, gambling, and narcotics all over town. As the commission's chief counsel Michael F. Armstrong told the story many decades later, the vast majority of beat cops, detectives, and special forces were "on the pad" in this period, regularly shaking down both criminal wrongdoers and honest bar and restaurant owners to protect them from arrest, prosecution, or day-to-day harassment (often in the form of time-consuming and expensive raids).

Not surprisingly, New York's infamous "Madam X," Xaviera Hollander, whose story is told in *The Happy Hooker* (1972) by herself and author of *The French Connection* and *The Green Berets* Robin Moore, paid off New York police on a regular basis in an attempt to curtail their endless raids on her brothel apartment and to protect her bid for a green card (per her pseudonym, she was a Dutch citizen). By Armstrong's account, the Knapp Commission was drastically underfunded throughout its course, such that it was ironically mainly the money obtained via Hollander's shakedowns that enabled it to do its work. Her bribes always went to "Patrolman P," who was so thoroughly implicated due to extensive bugging of Hollander's apartment that he became the commission's star witness. Xaviera was referred to by all involved as "the golden goose," and Armstrong observes that the crisis in their investigation came when Hollander simply refused to quit being squeezed: "So far we had been making payments with Xaviera Hollander's money. Now, in order to keep things moving, we would have to hand over $1500. It was a sum with which no law enforcement agency in those days was prepared to part" (100). Shortly thereafter, Phillips squealed, the hearings commenced, and Hollander, instead of being honored for her essential underwriting of the commission's success, was deported on a charge of "moral turpitude" and has lived outside the United States ever since.

Although Hollander describes a joyfully sexual lifestyle throughout the steamy, seamy chapters of *The Happy Hooker*, in fact her narration includes almost as many accounts of physical and emotional abuse, personal and legal hardship, and general grief at the hands exploiting men. As the golden goose of the Knapp Commission, she was indeed the "goose" in the situation, a sometimes duped and always victimized female—a tool herself in a trade between powerful men. She repeatedly denounced the appellation "hooker"—and hence the title of her book, which was Moore's idea—since she drew a sharp distinction between the hookers on the pavement outside her apartment and the high-class madams and call girls who populated the world she moved in and at one time ruled. And yet as Hollander's narrative also indicates, she was the rare "bird" in this second wave context, a professionally successful, financially independent woman whose resources were set upon by the men surrounding her in their ultimately successful attempt to put her out of business. Down on the much meaner streets, *Life* reporter James Mills's fictional rendition of a long-form exposé, *The Panic in Needle Park* (1965), presents a junkie couple with oddly traditional dreams and dilemmas. Bob avers that "I don't want her hustling. I'd rather her stay home and I go out and steal" (56), but as one in an endless line of working girls whose efforts go only to benefit men, it is Helen who "supported both our habits all the time" (57). Like a good housewife, she will even "wake [Bob] up and have [his] fix ready, like breakfast in bed" (63), though at a moment of bitter realization, she sees him as "just another arm to feed" (98).

Klute's call girl heroine Bree Daniels, played by Jane Fonda in an Oscar-winning role, walks the same fine line between self-determination and victimization. She has a few quick encounters with Xaviera-like madams but is otherwise in charge of her own destiny and that much more vulnerable to predators therefore. As original reviewers (e.g., Ebert and Greenspun) pointed out, the film is perversely named *Klute* since "Bree," who is clearly the audience's main identification point, would have been the more sensible title. Notably, Rossner's novel and Brooks's film feature a man's name, "Mr. Goodbar," implying the inevitable endpoint of the restless heroine, regardless of her attempt to live life on her own terms. In the same way, Bree comes home inevitably to John Klute, played by Donald Sutherland, despite her own deep ambivalence about life as the wife of a Pennsylvania police officer.

As someone who is herself caught on tape—she learns early in the film that her phone has been tapped and therefore faces possible arrest—Bree channels Madam X's story of bugged premises and victimization by men in all professional spheres. It is implied that Bree's tapes are made for the purposes of catching a killer, who may be one of her customers. But until and unless they pay off thus, the tapes simply situate Bree in an atmosphere of surveillance and crackdown akin to that created by the Knapp Commission or, as one reviewer of the film surmised, "Tricky Dick [Nixon] himself . . . for the FBI had been recording all of *Fonda's* phone calls in the early seventies" (Callahan 6, emphasis added; see also Gledhill 101–102). Notably, the large skylight in Bree's apartment, whence many-a spine-tingling shot of the killer's POV is made, recalls the ceiling cameras installed in the bedroom of Madam X. And though Bree fears (and often receives) trouble coming through her front door and telephone, she does not think to look up through the skylight until the eagle-eyed Klute arrives. In the same way, the typical prostitute of the era expected violence and larceny from her pimps and johns but may not have realized that cops, lawyers, and judges on the take, as well as reformers on a soapbox, would make her life even more hazardous.

Although "Mr. Goodbar," the good lay who would make no physical or emotional demands on independent Theresa Dunn, was ultimately nowhere to be found in Rossner's novel or in Rosanne Quinn's own tragic story, the upstanding John Klute is omnipresent. Even managing to rent a basement apartment in Bree's building, he is barely distinguishable from her several johns and stalkers: he stays up all night to watch over her sleep, gives her his twin bed the night she flees an attack, chases the killer around her building, and is miraculously on hand at the moment of mortal danger in the garment factory (see also Giddis 29–31). Despite its racy subject matter, gritty cinematography, improvised script, and violent thriller effects, *Klute* is as heavily constrained (verging on claustrophobic) a love story as tradition ever dictated, since almost every scene is another chance for Klute and Bree to spend time in each other's company, discovering their interdependence. In the view of Christine Gledhill, *Klute* departs from the noir conventions it elsewhere invokes by "disengage[ing] . . . the criminal problem from the relationship between detective and heroine" (103). It is notable that on their first meeting, Bree slams the door in Klute's face and fights her attraction to this unmitigated square for the duration of the film. As Russell Campbell remarks, "For Bree, it is a question of getting out of the city. . . . For the man, on the other hand . . . by 'rescuing' the prostitute, he creates for himself . . . the ideal love object, in whom are fused the erotic thrill of the woman who flaunts her sexuality with the nurturing care of the woman who is so grateful for being saved that she lavishes all her love on the instrument of her deliverance" (320). Of course, it is only the persisting presence of a rampaging murderer who brings them together in the first place, and Bree is rescued from the likely prospect of her own violent death only by making the choice—of traditional marriage in remote locale—that Theresa Dunn refused to make.

Conclusion: Elusive Equality

Though Xaviera Hollander enjoyed professional success sufficient to bankroll the Knapp Commission through its many salutary activities, even to her own undoing, she is the rare economically powerful "main character" in this discussion whose story demonstrates the importance of women's economic solvency. Liberal feminism's drive for economic parity looked like selling out to radical feminists, while modern commentators misread the difficult challenge it remains, as when Bradley repeatedly mistakes women's entry into the workforce—for example, the first woman police officer in a small town (251) and "working women" (285) now in many professions—with "equal pay for equal work." Neither the entrance of women into the workplace, nor whatever equal-pay laws are currently on the books, guarantee that women doing equal work earn anywhere near identical levels of income. As has been my thesis throughout, such equality achievements are always so intolerably expensive that they are never actually achieved: Equal Pay Day continues to be April 10 each year—the day when women dress in red to demonstrate that they have been "in the red" since January 1 and catching up to men's earning power three months late. Also, as suggested in my earlier readings of Greer and Firestone, romanticizing poverty as a political choice is a luxury only successful public intellectuals like themselves may enjoy. In the liberation era, economic solvency was achieved by some women not through plying the world's oldest trade but through writing best-selling narratives about this experience—or about middle-class women's diverse experiences of love, learning, triumph, and defeat.

In my discussion of the Black Power movement (see chapter 1), I distinguished between "talking" and "walking": speeches and manifestoes that enlarged the notoriety of movement leaders but did little to improve the plight of African Americans overall versus actions such as marches, pickets, and sometimes bloody confrontations that stung the national conscience and resulted in key political victories, even if economic gains rarely followed. Vital actions from this era's white middle-class women's movement made political inroads as well: early speak-outs on rape and abortion encouraged women (including Gloria Steinem; Cohen 225) to come out of their closets of shame, fear, and isolation, and the 26 August 1970 Women's Strike for Equality, largely organized by Betty Friedan, drew some forty thousand women marching down New York's Fifth Avenue. It was a dramatic media spectacle that presented to the nation sisterhood's power as a mass movement of unstoppable force. Elsewhere sit-ins and pickets of major media—in late 1967 the *New York Times* for posting in its classified section "jobs for women" and "jobs for men" (see Cohen 140, see also Bradley) and in March 1970 the office of *Ladies' Home Journal* editor John Mack Carter (see Cohen 190–194, Echols 195–197, and Bradley 68–71)—did improve women's economic picture: the desegregating of job ads opened career opportunities (even if not salary parity) for women, and the *Journal* replaced Carter (who later professed that the sit-in was a turning point in his own feminist consciousness; see Kaufman) with a woman editor in 1973. Across the media spectrum, magazines, newspapers, TV stations, and advertising moved to include not just women's interests in respectful, realistic ways but women producers of media content themselves (see also Bradley).

Yet as noted at the start of this chapter, women "in media" is yet another double-edged sword: staged actions such as the Miss America protest risked (or exploited) the spectacle of women's sexuality in the attention-seeking bodies, voices, and paraphernalia (posters of nude women, flying brassieres) of the protesters themselves. Many such actions with comic, theatrical, or improvisational undertones were stunts or goofs verging on pure spectacle with little if any political payoff: within the pageant that same day, a protester was arrested for "emanating a noxious odor" (see, e.g., Echols 94–95) when she sprayed a can of Toni Home Permanent into the crowd, and at a bridal fair in February 1969, a radical group known as WITCH let loose a flock of white mice (see, e.g., Echols 97–98 and Bradley 63–66).

Even in more serious-minded efforts to "walk the walk," the white middle-class women's movement risked enlarging the oppression stemming from the to-be-looked-atness that has constituted women's plight for centuries; more attractive movement members like the gorgeous radical Germaine Greer, the lovely liberal Gloria Steinem, "the good-looking television reporter" (Cohen 130) Marlene Sanders, and the "classically attractive" (Bradley 35) Muriel Fox opened doors—for themselves if for no other women—based in part on their good looks, while dowdier sisters were ignored by the press or vilified by the man on the street. An Ivy League college president, of all people, once told *New York* reporter Sheila Tobias that he could "readily accept . . . the part of the movement represented by Gloria Steinem, namely the part that accepts men and wishes to work with us." What he could not countenance (pun intended) was "the part of the movement represented by Betty Friedan, namely hate-male separatism" (qtd. in Cohen 321). As Tobias immediately recognized, this intelligent man had diametrically transposed the two women's opinions because "Steinem was so good looking. It never dawned on him that a woman with that kind of face and figure would be bitter or resentful of men" (321). The somewhat frumpy and harshly featured Betty Friedan, a married mother of three, "loved men" (Quinn C01) and once attacked Steinem for "fostering 'a female chauvinism that makes a woman apologize for loving her husband and children" (qtd. in Horowitz 235). Friedan preached men's inclusion in the movement every chance she got, while Steinem's most famous "Steinemism"—"a woman needs a man like a fish needs a bicycle"—was literally inaudible to the men who could not get past her loveliness and who perhaps were not listening that closely in the first place: an especially demoralizing comment comes from an early political mentor, John Kenneth Galbraith, who took Steinem under his wing mainly because of her "terrific good looks. . . . 'If Gloria says it's otherwise,' he would add, 'she's wrong'" (Cohen 115).

Most of the second wave's efforts to draw attention to itself pale in comparison to the confrontational impact of, for instance, a group of Black Panther men and women marching in formation with weapons in full view. NOW's 1969 "integration" of the Oak Room at the Plaza Hotel, which refused to seat women during the indeed vital businessman's lunch hour (see Cohen 13–22 and Bradley 43), is in telling contrast to the bravery of four North Carolina A&T students sitting down at a lunch counter in Greensboro nine years earlier. Aside from the protester with the can of Toni and various marchers pulled into police stations for, to be sure, harassment-filled overnight stays in the stir (see Cohen 198–200), few arrests were ever made and not a single injury or death occurred at the hands of police throughout the feminist movement's heyday from the late 1960s to mid-1970s—yet another sharp contrast to the copious blood lost in the fight for civil rights. Madhu Dubey describes the disconnect that divided the white and black women's movements in this period: "When in the 1970s, white women began to seek employment as a means of escaping the confinement of middle-class domesticity, they could not possibly strike a sympathetic chord in most black women, who historically had been workers out of economic necessity and whose experience of oppression in the labor market simply did not square with the white feminist conception of labor as a liberating experience." (16). Angela Davis adds that "as a direct consequence of their outside work—as 'free' women no less than as slaves—housework has never been the focus of Black women's lives [as it is for white feminists]. They have largely escaped the damage industrial capitalism inflicted on white middle-class housewives" (*Women* 130–131). Challenging Xaviera Hollander's snobbish distinctions, Kay Lindsey discerns that "where the white woman is the call girl or mistress, the Black woman is the street prostitute. . . . While white females are sexual objects, Black women are sexual laborers" (108).

In fact, as historians (e.g., Rosen 227–235) show time and again, most of the damage done to second-wave feminists occurred due to constant infighting with their movement sisters (see also Cohen and esp. Echols). Conferences, living room discussions, and phone calls devolved into rampant "conceptual confusion"

(Echols 7) over who was a radical, liberal, cultural, or socialist feminist; who was an NYRW member, Redstocking, or WITCH; and the proper ratio of consciousness-raising (talking) to mass action (walking) for fomenting revolution. Notably, it was the successful writers and speakers who drew the most resentment from the rank and file. Best-selling authors such as Susan Brownmiller (who led and was later harshly criticized for her role in the *Journal* sit-in) and Kate Millett (see Cohen 237–243) were attacked during widely attended feminist conferences for appending their own names to their written work.

Greer's celebration of female sexuality as its own political choice may have excused her flaunted beauty to some extent, while her Australian background, ensconcement in the U.K. academic setting, and loose to nonexistent affiliation with New York women's groups set her somewhat above the political fray in the U.S. Steinem, though she also "did not join a women's liberation group" (Cohen 225), was not as lucky, as she was resented and envied by her less photogenic sisters for stealing the limelight, being constantly in the company of glamorous men, and living luxuriously on New York's Upper East Side. Steinem wrote persuasively in favor of women's rights in dozens of landmark essays and columns, but her lifestyle ran so counter to the low-rent trenches in which most feminists found themselves battling toward revolution that almost every public appearance garnered suspicion of hypocrisy and opportunism. Indeed quite gallingly, despite her lack of affiliation with any organized feminist group, she was hailed as "The New Woman" in a flattering *Newsweek* cover story in 1971, as "Woman of the Year" in *McCall's* a year later, and as "the princess of the movement" (qtd. in Cohen 370) by *Ladies' Home Journal* in the rather unradical year of 1981. As a woman so glamorous and talented that she could have easily made it without feminism, her example proved to both women and men that there was serious political meaning in this movement.

Philosophically, Steinem favored the younger, more media-savvy radical feminists and regarded Betty Friedan's liberal feminist NOW as a middle-class organization from yesteryear (see "After Black Power"); in the pages of *Ms.*, Friedan and NOW were given minimal if any attention (see Cohen 331), and she regarded herself as "a feminist" foremost but if pressed, a "radical" one ("Far from" 381; see also Bradley 179). And yet Steinem's enmeshment in mainstream media (especially Clay Felker's *New York* and her own Felker-sponsored *Ms.*) and politics (especially George McGovern's 1972 presidential campaign) cast her very much in the liberal mode. In this way, she called for pay for "all productive work . . . including child rearing and other jobs done in the home" ("The Importance of Work" 182) and lamented women's tendency toward "too much reaction and living from one emergency to the next, with too little initiative and planned action of our own" ("The Time Factor" 190).

Her admiring profiles of women at work included Marilyn Monroe and the dreadfully exploited Linda Lovelace; her focus on working women's beleaguered bodies is just as disturbing in her first major piece for publication, "I Was a Playboy Bunny," appearing in the *Esquire*-affiliated *Show* in 1963. Despite its comic title and tone, the article's lengthy rehearsal of work conditions at the Playboy Club in New York—long, undercompensated shifts; starvation rations snatched from the buffet;

arms numbed from carrying heavy drink trays; dropped arches from these same stresses in three-inch heels; her ribcage crushed inside tight costumes; and the full panoply of sexual harassment from customers—is muckraking at its most effective. In a distant echo of the infantryman slogging through Vietnam in that same period, Steinem is "totally absorbed with my feet. They ache like bad teeth. They are so swollen that I can't even get sneakers on" ("I Was a Playboy Bunny" 63). Though enlarged feet cannot be regarded as disfigurement or disability of the proportion suffered by the Vietnam vet, they readily evoke the plight of laborers under less tricked-out but no less physically punishing circumstances throughout the blue-collar sector. Writing such as this anticipates later feminist landmarks such as Barbara Ehrenreich's *Nickeled and Dimed* (2001), although only a beauty such as Gloria Steinem could have infiltrated this early-1960s epicenter of sexual exploitation that was Hefner's Playboy empire. *Show*'s managing editor once asked, "If it hadn't been for the Playboy Bunny story, who would [Steinem] have become?" (qtd. in Cohen 219). But in fact it is as if Steinem's beauty had come between this editor's male gaze and the sharp-eyed, astutely phrased talent she might have presented her reader without such patronizing questions had she looked like a more ordinary woman.

Regretting that "in the 1960s and 1970s, many of us had spurned such legislative measures as the Equal Rights Amendment precisely because they didn't sound radical enough" ("Far from" 376), an older and wiser Steinem named the ERA for what it had tried to be—an aim toward salary "equity . . . introduced into systems that depend on inequity (in the workplace and in the home) [that] can turn out to be very radical indeed" ("Far from" 376). As Steinem dissolves the opposition between radical freedom and liberal equality that configured the second wave, she closes in on the thesis of this chapter as well: that narratives of women working every job from professor to prostitute and searching for (but always failing to find) the "work-life balance" that remains an elusive ideal are themselves radical tools of a trade whose secrets liberation-era and modern female audiences would gain from.

CONCLUSION

POSTSCRIPT FROM THE PRESENT DAY

By the time Lee Greenwood's "God Bless the USA" inspired cheers and tears at the 1984 Republican Convention, such hymns to freedom had traveled in the thirty years since the modern civil rights era 180 degrees on the American political-cultural spectrum, following the route taken by freedom itself in almost all political permutations. Greenwood told a country music website in the early 2010s that the cities mentioned in the song, specifically Detroit and Houston, "were both economically part of the basis of our economy—Motown and the oil industry" (Gallagher). Notably, by 1984, Detroit's economy was in shambles, and many of its neighborhoods had never recovered from the riots of the late 1960s. And though the barons of Houston's oil industry might have enjoyed bigger and bigger shares of our economy's blessings throughout the 1980s and since, the phrasing in Greenwood's lyric—"at least I know I'm free"—says it all in postliberation-era America: if U.S. workers had less and less to crow about in terms of employment, education, wealth, and overall quality of life, "freedom" was (as it has ever been) a high-minded, low-cost scrap of patriotic currency that was to substitute for the rest (see also Cowie 368). "Freedom" magnificently disguised its own ideological role as chief perpetrator—as comedian (and Canadian) Jim Carrey told Bill Maher on a September 2018 episode of *Real Time*, "Sink or fucking swim!"—of most average Americans' ever-depleting economic circumstances.

Though I have focused throughout *Freedom's Ring* on events and writings meaningful to the liberation era of the mid-1950s to the mid-1970s, the sometimes deadly conflict between freedom and equality that shaped the national agenda then is just as pertinent today. In the introduction to this book, I commented on police violence against unarmed black citizens as a current-day political crisis that, however urgently requiring redress, has the regrettable side effect of pushing vital economic inequalities to the national back burner time and again. In their most cynical rendering, police shootings might be seen as purposely deployed at just sufficient intervals to keep progressively minded Americans from turning attention back to those economic-related, much more expensive, ever-unmet agenda items:

affordable housing, better schools, health care for all, among many others. And yet the right wing has no monopoly on the expediency of politics instead of economics; it is an evidently universal human tendency to prefer quick, simple, no-cost, deeply satisfying name-calling over doing whatever possible against intractable fiscal problems. Hence the national obsession regarding red state versus blue, while the much more vital divide (brought into even harsher relief by a global pandemic) between the annually salaried and hourly underwaged is rarely discussed, cutting as it does across intensely invested-in political lines. So enthralled are we by the political theater (debates, conventions, market-tested messaging, and inauguration) that is the U.S. presidency that we fail to consider with equal care or turn over with equal frequency the membership of the U.S. legislature, where almost all of the economic harm to unions, workers' rights, and even campaign finance, ostensibly keeping lawmakers in the clutches of corporate lobbyists, has occurred. The Left is quick (and correct) to challenge cultural conservatives' deep reservoirs of racism and xenophobia, but the Left is also just as quick to minimize its own investment of time and resources by these same lights—to write off the electorate of Donald Trump as racists and fascists whose own intensive economic crises can therefore be conveniently ignored.

Who can care, after all, whether a racist puts food on his table, manages his opioid addiction, or sends his kids to college? This is the kind of question many of us might ask in our desire to improve the social landscape by calling out hate and hostility, daily if needed, but to not wrestle nearly as often with complicated monetary issues: Should my stock portfolio (or my payroll taxes) take a hit in the name of a guaranteed universal income, national health care, or an increased minimum wage for U.S. workers in downtown Baltimore *and* in rural Ohio? (Even if the answer to this question is yes, what does the Left do to realize such goals? Was there a discussion about improving society among well-meaning progressives during his presidential term that did not immediately devolve into a hate-fest against Donald Trump?) To quote from another episode of *Real Time*, host Bill Maher insisted, regarding Trump's popularity with working-class whites, that "I don't think it *is* an economic argument."

But how important is a good salary with health insurance and a retirement plan to Bill Maher (and to me), and how would my views on solving America's problems change if I suddenly and permanently lost all of those? Would I continue to think that the only national issue—and the only motivation for putting Trump in the White House—was the enabling of racist attitudes, or would a host of much more urgent matters prevent me from thinking in those terms at all? Regarding the massive (and eventually deadly) conflict regarding Civil War memorials in town squares throughout the South in 2017 and 2018, civil rights icon Andrew Young told NPR anchor Ailsa Chang on 23 August 2017, "And I'm saying that a minority can't be provoking a racist majority that is still underemployed, undereducated and dying faster than we are—that the issue is life and death—not some stupid monument." Lecturing at Spellman College in 2007, Black Power icon Elaine Brown called feminism's focus on reproductive rights an agenda for the "Gloria Steinem" contingent. But "Fannie Lou Hamer [among others] opposed abortion. We've gone far away from equal pay, remember that part? . . . [N]ow, we're talking about music videos, Vagina Monologues, looking at Oprah and Hillary Clinton as feminists" ("Speech")—that is, turning attention to contentious politics and popular culture, since "equal pay" proved impossible to achieve.

Claude Brown's mid-century masterwork, *Manchild in the Promised Land*, and related sociological studies of the heroin epidemic in 1950s New York (see chapter 2) crystalized the grievously inverse correlation between jobs and drugs in U.S. society: as cities rapidly deindustrialized in the immediate post-WWII period, highly addictive drugs rushed into that vacuum both as a career choice for former war workers who turned to dealing for a livelihood and as a daily occupation (or preoccupation or obsession) for the ordinary junkie on the street with nothing else to do. In the early twenty-first century, Middle America is beset by the same negative correlation that has ruined the lives of underemployed urban workers for decades (see, e.g., Kristoff and WuDunn, Quinones, and Reding), and the numbers of those now affected by joblessness/addiction resulted in a political upset in November 2016 that shocked the world. Ta-Nehisi Coates has recently made an incontrovertible "case for reparations," casting back over decades of unforgiveable assault on the solvency of African American families, and Thomas Sugrue corroborates these findings with his own thesis regarding "American metropolitan areas . . . [where] the ways of whites, through the combined advantages of race and residence, were able to hoard political and economic resources—jobs, public services, education, and other goods—to their own advantage" (xviii).

But it is notable that both Coates and Sugrue focus on cities, Chicago and Detroit, respectively, where indeed economic disparity is profoundly racially marked since almost the only wealthy whites left in America live in and around urban areas. Midessay, Coates remarks, "An unsegregated America might see poverty, and all its effects, spread across the country with no particular bias toward skin color" (60). Although the country indeed remains intensely segregated, poverty and its effects now suffuse thousands of small towns across the great "flyover" zone between urban centers. In addition to favorite national political lightning rods, Joan C. Williams has recently advised, "You better care, too, about good jobs and social dignity for Americans of all races without college degrees. Because if you don't, racialized economic populism is what you get" (xxi). Thus the presidency of Donald Trump was not only a symptom of an ongoing jobs/wage crisis too many decades ignored but also the bad medicine we *all* deserved: of course, Trump did nothing to turn back the clock to the mid-1970s, de-automating or de-outsourcing the jobs and salary wealth that have flowed offshore since the early 1960s. But his presidency must be the wake-up call to all of us "haves" (politically right, left, and center) who enjoy the economic security that *all* U.S. workers—urban and rural, black and white, semiskilled and unskilled, Democratic and Republican—crave and deserve, if we are not to see someone even less qualified succeed him in future years.

It is incorrect (or at least amnesiac) to insist as we do constantly that Trump during his term ruinously "divided the country." As we must recall, the political

Right led by the Tea Party felt outraged and alienated throughout Barack Obama's presidency, just as the Left felt during the tumultuous election and double-term of George W. Bush—on and on back through the decades. This book's prioritizing of the economic perspective asks us to realize that politics are inherently (and let us admit it, often greatly enjoyably) divisive no matter who lives in the White House, with the winner's party feeling a sense of united purpose and proper direction and the out party wringing its hands and shaking its fists. But economically speaking, well-paid members of America's upper classes (again, regardless of political affiliation) share vital interests—including all of those devoted to maximizing the retirement portfolio—and share blame for arguing politics when dollars and cents need vital attention instead. Prioritizing the economic also dissolves the utterly spurious divide between the "U.S. worker" (always pictured as a white, middle-aged, conservative male; see also Cowie 237–238) and residents of the "inner city"—as if cities since World War II were not bursting with equally willing but equally underemployed and undercompensated working people. These racially and politically diverse U.S. wage-workers also share vital interests and concerns: many cannot compete in today's high-tech, high-skilled, evermore automated, global/low-wage economy, and like the overvalued assets they are, they have been swept from the balance sheet of our capitalist system—no longer "free at last" but only "free at least"—and left to figure things out for themselves. One recent solution has been to put in charge of the problem the most unqualified person in national history in the hopes that such desperate measures will make an actual difference. Progressive America must come up with better alternatives by avoiding the overwhelming temptation to substitute politics for economics, freedom for equality, as has been the default since at least the dawn of the liberation era.

ACKNOWLEDGMENTS

This book was essentially enabled by the staff at UNT's Willis Library, who found me every title requested, no matter how obscure, far-flung, or immediately required. My thanks to Associate Dean for Public Services Mary Ann Venner, Collection Development Liaison Librarian Coby Condrey, Cataloging and Metadata Associate Kelly Evans, Cataloging and Metadata Associate (Interlibrary Loan) Lynne Wright, Scholarly Communication Librarian John Edward Martin, Humanities and Instruction Librarian Carol Hargis, Document Delivery Manager Rebecca Brand, and Remote Storage Supervisor, the inestimable James Flowers. I could not have gotten through a week's worth of work on this project without their expert skills and affirming good cheer. At Rutgers University Press, sincerest thanks to Executive Editor Nicole Solano, Production Editor Vincent Nordhaus, Production Assistant Veronica Meliksetian, Editorial Intern Malaika Jawed, Scribe Inc.'s Electronic Book Developer Bradley Cox, and all those involved in the production of this book. Special thanks to the invaluable support provided by my anonymous readers and to Thomas Doherty and Erika Doss for graciously endorsing this text. Thanks also to the editors of and readers for *CEA Critic* and *Journal of American Culture*, where parts of this work appeared in article form.

This book was sublimely inspired by the distinguished visitors and talented area researchers constituting UNT's Postwar Faculty Colloquium. Special thanks to Andrew Rubin, Ned O'Gorman, Thomas Doherty, Laura McEnaney, Debra Jaramillo, Christopher Loss, Malik Gaines, and Steven Cohan, whose keynote addresses have been scintillating high points over the years, and to Erika Doss and Amy Abugo Ongiri, whose presentations will surely scintillate when we can all be together in the same room again. More special thanks to local presenters, steering committee members, university sponsors, and friends-of: CVAD Associate Dean Denise Baxter, Agatha Beins, Harry Benshoff, CLASS Executive Dean Tamara Brown, Bryan Conn, Diane Culpin, Joseph Darda, Joanna Davis-McElligatt, Darryl Dickson-Carr, Jay Axline Gentry, Mark Hlavacik, Kyle Jensen, Holly Karibo, John Kinder, George Larke-Walsh, Sean Griffin, Liz Kim, Anna Lovatt, Jeff Menne,

Andrew McGregor, Drew McKevitt, VPRI Mark McLellan, Rachel Louise Moran, the marvelous and much-loved Marilyn Morris, Wesley Phelps, Clark Pomerleau, Jennifer Porst, Ben Rogerson, Stacy Takacs, Lee Demetrius Walker, Jacqueline Walker, Rick Worland, James Zeigler, and the UNT department chairs who have generously supported our endeavors. Harry Benshoff and Kyle Jensen have been key to mounting the meeting each year, as well as incisive respondents to my work in progress and dear friends.

This book was written for (and with) wonderful friends and family, whose ever-willingness to ask how it's going ever-encouraged me toward the pages that answered their question. Thank you, April Aguayo, Diana Treviño Benet, Kathryn Duncan, Christie Roden, and Annette Trefzer and beloved family Mom and Dad in Chicagoland and Christine Foertsch and Mike McKee in upstate New York. As ever, this book is dedicated to Aurora McKee and Solana McKee, who light my way, and to Terence Donovan, my heart and home.

NOTES

INTRODUCTION

1. Freedom, of course, is mainstream American politics' name for capitalism, as politicians are as loath to discuss this term, and the total disregard for humanity designated its fiduciary duty, as they are its feared opposite, *socialism*. Neither word is ever spoken, the latter banished to the national underworld and the former enshrined as the god that shall not be looked upon, nor even named.

2. Perhaps not surprisingly, Thurgood Marshall, famed for winning the Supreme Court's 1954 *Brown v. Board of Education* decision, was an early adversary: "Marshall visited the New York offices of the FBI on June 4, 1959, and urged agents to investigate Williams 'in connection with [Marshall's] efforts to combat Communist attempts to infiltrate the NAACP'" (Tyson 558).

3. Even the noted African American sociologist E. Franklin Frazier critiqued the "alien culture" of "Gandhism" as not "really applicable to the Negro's situation in the United States" (63).

4. Singh attaches the concept of freedom to economics via theories of the free market and equality to politics via theories of equality before the law: "If the ideal inhabitants of the nation-state are citizen-subjects, . . . formally equivalent participants in a common civic enterprise, then the ideal inhabitants of the market are private individuals . . . engaged in competition and personal advancement" (25). As useful as these formulations are, they are readable as universal in theory only—for example, how free is the free market when legislative and cultural effects come into play?—and thus may be said to allow for alternate formulations such as those advanced throughout this project.

5. In early 1970, Moynihan in his role as advisor to President Nixon advised in yet another infamous memo that "the time may have come when the issue of race could benefit from a period of 'benign neglect'" (qtd. in Kihss 1), due to progress deemed achieved on several fronts. Once made public, this comment again stirred controversy.

CHAPTER 1 — TALKING FIRST AND SHOOTING LATER IN THE BLACK POWER ERA

1. In spring 1964, Carmichael and a group of activists marched toward the Justice Department to protest the murder of Louis Allen, a Mississippi man who was killed for trying to register to vote. One in the group called out, "'Hey, there's Bro Malcolm.' And sho nuff, there was the brother standing on the sidewalk reading our signs. He was by himself and we shouted at him to come join us. He merely smiled and shook his head. But I could sense that a part of him wanted to" (Carmichael, *Ready* 355). Ed Brown, Rap's older brother and a member of the group, adds, "I did feel that the brother looked a little lonely standing there by himself. I know he had been getting a little tired of standing on the sidelines because of the Nation [of Islam]'s strict ban on political activity. . . . Malcolm was fundamentally an activist" (356).

2. Later Axelrod sued Cleaver for proceeds from his book sales due to inclusion of this letter.

3. Newton's attitudes toward women come from the same questionable perspective: "I would sleep with more than one woman, to see if they could deal with this without regressing to their old values, which [I] . . . considered outdated and bourgeois" (95). Facing the prospect of marriage, and the regular job necessary to support a wife and family, "I balked. By rejecting marriage and family, I held on to my 'freedom'" (97), even though he later realizes that such "intimacy and companionship . . . is probably as great as, perhaps greater than, the freedom I wanted" (96).

4. Pearson reports the statement of the man with Newton the night he died, regarding Newton's confession to the murder of Frey. Other witnesses comment on this and other deadly shootings and pistol-whippings confessed to by Newton but from which he escaped punishment due to hung juries in the early 1970s. C. Austin declares Pearson's treatment a "near-slanderous critique" (398) and adheres to Newton's own version of the events—that he fell unconscious shortly after the Frey shooting began only to awake in great agony, from abdominal bullet wounds, in the hospital later.

CHAPTER 2 — NOTHING LEFT TO LOSE

1. By 1991, Bullins was doubling down on his frequent return to the rape theme in early plays: "I've been interested in the ways that these people could touch one another or to get to know one another. . . . One of those ways is through violence, and violence can be verbal or physical. But also violence is an exciting spectacle in the theater" (qtd. in Menson-Furr 74).

2. Courtwright regards the early-1970s heroin epidemic as another "baby-boom phenomenon. . . . 42 million baby boomers, born between 1946 and 1956, were entering their most heroin-susceptible years between the mid-1960s and mid-1970s" (*Dark Paradise* 165).

CHAPTER 3 — TOOLS OF THE TRADE

1. Behrent hears a note of hope at the end of Dorothy Bryant's *Ella Price's Journal* (1972)—"not an end but a beginning" (270)—but my own view is that this text follows the same depressing course as French's: focused at first on the joys of learning and expanded consciousness, it shifts into melodrama when the heroine has a failed love affair with a professor, is counseled by an intensely lonely divorced friend not to leave her own marriage, but then does so on the eve of her planned abortion on Christmas Day. Instead of congratulating herself on this necessary, however difficult, move, Ella records in her journal feeling "like a plucked chicken about to be gutted" (227). In an early review, Martin Levin regarded the title character to conclude her experience having "exchange[d] her special brand of unhappiness for another of its infinite varieties" (BR14).

2. Levin's novel presents a striking racial angle, largely excised from the film. An African American children's author, Ruthanne Hendry, and her family move to Stepford late in the story; Levin allegorizes this group's "late" arrival to the suburbs and the stultification of professional womanhood that this move entailed. As sociologist Joyce Ladner suggested that African American women made better feminists because they were always already liberated, so Ruthanne is the sole survivor after the violent demise of Joanna. She links the Stepford crisis, what Friedan just as mysteriously termed "the feminine mystique," with racial identity: "The way they shopped so languidly, gliding along as if they never sweated. How white could you get?" (121). Ironically, the Hendrys' achieving the integrationist goal of suburban living means that Ruthanne's husband is instantly welcomed into the Men's Association. He chairs the sociology department of a university in the city, and when in the novel's final scene he sets down a classic from the late 1960s (Lionel Tiger's *Men in Groups*) to grudgingly take the kids to McDonald's, his academic reading matter portends Ruthanne's own fate.

3. As Nystrom points out, Bruce (13) and Kael (147) have read Theresa as a *gay* man cruising in bars, but Theresa's self-interested behavior is readable as masculine regardless of sexual orientation. To the degree that straight men only temper their own cruising instincts in order to attract women, who may tend more toward monogamy and nesting, gay men may model truer male behavior since they do so in contexts where feminine constraints are absent.

4. As Hollander relates the story, the installation of cameras and recorders throughout her apartment was the idea of her coauthor Moore, who suggested that such data collection would allow them to tell a more accurate story. The man hired to do the wiring wound up in the employ of the Knapp Commission, and without Hollander's knowing it, the archive she established to help her sell more books later entrapped her into prosecution and deportation.

WORKS CITED

Alghawas, Eman. "Looking Past the Hate: From Malcolm X to El-Shabazz." *Young Scholars in Writing*, vol. 3, 2005, pp. 61–67.

Araiza, Lauren. "'In Common Struggle against a Common Oppression': The United Farm Workers and the Black Panther Party, 1968–1973." *Journal of African American History*, vol. 94, no. 2, 2009, pp. 200–223.

Arendt, Hannah. "Reflections on Little Rock." *Dissent*, Winter 1959, pp. 45–56.

Armstrong, Michael F. *They Wished They Were Honest: The Knapp Commission and New York Police Corruption*. New York, Columbia UP, 2012.

Aubry, Timothy. "Erica Jong's Textual Bulimia: *Fear of Flying* and the Politics of Middlebrow Consumption." *Journal of Popular Culture*, vol. 42, no. 3, 2009, pp. 419–441.

Austin, Curtis J. *Up against the Wall: Violence in the Making and Unmaking of the Black Panther Party*. Fayetteville, U of Arkansas P, 2006.

Austin, Joe. *Taking the Train: How Graffiti Art Became an Urban Crisis in New York City*. New York, Columbia UP, 2001.

Avril, Chloé. "Race, Gender, and Class in the Autobiography of Huey P. Newton." *Nordic Journal of English Studies*, vol. 11, no. 2, 2012, pp. 5–35.

Bain, Donald. *Coffee, Tea, or Me?* 1968. New York, Penguin, 2003.

Baraka, Imamu Amiri. *Junkies Are Full of SHHH. Black Drama Anthology* (1970), edited by Woodie King and Ron Milner, New York, Penguin/Meridian, 1986, pp. 11–23.

Barnett, Pamela E. *Dangerous Desire: Literature of Sexual Freedom and Sexual Violence since the Sixties*. New York, Routledge, 2004.

Behrent, Megan. "Suburban Captivity Narratives: Feminism, Domesticity, and the Liberation of the American Housewife." *Journal of Narrative Theory*, vol. 49, no. 2, 2019, pp. 247–286.

Bell, Daniel. *The End of Ideology: On the Exhaustion of Political Ideas in the Fifties*. Glencoe, Ill., Free P, 1960.

Bell, Malcolm. *The Turkey Shoot: Tracking the Attica Cover-Up*. New York, Grove, 1985.

Benson, Thomas W. "Rhetoric and Autobiography: The Case of Malcolm X." *Quarterly Journal of Speech*, vol. 60, no. 1, 1974, pp. 1–13.

Berg, Peter. "San Francisco Mime Troupe: Risk and Frontal Assault." *The Digger Archives*, 1966, https://www.diggers.org/SFMT_Risk_by_Berg_1966.htm.

Berlin, Isaiah. *Four Essays on Liberty*. London, Oxford UP, 1969.

Black Panther, 23 Nov. 1967, http://freedomarchives.org/Documents/Finder/DOC513_scans/BPP_Intercommunal/513.Black%20Panther%20%28New%29%20Intercommunal%20News%20Service.The_Black_Panther_1967.pdf.

Black Panther, 2 Jan. 1971, http://freedomarchives.org/Documents/Finder/DOC513_scans/BPP_Paper/513.BPP.ICN.V5.N27.Jan.2.1971.pdf.

Black Women's Liberation Movement. "Statement on Birth Control." *Sisterhood Is Powerful: An Anthology of Writings from the Women's Liberation Movement*, edited by Robin Morgan, New York, Random/Vintage, 1970, pp. 404–406.

Blauner, Robert. "Whitewash over Watts: The Failure of the McCone Commission Report." *Mass Violence in America: The Los Angeles Riots*, edited by Robert M. Fogelson, New York, Arno Press / New York Times, 1969, pp. 165–188.

Blue, Gary. "Bring It Down Front / Drug Users Are Traitors." *Essence*, Nov. 1970, p. 40.

Boggs, Grace Lee. "The Black Revolution in America." 1968. *The Black Woman: An Anthology* (1970), edited by Toni Cade Bambara, New York, Washington Square, 2005, pp. 269–285.

Booker, Chris. "Lumpenization: A Critical Error in the Black Panther Party." *The Black Panther Party Reconsidered*, edited by Charles E. Jones, Baltimore, Black Classic, 1998, pp. 337–362.

Bosnicova, Nina. "God Is an Activist: Religion in *Narrative of the Life of Frederick Douglass* and *The Autobiography of Malcolm X*." *Americana: E-Journal of American Studies in Hungary*, vol. 5, no. 1, 2009. http://americanaejournal.hu/vol5no1/bosnicova.

Bradley, Patricia. *Mass Media and the Shaping of American Feminism, 1963–1975*. Jackson, UP of Mississippi, 2003.

Brewer, Brad. "Revolutionary Artist or Revisionist Al Capp?" *Right On!*, vol. 3, Apr. 1971, p. 15.

Brooks, Richard, director. *Looking for Mr. Goodbar*. Paramount, 1977.

Brown, Claude. *The Children of Ham*. 1973. New York, Stein and Day, 1976.

———. *Manchild in the Promised Land*. New York, Macmillan, 1965.

Brown, Elaine. "Speech on Feminism." Educational Video Group/Alexander Street, 2007. https://search.alexanderstreet.com/view/work/bibliographic_entity%7Cvideo_work%7C2787210.

———. *A Taste of Power: A Black Woman's Story*. New York, Anchor, 1992.

Brown, Helen Gurley. *Sex and the Single Girl*. New York, B. Geis / Pocket, 1962.

Brown, H. Rap. *Die Nigger Die!* New York, Dial, 1969.

Brown, Norman O. *Life against Death: The Psychoanalytic Meaning of History*. New York, Vintage, 1959.

Brownmiller, Susan. *Against Our Will: Men, Women, and Rape*. New York, Fawcett, 1975.

Bruce, Bryan. "Madness, Pleasure, and Transgression: *Looking for Mr. Goodbar*." *CineAction!*, vol. 2, 1985, pp. 7–13.

Bryant, Dorothy. *Ella Price's Journal*. New York, Lippincott, 1972.

Buchwald, Art. "The Bra-Burners." *New York Post*, 12 Sept. 1968, p. 42.

Bullins, Ed. *The Corner*. *Black Drama Anthology*, edited by Woodie King and Ron Milner, New York, Penguin/Meridian, 1986, pp. 77–88.

———. "A Short Statement on Street Theater." *The Drama Review*, vol. 12, no. 4, 1968, p. 93.

Burris, Greg. "Prometheus in Chicago: Film Portrayals of the Chaining and Gagging of Bobby Seal and the Real-ization of Resistance." *Cinema Journal*, vol. 54, no. 4, 2015, pp. 26–49.

Burroughs, William S. *Junky*. 1953, edited by Oliver Harris, New York, Grove, 2003.

Butler, Robert J. "The Woman Writer as American Picaro: Open Journeying in Erica Jong's *Fear of Flying*." *The Centennial Review*, vol. 31, no. 3, 1987, pp. 308–329.

Cade Bambara, Toni. "The Pill: Genocide or Liberation?" *The Black Woman: An Anthology* (1970), edited by Toni Cade Bambara, New York, Washington Square, 2005, pp. 203–212.

Caldwell, Ben. *The Job. The Drama Review*, vol. 12, no. 4, 1968, pp. 43–46.

———. *Prayer Meeting; or, the First Militant Minister*. 1967, 1969. *A Black Quartet: Four New Black Plays*, New York, NAL, 1970, pp. 27–36.

———. *Riot Sale; or, Dollar Psych Fake Out. The Drama Review*, vol. 12, no. 4, 1968, pp. 41–42.

———. *Top Secret; or, a Few Million after B.C. The Drama Review*, vol. 12, no. 4, 1968, pp. 47–50.

———. *The Wall. The Drama Review*, vol. 12, no. 4, 1968, pp. 91–92.

Callahan, Dan. "Hooker with a Heart of Darkness: Jane Fonda in *Klute*." *Bright Lights Film Journal*, 30 Apr. 2005, pp. 1–14. https://brightlightsfilm.com/hooker-with-a-heart-of-darkness-jane-fonda-in-klute/#.X5B1MOdOmUk.

Campbell, Russell. *Marked Women: Prostitutes and Prostitution in the Cinema*. Madison, U of Wisconsin P, 2006.

Cannato, Vincent J. *The Ungovernable City: John Lindsay and His Struggle to Save New York*. New York, Basic, 2001.

Carew, Jan. "Between Apocalypse and the Moon." *Globe and Mail*, 17 May 1969, p. A23.

Carmichael, Stokely. *Ready for Revolution: The Life and Struggles of Stokely Carmichael (Kwame Ture)*. With Ekwueme Michael Thelwell. New York, Scribner, 2003.

———. *Stokely Speaks: From Black Power to Pan-Africanism*. 1971. Chicago, Chicago Review Press, 2007.

———. "What We Want." *New York Review of Books*, 22 Sept. 1966, pp. 5+.

Carmichael, Stokely, and Charles V. Hamilton. *Black Power: The Politics of Liberation in America*. New York, Random House, 1967.

Carpenter, John. "Director's Special Edition Interview." *Escape from New York*, New Line Home Video, 1994.

Carrey, Jim. *Real Time*, HBO, 7 Sept. 2018.

Carroll, Jim. *Forced Entries: The Downtown Diaries, 1971–1973*. New York, Penguin, 1987.

Carson, Clayborne. *In Struggle: SNCC and the Black Awakening of the 1960s*. Cambridge, Harvard UP, 1981.

Castle, Terry. *The Apparitional Lesbian: Female Homosexuality and Modern Culture*. New York, Columbia UP, 1993.

Churchill, Ward. "To Disrupt, Discredit, and Destroy: The FBI's Secret War against the Black Panther Party." *Liberation, Imagination, and the Black Panther Party: A New Look at the Panthers and Their Legacy*, edited by Kathleen Cleaver and George Katsiaficas, New York, Routledge, 2001, pp. 78–117.

Clark, Joanna. "Motherhood." *The Black Woman: An Anthology* (1970), edited by Toni Cade Bambara, New York, Washington Square, 2005, pp. 75–86.

Clark, Richard X. *The Brothers of Attica*. New York, Links, 1973.

Cleaver, Eldridge. "Crackers to Spare." *Black Panther*, 23 Nov. 1967, p. 9.

———. "On the Contradictions within the Black Panther Party." *Right On!*, 3 April 1971, pp. 9–11.

———. *Soul on Ice*. New York, Delta, 1968.

Coates, Ta-Nehisi. "The Case for Reparations." *The Atlantic*, June 2014, pp. 54–71.

Cohen, Marcia. *The Sisterhood: The Inside Story of the Women's Movement and the Leaders Who Made It Happen*. New York, Fawcett, 1988.

Coleman, Kate. "Carnal Knowledge: A Portrait of Four Hookers." *Ramparts*, Dec. 1971, pp. 16+.

Cook, Ann. "Black Pride? Some Contradictions" 1969. *The Black Woman: An Anthology* (1970), edited by Toni Cade Bambara, New York, Washington Square, 2005, pp. 187–201.

Couch, William, Jr. Introduction. *New Black Playwrights*, edited by William Couch Jr., Baton Rouge, Louisiana State UP, 1968, pp. ix–xiii.

Courtwright, David T. *Dark Paradise: A History of Opiate Addiction in America*. Cambridge, Harvard UP, 2001.

———. *Violent Land: Single Men and Social Disorder from the Frontier to the Inner City*. Cambridge, Harvard UP, 1996.

Covington, Francee. "Are the Revolutionary Techniques Employed in *The Battle of Algiers* Applicable to Harlem?" *The Black Woman: An Anthology* (1970), edited by Toni Cade Bambara, New York, Washington Square, 2005, pp. 313–322.

Cowie, Jefferson. *Stayin' Alive: The 1970s and the Last Days of the Working Class*. New York, New Press, 2012.

Critchlow, Donald T. *Intended Consequences: Birth Control, Abortion, and the Federal Government in Modern America*. New York, Oxford UP, 1999.

Cruse, Harold. *The Crisis of the Negro Intellectual*. 1967. New York, New York Review Books, 2005.

Daniel, Douglass K. *Tough as Nails: The Life and Films of Richard Brooks*. Madison, U of Wisconsin P, 2011.

Davenport, Christian A. "Reading the 'Voice of the Vanguard': A Content Analysis of the Black Panther Intercommunal News Service, 1969–1973." *The Black Panther Party Reconsidered*, edited by Charles E. Jones, Baltimore, Black Classic, 1998, pp. 193–209.

Davis, Angela. *Angela Davis: An Autobiography*. New York, Random House, 1974.

———. *Women, Race, and Class*. 1981. New York, Random House, 1983.

Davis, Kenneth C. *Two-Bit Culture: The Paperbacking of America*. Boston, Houghton Mifflin, 1984.

Deck, Alice A. "Review of *A Taste of Power*." *African American Review*, vol. 31, no. 2, 1997, pp. 367–369.

Densmore, Dana. "Independence from the Sexual Revolution." *Radical Feminism*, edited by Anne Koedt et al., New York, Quadrangle, 1973, pp. 107–118.

"The Digger Free Store." *The Digger Archives*, https://www.diggers.org/free_store.htm.

Dobbs, Michael. *One Minute to Midnight: Kennedy, Khrushchev, and Castro on the Brink of Nuclear War*. New York, Knopf, 2008.

Doherty, Thomas. "Malcolm X: In Print, On Screen." *Biography*, vol. 23, no. 1, 2000, pp. 29–48.

Doss, Erika. "'Revolutionary Art Is a Tool for Liberation': Emory Douglas and Protest Aesthetics at the *Black Panther*." *Liberation, Imagination, and the Black Panther Party: A New Look at the Panthers and Their Legacy*, edited by Kathleen Cleaver and George Katsiaficas, New York, Routledge, 2001, pp. 175–187.

Dubey, Madhu. *Black Women Novelists and the Nationalist Aesthetic*. Bloomington, Indiana, 1994.

Dubois, Ellen. "Sisters and Brothers." *The Nation*, 6/13 Sept. 1993, pp. 251–253.

Dunbar, Roxanne. "Brainwashing and Women." *Radical Therapist*, vol. 1, no. 3, Aug.–Sept. 1970, p. 5.

———. "'Sexual Liberation': More of the Same Thing." *No More Fun and Games: A Journal of Female Liberation*, Nov. 1969, pp. 49–56.

Eakin, Paul John. "Malcolm X and the Limits of Autobiography." *Criticism*, vol. 18, no. 3, 1976, pp. 230–242.

Ebert, Roger. "Klute." *Chicago Sun-Times*, 1 Jan. 1971, https://www.rogerebert.com/reviews/klute-1971.

Echols, Alice. *Daring to Be BAD: Radical Feminism in America, 1967–1975*. Minneapolis, U of Minnesota P, 1989.

Ehrenreich, Barbara, et al. *Re-making Love: The Feminization of Sex*. New York, Anchor, 1986.

Eisenstein, Zillah R. *The Radical Future of Liberal Feminism*. 1981. Boston, Northeastern UP, 1993.

English, T. J. *The Savage City: Race, Murder, and a Generation on the Edge*. New York, William Morrow, 2012.

Escape from New York. Directed by John Carpenter. Avco Embassy, 1981.

Evans, Don. "The Theater of Confrontation: Ed Bullins, Up against the Wall." *Black World*, Apr. 1974, pp. 14–18.

Faludi, Susan. "Death of a Revolutionary." *New Yorker*, 15 Apr. 2013, pp. 52+.

Farber, David. *Chicago '68*. Chicago, U of Chicago P, 1988.

Fiddle, Seymour. *Portraits from a Shooting Gallery: Life Styles from the Drug Addict World*. New York, Harper & Row, 1967.

Fife, Lucy. "Human Monstrosity: Rape, Ambiguity, and Performance in *Rosemary's Baby*." *Hosting the Monster*, edited by Holly Lynn Baumgartner and Roger Davis, Amsterdam, Rodopi, 2008, pp. 43–62.

Firestone, Shulamith. *The Dialectic of Sex: The Case for Feminist Revolution*. New York, Morrow Quill, 1970.

Fischer, Lucy. "Birth Traumas: Parturition and Horror in *Rosemary's Baby*." *Cinema Journal*, vol. 31, no. 3, 1992, pp. 3–18.

Fishbein, Leslie. "*Looking for Mr. Goodbar*: Murder for the Masses." *International Journal of Women's Studies*, vol. 3, 1980, pp. 173–182.

Fogelson, Robert M. "White on Black: A Critique of the McCone Commission Report on the Los Angeles Riots." *Mass Violence in America: The Los Angeles Riots*, edited by Robert M. Fogelson, New York, Arno Press / New York Times, 1969, pp. 111–143.

Foner, Eric. *Reconstruction: America's Unfinished Revolution, 1863–1877*. New York, Harper & Row, 1988.

Fosburgh, Lacey. *Closing Time: The True Story of the Goodbar Murder*. 1975. New York, Dell, 1977.

Fox, Cristi A. "Ben Caldwell (1937–)." *African American Dramatists: An A-to-Z Guide*, edited by Emmanuel S. Nelson, Westport, Conn., Greenwood, 2004, pp. 78–87.

Fox, Margalit. "Helen Gurley Brown, Who Gave *Cosmo* Its Purr, Is Dead at 90." *Akron Beacon Journal*, 14 Aug. 2012.

Frazier, E. Franklin. "The Failure of the Negro Intellectual." 1962. *The Death of White Sociology: Essays in Race and Culture*, edited by Joyce Ladner, Baltimore, Black Classic, 1973, pp. 52–67.

French, Marilyn. *The Women's Room*. New York, Harcourt Brace Jovanovich, 1977.

Freud, Sigmund. "The 'Uncanny" (1919). *The Standard Edition of the Complete Psychological Works of Sigmund Freud, Volume XVII (1917–1919): An Infantile Neurosis and Other Works*, edited and translated by James Strachey, London, Hogarth, 1925, pp. 217–256.

Friedan, Betty. *The Feminine Mystique*. 1963. New York, W. W. Norton, 2010.

Frost, Laura. "'Every Woman Adores a Fascist': Feminist Visions of Fascism from *Three Guineas* to *Fear of Flying*." *Women's Studies*, vol. 29, 2000, pp. 37–69.

Gaines, Malik. *Black Performance on the Outskirts of the Left: A History of the Impossible*. New York, New York UP, 2017.

Gallagher, Pat, with Angela Stefano. "Story behind the Song: Lee Greenwood, 'God Bless the USA.'" *The Boot*, theboot.com.

Gardner, Sean. "Freeze Frame on a Bad Cop." *Village Voice*, 8 Aug. 2006, https://www.villagevoice.com/2006/08/08/freeze-frame-on-a-bad-cop/.

Garrett, Jimmy. *And We Own the Night: A Play of Blackness*. *The Drama Review*, vol. 12, no. 4, 1968, pp. 61–69.

Geary, Daniel. *Beyond Civil Rights: The Moynihan Report and Its Legacy*. Philadelphia, U of Pennsylvania P, 2015.

Gerhard, Jane. *Desiring Revolution: Second-Wave Feminism and the Rewriting of American Sexual Thought, 1920 to 1982*. New York, Columbia UP, 2001.

———. "Revisiting 'The Myth of the Vaginal Orgasm': The Female Orgasm in American Sexual Thought and Second-Wave Feminism." *Feminist Studies*, vol. 26, no. 2, 2000, pp. 449–476.

Giddis, Diane. "The Divided Woman: Bree Daniels in *Klute*." *Women and the Cinema: A Critical Anthology*, edited by Karyn Kay and Gerald Peary, New York, Dutton, 1977, pp. 26–36.

Gitlin, Todd. *The Sixties: Years of Hope, Days of Rage*. 1987. New York, Bantam, 1993.

———. *The Whole World Is Watching: Mass Media in the Making and Unmaking of the New Left*. Berkeley, U of California P, 1980.

Gledhill, Christine. "*Klute* 2: Feminism and *Klute*." *Women in Film Noir*, edited by E. Ann Kaplan, London, BFI, 1980, pp. 112–128.

Goines, Donald. *Dopefiend*. 1971. New York, Holloway/Kensington, 2009.

Goode, Erich. *Drugs in American Society*. New York, Knopf, 1972.

Goode, Greg. "From *Dopefiend* to *Kenyatta's Last Hit*: The Angry Black Crime Novels of Donald Goines." *MELUS*, vol. 11, no. 3, 1984, pp. 41–48.

Gordon, Milton. *Assimilation in American Life*. New York, Oxford UP, 1964.

Gorfinkel, Elena. *Lewd Looks: American Sexploitation Cinema in the 1960s*. Minneapolis, U of Minnesota P, 2015.

Gottehrer, Barry. *New York: City in Crisis*. New York, McKay, 1965.

Grant, Nathan L. "Ed Bullins (b. 1935)." *Concise Oxford Companion to African American Literature*, edited by William L. Andrews et al., New York, Oxford UP, 2001, https://www.oxfordreference.com/view/10.1093/acref/9780195138832.001.0001/acref-9780195138832-e-88#.

Greenspun, Roger. "Klute." *New York Times*, 24 June 1971, p. 35.

Greenwood, Lee. "God Bless the USA." MCA, 1984.

Greer, Germaine. "Down with Panties." *Ms.*, July 1972, p. 8. Originally published as "Going Without." *Sunday Times*, 19 Sept. 1971.

———. *The Female Eunuch*. 1970. New York, Harper Collins, 2006.

Gregory, Dick. *Dick Gregory's Frankenstein*. New York, MGM/Poppy, 1970.

Grogan, Emmett. *Ringolevio: A Life Played for Keeps*. 1972. New York, New York Review Books, 1990.

Gross, David. "Culture, Politics, and 'Lifestyle' in the 1960s." *Race, Politics, and Culture: Critical Essays on the Radicalism of the 1960s*, edited by Adolph Reed Jr., Westport, Conn., Greenwood, 1986, pp. 100–117.

Gustaitis, Rasa. *Turning On*. New York, Signet/NAL, 1969.

Hacker, Andrew. *The End of the American Era*. New York, Atheneum, 1970.

———. *The New Yorkers: A Profile of an American Metropolis*. New York, Mason/Charter, 1975.

Haley, Alex. "Epilogue." *The Autobiography of Malcolm X, as Told to Alex Haley*, New York, Random House, 1965, pp. 390–463.

Halliwell, Martin. *Therapeutic Revolutions: Medicine, Psychiatry, and American Culture, 1945–1970*. New Brunswick, N.J., Rutgers UP, 2013.

Harris, Fred. *Alarms and Hopes: A Personal Journey, a Personal View*. New York, Harper & Row, 1968.

Harris, Fred, and John Lindsay. *The State of the Cities: Report of the Commission on the Cities in the '70s*. New York, Praeger, 1972.

Harris, Oliver. *William Burroughs and the Secret of Fascination*. Carbondale, Southern Illinois UP, 2003.

Harrison, Isheka N. "Dream Defenders Host Former Black Panther." *South Florida Times*, 20 Apr. 2017, pp. 1B–2B.

Hartnell, Anna. "Between Exodus and Egypt: Malcolm X, Islam, and the 'Natural' Religion of the Oppressed." *European Journal of American Culture*, vol. 27, no. 3, 2008, pp. 207–225.

Hay, Samuel L. *Ed Bullins: A Literary Biography*. Detroit, Wayne State UP, 1997.

Hayden, Tom. *Rebellion in Newark: Official Violence and Ghetto Response*. New York, Vintage, 1972.

Healy, David. *Let Them Eat Prozac: The Unhealthy Relationship between the Pharmaceutical Industry and Depression*. New York, New York UP, 2004.

Helford, Elyce Rae. "*The Stepford Wives* and the Gaze: Envisioning Feminism in 1975." *Feminist Media Studies*, vol. 6, no. 2, 2006, pp. 145–156.

Himes, Chester. *Plan B*. Jackson, UP of Mississippi, 1993.

Hoffman, Abbie. *The Autobiography of Abbie Hoffman*. New York, Four Walls Eight Windows, 1980.

———. *Fuck the System*. Pamphlet. New York, 1967.

———. *Revolution for the Hell of It*. New York, Dial, 1968.

Hoffman, A. Robin. "How to See the Horror: The Hostile Fetus in *Rosemary's Baby* and *Alien*." *LIT: Literature, Interpretation, Theory*, vol. 22, no. 3, 2011, pp. 239–261.

Hogeland, Lisa Maria. *Feminism and Its Fictions: The Consciousness-Raising Novel and the Women's Liberation Movement*. Philadelphia, U of Pennsylvania P, 1998.

Hollander, Xaviera, et al. *The Happy Hooker*. New York, Dell, 1972.

Hood, Jay. "Desire and Fantasy in Erica Jong's *Fear of Flying*." *This Book Is an Action: Feminist Print Culture and Activist Aesthetics*, edited by Jaime Harker and Cecilia Konchar Farr, Urbana, U of Illinois P, 2016, pp. 149–162.

Horne, Gerald. *Fire This Time: The Watts Uprising and the 1960s*. Charlottesville, U of Virginia P, 1995.

Horowitz, Daniel. *Betty Friedan and the Making of* The Feminine Mystique: *The American Left, The Cold War, and Modern Feminism*. Amherst, U of Massachusetts P, 1998.

Houck, Davis W. "'By Any Means Necessary': Rereading Malcolm X's Mecca Conversion." *Communication Studies*, vol. 44, nos. 3–4, 1993, pp. 285–298.

Hudson, Taylor. "Annals of Addiction: Go Ask Alice Which '70s-Era Drug Film Is Her Favorite." *Bitch: Feminist Responses to Popular Culture*, Spring 2008, p. 96.

Hughes, Helen MacGill, editor. *The Fantastic Lodge: The Autobiography of a Girl Drug Addict*. Boston, Houghton Mifflin, 1961.

Jackson, Candice Love. "'Sinners Have Souls, Too': Spirituality in the Secular Text." *Xavier Review*, vol. 27, no. 1, 2007, pp. 104–115.

Jackson, Thomas F. *From Civil Rights to Human Right: Martin Luther King and the Struggle for Economic Justice*. Philadelphia, U of Pennsylvania P, 2007.

Jacobs, Jane. *The Death and Life of Great American Cities*. New York, Vintage/Knopf, 1961.

Jezer, Marty. *Abbie Hoffman: American Rebel*. New Brunswick, N.J., Rutgers UP, 1993.

Johnson, Davi. "The Rhetoric of Huey P. Newton." *Southern Communication Journal*, vol. 70, no. 1, 2004, pp. 15–30.

Johnson, Lyndon B. "Commencement Address at Howard University: 'To Fulfill These Rights.'" *University of Texas Johnson Archives*, 4 June 1965, lbjlib.untexas.edu.

Johnson, Rob. *The Lost Years of William S. Burroughs: Beats in South Texas*. College Station, Texas A&M P, 2006.

Jong, Erica. *Fear of Flying*. 1973. New York, NAL, 2003.

Joseph, Peniel E. *Waiting 'til the Midnight Hour: A Narrative History of Black Power in America*. New York, Henry Holt, 2006.

Kael, Pauline. "*Goodbar*, or How Nice Girls Go Wrong." *New Yorker*, 24 Oct. 1977, pp. 147–150.

Kahn, Tom. *The Economics of Equality*. New York, League for Industrial Democracy, 1964.

Kane, Paula, with Christopher Chandler. *Sex Objects in the Sky: A Personal Account of the Stewardess Rebellion*. Chicago, Follett, 1974.

Kaplan, E. Ann. *Women and Film: Both Sides of the Camera*. London, Routledge, 1983.

Katsoulis, Melissa. *Telling Tales: A History of Literary Hoaxes*. London, Constable and Robinsons, 2009.

Kaufman, Leslie. "John Mack Carter, 86, Is Dead; Led 'Big 3' Women's Magazines." *New York Times*, 26 Sept. 2014, p. D8.

Kelley, Robin D. G. *Freedom Dreams: The Black Radical Imagination*. Boston, Beacon, 2002.

Kerner Report. *Report of the National Advisory Commission on Civil Disorders*. New York, New York Times, 1968.

Kihss, Peter. "'Benign Neglect' on Race Is Proposed by Moynihan." *New York Times*, 1 Mar. 1970, p. 1.

King, Martin Luther, Jr. *Where Do We Go from Here: Chaos or Community?* New York, Harper & Row, 1967.

Klemesrud, Judy. "Feminists Recoil at Film Designed to Relate to Them." *New York Times*, 26 Feb. 1975, p. 28.

Kleps, Art. *Millbrook: A Narrative of the Early Years of American Psychedelism*. 1975. Austin, Tex., Original Kleptomanian Neo-American Church, 2005.

Klute. Directed by Alan J. Pakula. Warner Brothers, 1971.

Knowles, Claire. "Working Girls: Femininity and Entrapment in *Peyton Place* and *Valley of the Dolls*." *Women: A Cultural Review*, vol. 27, no. 1, 2016, pp. 62–78.

Koedt, Anne. "The Myth of the Vaginal Orgasm." *CWLU Herstory Archive*, 1970, https://www.cwluherstory.org/classic-feminist-writings-articles/myth-of-the-vaginal-orgasm.

Koerner, Brendan I. *The Skies Belong to Us: Love and Terror in the Golden Age of Hijacking*. New York, Broadway Books, 2013.

Kristoff, Nicolas D., and Sheryl WuDunn. *Tightrope: Americans Reaching for Hope*. New York, Penguin/Random House, 2020.

Ladner, Joyce A. *Tomorrow's Tomorrow: The Black Woman*. Garden City, Anchor, 1971.

Langan, John. "A Devil for the Day: William Peter Blatty, Ira Levin, and the Revision of the Satanic." *The American Exorcist: Critical Essays on William Peter Blatty*, edited by Benjamin Szumskyj, Jefferson, N.C., McFarland, 2008, pp. 45–70.

Langum, David J. *William M. Kunstler: The Most Hated Lawyer in America*. New York, New York UP, 1999.

Larner, Jeremy, with Ralph Tefferteller. *The Addict in the Street*. New York, Grove, 1964.

Lauret, Maria. *Liberating Literature: Feminist Fiction in America*. New York, Routledge, 1994.

Lavelle, Ashley. "From 'Soul on Ice' to 'Soul for Hire'? The Political Transformation of Black Panther Eldridge Cleaver." *Race & Class*, vol. 54, no. 2, 2012, pp. 55–74.

Leary, Timothy. *Your Brain Is God*. 1988. Berkeley, Ronin, 2001.

Lee, Martin A., and Bruce Shlain. *Acid Dreams: The Complete Social History of LSD—the CIA, the Sixties, and Beyond*. 1985. New York, Grove, 1992.

Lehmann-Haupt, Christopher. "Books of the Times." *New York Times*, 27 Oct. 1977, p. 73.

Lester, Julius. *Look Out, Whitey! Black Power's Gon' Get Your Mama!* New York, Grove, 1968.

Leuci, Robert. *All the Centurions: A New York City Cop Remembers His Years on the Street, 1961–1981*. New York, HaperCollins, 2004.

Levin, Ira. *Rosemary's Baby*. 1967. New York, Penguin, 2010.

———. *The Stepford Wives*. 1972. New York, Perennial/Harper Collins, 2002.

Levin, Martin. "New and Novel: *Ella Price's Journal*." *New York Times*, 24 Dec. 1972, p. BR14.

Lindsey, Kay. "The Black Woman as a Woman." *The Black Woman: An Anthology* (1970), edited by Toni Cade Bambara, New York, Washington Square, 2005, pp. 103–108.

Lipsky, Michael, and David J. Olson. "Civil Disorders and the American Political Process." *Violence as Politics: A Series of Original Essays*, edited by Herbert Hirsch and David C. Perry, New York, Harper & Row, 1973, pp. 161–186.

Looking for Mr. Goodbar. Directed by Richard Brooks. Paramount, 1977.

Loudermilk, Kim A. *Fictional Feminism: How American Bestsellers Affect the Movement for Women's Equality*. New York, Routledge, 2004.

Lueck, Thomas J. "Officer Jailed for 32 Years Wins Parole." *New York Times*, 23 Sept. 2007, p. 40.

Lupsha, Peter A., and Catherine MacKinnon. "Domestic Political Violence, 1965–1971: A Radical Perspective." *Violence as Politics: A Series of Original Essays*, edited by Herbert Hirsch and David C. Perry, New York, Harper & Row, 1973, pp. 5–40.

Lytle, Mark Hamilton. *America's Uncivil Wars: The Sixties Era from Elvis to the Fall of Richard Nixon*. New York, Oxford UP, 2006.

Maas, Peter. *Serpico*. 1973. New York, Bantam, 1974.

MacLean, Nancy. *Freedom Is Not Enough: The Opening of the American Workplace*. Cambridge, Harvard UP, 2008.

Maher, Bill. *Real Time*, HBO, 10 Aug. 2018.

Mainardi, Patricia. "The Politics of Housework." 1970. *The American Women's Movement, 1945–2000: A Brief History with Documents*, edited by Nancy MacLean, Boston, Bedford/St. Martin's, 2009, pp. 94–96.

Malcolm X. *The Autobiography of Malcolm X, as Told to Alex Haley*. New York, Random House, 1965.

———. "The Ballot or the Bullet." 3 and 12 Apr. 1964. Rpt. in *Malcolm X Speaks: Selected Speeches and Statements*, edited by George Breitman, New York, Grove, 1965, pp. 23–44.

Marcus, Sharon. "Placing *Rosemary's Baby*." *Differences: A Journal of Feminist Cultural Studies*, vol. 5, no. 3, 1993, pp. 121–153.

Marcuse, Herbert. *Eros and Civilization: A Philosophical Inquiry in Freud*. Boston, Beacon Press, 1969.

Marks, Lara V. *Sexual Chemistry: A History of the Oral Contraceptive Pill*. New Haven, Yale UP, 2001.

Martin, Bradford D. *The Theater Is in the Street: Politics and Performance in Sixties America*. Amherst, U of Massachusetts P, 2004.

May, Rollo. *Love and Will*. New York, W. W. Norton, 1969.

McAlister, Melanie. "One Black Allah: The Middle East in the Cultural Politics of African American Liberation, 1955–1970." *American Quarterly*, vol. 51, no. 3, 1999, pp. 622–656.

McCone Report. *Violence in the City—an End or a Beginning: A Report by the Governor's Commission on the Los Angeles Riots*. Los Angeles, College Bookstore, 2 Dec. 1965.

McKay Report. *Attica: The Official Report of the New York State Special Commission on Attica*. New York, Praeger, 1972.

McKay, Robert B. "Attica: The Anatomy of an Investigation." *Chicago-Kent Law Review*, vol. 49, no. 2, 1972, pp. 139–160.

McKissick, Floyd. "Book Reviews." *California Law Review*, vol. 57, 1969, pp. 547–550.

———. *3/5 of a Man*. New York, Macmillan, 1969.

McKnight, Gerald D. *The Last Crusade: Martin Luther King, Jr., the FBI, and the Poor People's Campaign*. Boulder, Westview Press, 1998.

McManis, Jo Agnew. "*Rosemary's Baby*: A Unique Combination of Faust, Leda, and 'The Second Coming.'" *McNeese Review*, vol. 20, 1971–1972, pp. 33–36.

Menson-Furr, Ladrica. "Ed Bullins (1935–)." *African American Dramatists: An A-to-Z Guide*, edited by Emmanuel S. Nelson, Westport, Conn., Greenwood, 2004, pp. 64–77.

Miles, Barry. *William Burroughs: El Hombre Invisible*. New York, Hyperion, 1992.

Miller, D. Quentin. "Lost and . . . Found? James Baldwin's Script and Spike Lee's *Malcolm X*." *African American Review*, vol. 46, no. 4, 2013, pp. 671–685.

Miller, Henry. "On *Fear of Flying*." *New York Times*, 1973. Reprinted in *Fear of Flying* by Erica Jong, New York, NAL, 2003, pp. 439–443.

Miller, Loren. "Farewell to Liberals: A Negro View." *The Nation*, 20 Oct. 1962, pp. 235–238.

Millett, Kate. *Sexual Politics*. 1969. Urbana, U of Illinois P, 2000.

Milliken, Christie. "Rate It X? Hollywood Cinema and the End of the Production Code." *Sex Scene: Media and the Sexual Revolution*, edited by Eric Schaefer, Durham, Duke UP, 2014, pp. 25–52.

Mills, James. *The Panic in Needle Park*. 1965. New York, Signet, 1971.

Mills, Nathaniel. "Cleaver/Baldwin Revisited: Naturalism and the Gendering of Black Revolution." *Studies in American Naturalism*, vol. 7, no. 1, 2012, pp. 50–79.

Moody, Anne. *Coming of Age in Mississippi*. New York, Dial, 1968.

Morgan, Jo-Anne. "Huey Newton Enthroned: Iconic Image of Black Power." *Journal of American Culture*, vol. 37, no. 2, 2014, pp. 129–148.

Morgan, Robin. "No More Miss America!" Press Release, 22 Aug. 1968. Reprinted in *Sisterhood Is Powerful: An Anthology of Writings from the Women's Liberation Movement*, New York, Random/Vintage, 1970, pp. 584–588.

Morgan, Ted. *Literary Outlaw: The Life and Times of William S. Burroughs*. New York, Henry Holt, 1988.

Morrison, Toni. "What the Black Woman Thinks about Women's Lib." *New York Times*, 22 Aug. 1971, pp. 14+.

Moynihan, Daniel Patrick. *The Negro Family: The Case for National Action*. Washington, D.C.: Office of Policy, Planning, and Research / Department of Labor, Mar. 1965.

———. "The President and the Negro: The Moment Lost." *Commentary*, 1 Feb. 1967, pp. 31–45.

Neal, Larry. "The Black Arts Movement." *The Drama Review*, vol. 12, no. 4, 1968, pp. 28–39.

Newton, Huey, with J. Herman Blake. *Revolutionary Suicide*. 1973. New York, Penguin, 2009.

Newton, Michael. *Bitter Grain: Huey Newton and the Black Panther Party*. 1980. Los Angeles, Holloway House, 1991.

Norton, Anne. "Heart of Darkness: Africa and African Americans in the Writings of Hannah Arendt." *Feminist Interpretations of Hannah Arendt*, edited by Bonnie Honig, University Park, Pennsylvania State UP, 1995, pp. 247–262.

Nowsreal. Directed by Diggers, 1968, https://www.diggers.org/nowsreal.htm.

Nystrom, Derek. *Hard Hats, Rednecks, and Macho Men: Class in 1970s American Cinema*. Oxford, Oxford UP, 2009.

Ohmann, Carol. "*The Autobiography of Malcolm X*: A Revolutionary Use of the Franklin Tradition." *American Quarterly*, vol. 22, no. 2, 1970, pp. 131–149.

Ongiri, Amy Abugo. *Spectacular Blackness: The Cultural Politics of the Black Power Movement and the Search for a Black Aesthetic*. Charlottesville, U of Virginia P, 2010.

"On the Assassination of Deputy Field Marshall Robert Webb." *Right On!*, 3 April 1971, p. 3.

Patterson, James T. *Freedom Is Not Enough: The Moynihan Report and America's Struggle over Black Family Life from LBJ to Obama*. New York, Basic, 2010.

Pearson, Hugh. *The Shadow of the Panther: Huey Newton and the Price of Black Power in America*. Cambridge, Mass., Perseus, 1996.

Peavy, Charles D. "Satire and Contemporary Black Drama." *Satire Newsletter*, vol. 7, Fall 1969, pp. 40–49.

Peirce, Neal R. *The Megastates of America: People, Politics, and Power in the Ten Great States*. New York, Norton, 1972.

Perkins, Margo V. *Autobiography as Activism: Three Black Women of the Sixties*. Jackson, UP of Mississippi, 2000.

Perry, Charles. *The Haight-Ashbury: A History*. 1984. New York, Wenner Books, 2005.

Pitkin, Hanna Fenichel. "Conformism, Housekeeping, and the Attack of the Blob: The Origins of Hanna Arendt's Concept of the Social." *Feminist Interpretations of Hannah Arendt*, edited by Bonnie Honig, University Park, Pennsylvania State UP, 1995, pp. 51–82.

"The Post-competitive, Comparative Game of a Free City." *The Realist / The Digger Papers*, Aug. 1968, p. 15, https://www.diggers.org/digpaps68/postcomp.html.

Preble, Edward, and John J. Casey Jr. "Taking Care of Business: The Heroin User's Life on the Street." *International Journal of Addictions*, vol. 4, no. 1, 1969, pp. 1–24.

Quashie, Kevin Everod. "Black Feminisms and *The Autobiography of Malcolm X*." *Journal X*, vol. 4, no. 1, 1991, pp. 41–70.

Quinn, Sally. "Once Again, Feminists Take Up a Fight We Shouldn't Have." *Washington Post*, 14 Mar. 2013, p. C01.

Quinones, Sam. *Dreamland: The True Tale of America's Opiate Epidemic*. New York, Bloomsbury, 2015.

Rader, Dotson. *I Ain't Marchin' Anymore*. New York, Paperback, 1969.

Raiford, Leigh. *Imprisoned in a Luminous Glare: Photography and the African American Freedom Struggle*. Chapel Hill, U of North Carolina P, 2011.

Rainwater, Lee, and William L. Yancey. *The Moynihan Report and the Politics of Controversy*. Cambridge, Mass., MIT P, 1967.

Reding, Nick. *Methland: The Death and Life of an American Dream*. New York, Bloomsbury, 2010.

Reich, Wilhelm. *The Function of the Orgasm: Sex-Economic Problems and Biological Energy*. 1942. London, Panther, 1968.

———. *The Sexual Revolution*. 1945. Translated by Theodore P. Wolfe. New York, FSG/ Noonday, 1962.

Rhodes, Jane. *Framing the Black Panthers: The Spectacular Rise of a Black Power Icon*. New York, New Press, 2007.

Riley, Clayton. Introduction. *A Black Quartet: Four New Black Plays*. New York, NAL, 1970, pp. vii–xxiii.

Rosen, Ruth. *The World Split Open: How the Modern Women's Movement Changed America*. New York, Viking, 2000.

Rossman, Michael. *The Wedding within the War*. New York, Anchor, 1971.

Rossner, Judith. *Looking for Mr. Goodbar*. 1975. New York, Simon and Schuster, 2014.

Rout, Kathleen. *Eldridge Cleaver*. Boston, Twayne, 1991.

Rubin, Jerry. *Do It! Scenarios of the Revolution*. New York, Ballantine, 1970.

Rustin, Bayard. "The Watts 'Manifesto' and the McCone Report." *Mass Violence in America: The Los Angeles Riots*, edited by Robert M. Fogelson, New York, Arno Press / New York Times, 1969, pp. 145–164.

Sanchez, Sonia. *The Bronx Is Next*. *The Drama Review*, vol. 12, no. 4, 1968, pp. 78–84.

Scahill, Andrew. "Deviled Eggs: Teratogenesis and the Gynecological Gothic in the Cinema of Monstrous Birth." *Demons of the Body and Mind: Essays on Disability in Gothic Literature*, edited by Ruth Bienstock Anolik, Jefferson, N.C., McFarland, 2010, pp. 197–216.

Scanlon, Jennifer. *Bad Girls Go Everywhere: The Life of Helen Gurley Brown*. New York, Oxford UP, 2009.

Schaefer, Eric. "Pandering to the 'Goon Trade': Framing the Sexploitation Audience through Advertising." *Sleaze Artists: Cinema at the Margins of Taste, Style, and Politics*, edited by Jeffrey Sconce, Durham, Duke UP, 2007, pp. 19–46.

Scharine, Richard G. "Ed Bullins Was Steve Benson (But Who Is He Now?)." *Black American Literature Forum*, vol. 13, no. 3, 1979, pp. 103–109.

Schjeldahl, Peter. "The Outlaw." *New Yorker*, 3 Feb. 2014, pp. 70–74.

Schlesinger, Arthur M., Jr. *The Vital Center: The Politics of Freedom*. Boston, Houghton Mifflin, 1949.

Schneider, Eric C. *Smack: Heroin and the American City*. Philadelphia, U of Pennsylvania P, 2008.

Sconce, Jeffrey. "Altered Sex: Satan, Acid, and the Erotic Threshold." *Sex Scene: Media and the Sexual Revolution*, edited by Eric Schaefer, Durham, Duke UP, 2014, pp. 235–261.

Seale, Bobby. "Chairman Bobby Speaks at Boycott Site." *Black Panther*, 9 Aug. 1971, p. B+.

———. *Seize the Time: The Story of the Black Panther Party and Huey Newton*. 1970. Baltimore, Black Classics, 1991.

Seaman, Barbara. *Free and Female: The New Sexual Role of Women*. New York, Fawcett Crest, 1972.

———. *Lovely Me: The Life of Jacqueline Susann*. 1987. New York, Seven Stories Press, 1996.

Segal, Lynne. *Straight Sex: Rethinking the Politics of Pleasure*. Berkeley, U of California P, 1994.

Shakur, Assata. *Assata: An Autobiography*. Westport, Conn., Lawrence Hill, 1987.

———. "Assata Shakur: Profiled and on the Run." *Crisis*, Nov./Dec. 2000, pp. 23–25.

Shecter, Leonard, with William Phillips. *On the Pad: The Underworld and Its Corrupt Police*. New York, G. P. Putnam's Sons, 1973.

Sheehy, Gail. *Hustling: Prostitution in Our Wide Open City*. New York, Delacorte, 1973.

———. "Wide Open City." *New York*, 26 July 1971, pp. 24–35.

Sher, Louis K. *The Stewardesses*. Directed by Allan Silliman. Sherpix, 1969–1971.

Showalter, Elaine. "Rethinking the Seventies: Women Writers and Violence." *The Antioch Review*, vol. 39, no. 2, 1981, pp. 156–170.

Silver, Anna Krugovoy. "The Cyborg Mystique: *The Stepford Wives* and Second Wave Feminism." *Arizona Quarterly*, vol. 58, no. 1, 2002, pp. 109–126.

Singh, Nikhil Pal. *Black Is a Country: Race and the Unfinished Struggle for Democracy*. Cambridge, Harvard UP, 2004.

Slater, Philip E. *The Pursuit of Loneliness: American Culture at the Breaking Point*. Boston, Beacon, 1970.

Slobodkin, Marvin. *Inside Dope*. New York, Dutton, 1971.

Slotkin, Richard. *Gunfighter Nation: The Myth of the Frontier in Twentieth-Century America*. Norman, U of Oklahoma P, 1998.

Steinem, Gloria. "After Black Power, Women's Liberation." *New York*, 7 Apr. 1969, pp. 8–10.

———. "Campaigning." *Outrageous Acts and Everyday Rebellions*. New York, Holt, 1995, pp. 76–120.

———. "Far from the Opposite Shore." 1978. *Outrageous Acts and Everyday Rebellions*. New York, Holt, 1995, pp. 370–392.

———. "The Importance of Work." *Outrageous Acts and Everyday Rebellions.* New York, Holt, 1995, pp. 189–194.

———. "I Was a Playboy Bunny." 1963. *Outrageous Acts and Everyday Rebellions.* New York, Holt, 1995, pp. 32–75.

———. "The Moral Disarmament of Betty Coed." *Esquire,* Sept. 1962, pp. 97+.

———. "The Real Linda Lovelace." 1980. *Outrageous Acts and Everyday Rebellions.* New York, Holt, 1995, pp. 266–276.

———. "The Time Factor." *Outrageous Acts and Everyday Rebellions.* New York, Holt, 1995, pp. 195–197.

The Stepford Wives. Directed by Bryan Forbes. Columbia, 1975.

Stephenson, Donald Grier, Jr. *The Right to Vote: Rights and Liberties under the Law.* Santa Barbara, ABC-CLIO, 2004.

Stevens, Jay. *Storming Heaven: LSD and the American Dream.* New York, Grove, 1987.

Stewart, Charles J. "The Evolution of a Revolution: Stokely Carmichael and the Rhetoric of Black Power." *Quarterly Journal of Speech,* vol. 83, 1997, pp. 429–446.

Sugrue, Thomas J. *The Origins of the Urban Crisis: Race and Inequality in Postwar Detroit.* Princeton, Princeton UP, 2005.

Susann, Jacqueline. *Valley of the Dolls.* 1966. New York, Grove, 1997.

"Talk of the Town." *New Yorker,* 14 Oct. 1976, p. 49, https://www.diggers.org/free_store1.htm.

Taylor, Douglas. "Three Lean Cats in a Hall of Mirrors: James Baldwin, Norman Mailer, and Eldridge Cleaver on Race and Masculinity." *Texas Studies in Literature and Language,* vol. 52, no. 1, 2010, pp. 70–101.

Thomas, Pat. *Listen, Whitey! The Sights and Sounds of Black Power, 1965–1975.* Seattle, Fantagraphics, 2012.

Thompson, Heather Ann. *Blood in the Water: The Attica Prison Uprising of 1971 and Its Legacy.* New York, Pantheon, 2016.

Tone, Andrea. "Tranquilizers on Trial: Psychopharmacology in the Age of Anxiety." *Medicating Modern America: Prescription Drugs in History,* edited by Andrea Tone and Elizabeth Siegel Watkins, New York, New York UP, 2007, pp. 156–182.

Tremblay, Jean-Thomas. "Room for Critique: The Spaces of Institutional Disillusionment in 1970s US Feminist Fiction." *Post-45,* 8 Oct. 2016.

Tyler, Anne. "Starting Out Submissive." *New York Times Book Review,* 16 Oct. 1977, pp. 7+.

Tynan, Kenneth. "Preface." *The Connection* by Jack Gelber. New York, Grove, 1957.

Tyson, Timothy B. "Robert F. Williams, 'Black Power,' and the Roots of the African American Freedom Struggle." *Journal of American History,* vol. 85, no. 2, 1998, pp. 540–570.

Updike, John. "Jong Love." *New Yorker,* 17 Dec. 1973. Reprinted in *Fear of Flying* by Erica Jong, New York, NAL, 2003, pp. 445–451.

Valerius, Karyn. "*Rosemary's Baby,* Gothic Pregnancy, and Fetal Subjects." *College Literature,* vol. 32, no. 3, 2005, pp. 116–135.

Van Deburg, William L. *Hoodlums: Black Villains and Social Bandits in American Life.* Chicago, U of Chicago P, 2004.

———. *New Day in Babylon: The Black Power Movement and American Culture, 1965–1975.* Chicago, U of Chicago P, 1992.

Van Gelder, Lindsy. "A Year Later: The Lure of the Women's Room." *Ms.,* Apr. 1979, pp. 42–44.

Wallace, Christine. *Germaine Greer: Untamed Shrew.* London, Richard Cohen, 1999.

Wallace, Michele. *Black Macho and the Myth of the Superwoman.* New York, Dial, 1978.

Ward, Douglas Turner. *Happy Ending.* New York, Dramatists Play Services, 1966.

Watkins, Rychetta. *Black Power, Yellow Power, and the Making of Revolutionary Identities.* Jackson, UP of Mississippi, 2012.

Watson, Jamal E. "Former Black Panther Leader Runs for Brunswick, Georgia, Mayor." *New York Amsterdam News*, 28 July 2005, pp. 1+.

Wexman, Virginia Wright. "The Trauma of Infancy in Roman Polanski's *Rosemary's Baby*." *American Horrors: Essays on the Modern American Horror Film*, edited by Gregory A. Waller, Urbana, U of Illinois P, 1987, pp. 30–43.

Wicker, Tom. *A Time to Die*. New York, Quadrangle/New York Times, 1975.

Wilderson, Frank, III. "Gramsci's Black Marx: Whither the Slave in Civil Society?" *Social Identities*, vol. 9, no. 2, 2003, pp. 225–240.

Willbern, David. *The American Popular Novel after World War II: A Study of 25 Bestsellers, 1947–2000*. Jefferson, NC, McFarland, 2013.

Williams, Anne. "*The Stepford Wives*: What's a Living Doll to Do in a Postfeminist World?" *Postfeminist Gothic: Critical Interventions in Contemporary Culture*, edited by Benjamin A. Brabon and Stéphanie Genz, Houndmills, Palgrave Macmillan, 2007, pp. 85–98.

Williams, Joan C. *White Working Class: Overcoming Class Cluelessness in America*. Boston, Harvard Business Review, 2020.

Williams, Mabel. *Robert F. Williams: Self Defense, Self-Respect, and Self-Determination, as Told by Mabel Williams. Freedom Archives*, https://www.freedomarchives.org/RFW.html.

Williams, Robert F. "Can Negroes Afford to Be Pacifists?" *African American Political Thought: Confrontation vs. Compromise: 1945 to the Present*, edited by Marcus D. Pohlmann, New York, Routledge, 2003, pp. 69–76.

———. *Negroes with Guns*. New York, Marzani and Munsell, 1962.

———. "Speech: Delivered at the International Conference for Solidarity with the People of Vietnam against US Imperialist Aggression for the Defense of Peace. Hanoi, Democratic Republic of Vietnam, Nov. 25–29, 1965." *The Crusader*, vol. 6, no. 3, Mar. 1965, pp. 1–5, http://www.aavw.org/protest/early_rfw_abstract21.html.

———. "USA: The Potential of a Minority Revolution." *The Crusader*, May–June 1964, pp. 1–7.

Wilson, James Q., and George L. Kelling. "Broken Windows." *Atlantic Monthly*, Mar. 1982, pp. 29–38.

Winstead, Antoinette F. "The Devil Made Me Do It: The Devil in 1960–1970s Horror Film." *Vader, Voldemort, and Other Villains: Essays on Evil I Popular Media*, edited by Jamey Heit, Jefferson, N.C., McFarland, 2011, pp. 28–45.

Wolfe, Tom. *The Electric Kool-Aid Acid Test*. 1968. New York, Picador, 2008.

Wolff, Cynthia Griffin. "The Radcliffean Gothic Model: A Form of Feminine Sexuality." *Modern Language Studies*, vol. 9, no. 3, 1979, pp. 98–113.

Woo, Elaine. "Marilyn French Dies at 79; Author of Feminist Classic 'The Women's Room.'" *Los Angeles Times*, 5 May 2009, https://www.latimes.com/local/obituaries/la-me-marilyn-french5-2009may05-story.html.

Young, Andrew. "Civil Rights Activist Argues to Keep Confederate Monuments." National Public Radio, 23 Aug. 2017, https://www.npr.org/transcripts/545435024.

Yuill, Kevin L. "The 1966 White House Conference on Civil Rights." *The Historical Journal*, vol. 41, no. 1, 1998, pp. 259–282.

Zelizer, Julian E. Introduction. *The Kerner Report*. 50th anniversary edition, Princeton, Princeton UP, 2016, pp. xiii–xxxvi.

Zepp, Ira G., Jr. *The Social Vision of Martin Luther King, Jr.* Brooklyn, Carlson, 1989.

Zieger, Susan. "Queering the Drug Diary: *Go Ask Alice* and Its Victorian Genealogies." *Genre*, vol. 39, no. 1, 2006, pp. 89–113.

Zita, Jacquelyn N. "Pornography and the Male Imaginary." *Enclitic*, vol. 9, nos. 1–2, 1988, pp. 28–44.

INDEX

1964 Democratic Convention, 2, 35
1968 Democratic Convention, 57, 89, 93–94
1970 Women's Strike for Equality / March, 111, 146
3/5 of a Man (Floyd McKissick), 22, 36, 117

Albee, Edward, 85
Algren, Nelson, 98
Allen, Ivan, 42
Altamont free concert (Rolling Stones), 96
amphetamine (a.k.a. speed), 97, 121–122, 123
And We Own the Night (Jimmy Garrett), 86, 88
Arendt, Hannah, 16, 21, 23
Armstrong, Michael, 83, 143
Artists Liberation Front, 6
Attica Prison/riot, 69, 75–80, 90, 107, 108
Autobiography of Abbie Hoffman (Abbie Hoffman), 92, 94
Autobiography of Malcolm X (Malcolm X and Alex Haley), 34, 37, 39–41, 49, 97, 124
Axelrod, Beverly, 47, 158n2 (chap. 1)

Bain, Donald, 113, 130–131, 132–133
Baldwin, James, 46
"Ballot or the Bullet, The" (Malcolm X), 4, 38
Baraka, Amiri, 85, 97
Berg, Peter, 7, 8, 9
Berger, John, 44
Bernard Geis publishing company, 126–127
Bill of Rights, 3, 51, 53
Bishop, Leonard, 98, 99
Black Liberation Army (BLA), 4
Black Panther newspaper, 32, 45, 54–56, 62, 117
Black Panther Party (BPP), 3, 10, 38, 45, 50–54, 59–62, 63, 75, 85, 91, 96, 147
Black Women's Liberation Movement, 118
Blue, Gary, 11
Boyette, Bill, 59–60
"Bra-Burners, The" (Art Buchwald), 109–110
Breakfast for Children program, 10, 27, 36, 55, 59, 62, 64
Bronx Is Next, The (Sonia Sanchez), 88
Brooks, Richard, 141, 144
Brown, Claude, 36, 92, 97, 98, 99, 101–103, 105–106, 152
Brown, Ed, 157–158n1
Brown, Edmund "Pat," 70, 72
Brown, Elaine, 25, 36, 62–63, 151
Brown, Helen Gurley, 126–128
Brown, H. Rap, 4, 31, 33, 37, 42–45, 54, 63, 75, 94, 104
Brown, Norman O., 114–115
Brownmiller, Susan, 93, 125, 140, 148
Brown v. Board of Education, 22, 157n2
Bryant, Dorothy, 158n1 (chap. 3)
Buchwald, Art, 109–110
Buckley, William F., 22, 24
Bullins, Ed, 65, 86–88, 158n1 (chap. 2)
Burroughs, William S., 97, 98–101, 114
Bush, George W., 153

Caldwell, Ben, 27, 66–67, 69, 85, 86, 105, 117
California State Capitol/Assembly, 3, 10, 48, 52, 63
Cambridge, Maryland, 43, 67
Canton, Mississippi, 36
Capote, Truman, 140
Carmichael, Stokely, 2, 7, 31–33, 35, 37–38, 41–43, 44, 54, 63, 93, 157–158n1
Carpenter, John, 13, 28, 106–108
Carrey, Jim, 150
Carroll, Jim, 103–104
Carter, John Mack, 146

Cassavetes, John, 134
Chicago 8 (7) Trial, 53, 57–59
Children of Ham (Claude Brown), 102, 105–106
Chisolm, Shirley, 16
Choice, 66
Civil Rights Act of 1964, 24
Civil Rights Acts of 1866–1875, 22
Clark, Kenneth, 19, 102
Clark, Mark, 59
Clark, Richard X., 76–77
Clark, Sonny, 11
Cleaver, Eldridge, 6, 13, 32, 38, 45–48, 49, 54, 56, 60–61, 63, 89, 158n2 (chap. 1)
Cleaver, Kathleen Neal, 48, 53, 60
Closing Time (Lacey Fosburgh), 140
Clutter, Nancy, 140
Cockettes, 8
Coffee, Tea, or Me? (Donald Bain), 113, 130–131, 132–134
Coming of Age in Mississippi (Anne Moody), 35–36
Congress of Racial Equality (CORE), 34, 42, 44
Connection, The (Jack Gelber), 99, 103
Constitution (U.S.), 3, 20–24, 42, 46, 50–51, 53, 63
Corner, The (Ed Bullins), 86–87
"Crackers to Spare" (Eldridge Cleaver), 32
Crisis of the Negro Intellectual (Harold Cruse), 21, 24, 33
Cruse, Harold, 21, 24, 33

Daley, Richard J., 57, 93–94
Davis, Angela, 36, 41–42, 57, 61–62, 63, 107, 117, 119, 147
Deacons of Defense and Justice, 3
Declaration of Independence, 4, 10, 22, 53, 95
Del Mauro, James, 74
Detroit riots, 20, 66, 68, 70, 73, 78, 83
Dexedrine, 121, 123
Dialectic of Sex, The (Shulamith Firestone), 118–119
Die Nigger Die! (H. Rap Brown), 43–45
Diggers of San Francisco, 6–10, 60, 92, 94, 96, 110
Dohrn, Bernadine, 107
Do It! (Jerry Rubin), 89
Dopefiend (Donald Goines), 98–99
Douglas, Emory, 43, 55–56, 61
Down All Your Mean Streets (Leonard Bishop), 98
Dutchman (Amiri Baraka), 85

Ebony magazine, 44
Eighth Amendment, 58
Ella Price's Journal (Dorothy Bryant), 158n1 (chap. 3)
Eros and Civilization (Herbert Marcuse), 114
Escape from New York (John Carpenter), 13, 28, 106–108
Esquire magazine, 47, 116, 148

Fantastic Lodge, The (Helen MacGill Hughes), 98, 99
Farrow, Mia, 134
Fear and Loathing in Las Vegas (Hunter S. Thompson), 57
Fear of Flying (Erica Jong), 113, 126, 128–130, 131, 133
Felker, Clay, 148
Female Eunuch, The (Germaine Greer), 115–116
Fifteenth Amendment, 3, 22
Fifth Amendment, 53
Firestone, Shulamith, 118–119, 130, 145
First Amendment, 34, 43
Fonda, Jane, 144
Forbes, Bryan, 136
Fosburgh, Lacey, 140, 141, 142
Fourteenth Amendment, 3, 21–22, 50
Fox, Muriel, 146
Fox News, 1
Frazier, E. Franklin, 19, 157n3
Free and Female (Barbara Seaman), 116
Free DC Movement, 41
Freedom Budget, 15, 16
Freedom Center / Freedom House, 95
Freedom City, 41
Freedom Male Catheter, 1
Free Huey! campaign, 10, 27, 54–56, 61
Free Speech Movement (FSM), 2, 5, 46, 89
Free Stores, 7–8
French, Marilyn, 118, 120–121, 123–126, 129, 131, 133, 134, 158n1 (chap. 3)
Freud, Sigmund, 114–115, 127, 137, 138
Frey, John, 10, 53–54, 55, 158n4
Friedan, Betty, 14, 25, 26, 28, 111, 120, 124, 134, 146–147, 148, 159
Fuck the System (a.k.a. *Steal This Book*; Abbie Hoffman), 7, 9
Function of the Orgasm, The (Wilhelm Reich), 114

Galbraith, John Kenneth, 147
Gandhi, Mohandas, 4, 49, 157n3
Garland, Judy, 121, 122, 123
Garrett, Jimmy, 86, 88
Garry, Charles, 54
Geismar, Maxwell, 45
Gelber, Jack, 99, 103
Genovese, Kitty, 140

Gibson, Kenneth A., 16
Glazer, Nathan, 18, 19, 105, 106
Go Ask Alice (Muriel Sparks), 98
"God Bless the USA" (Lee Greenwood), 150
Goines, Donald, 98–99
Goldwater, Barry, 4, 24, 26, 66
Gordon, Milton, 20–21
Gordon, Ruth, 134
Gottlieb, Lou (*Morningstar Ranch*), 105
Grant, Cary, 96
Greene County, Alabama, 45
Greenwood, Lee, 150
Greenwood, Mississippi, 35
Greer, Germaine, 25, 26, 109, 115–116, 118, 119, 127–128, 134, 145, 146
Gregory, Dick, 9, 108
Griffith, D. W., 22
Grogan, Emmett, 7, 8, 9, 92

Haight Ashbury, 5, 6, 8, 96
Haley, Alex, 34, 40
Hamer, Fannie Lou, 152
Hamilton, Charles V., 35
Hampton, Fred, 59, 83
Happy Ending (Douglas Turner Ward), 85–86
Happy Hooker, The (Xaviera Hollander and Robin Moore), 143
Harris, Fred, 69, 73, 75, 103, 104
Hayes, Isaac, 107–108
Heanes, Herbert, 54
Hearst, Patty, 107
Hefner, Hugh (*Playboy*), 128, 149
heroin (opiates), 28, 77, 92, 95–103, 108
Hilliard, David, 54, 61, 62
Himes, Chester, 68
H Is for Heroin (David Hulburd), 98, 99
Hoffman, Abbie, 7–9, 26, 27, 29, 59, 90, 91–93, 94, 96, 103, 109
Hoffman, Julius, 53, 57–59
Holiday, Billie, 11
Hollander, Xaviera, 29, 143, 145, 147, 159n4
Howard University speech, 17, 19
Hughes, Helen MacGill, 98, 99
Hughes, Langston, 66, 85
Hughes, Richard, 68
Hulburd, David, 98, 99
Human Be-In, 6
Humphrey, Hubert, 93
Hutton, Lil' Bobby, 59, 61
Huxley, Aldous, 96

I Ain't Marchin' Anymore (Dotson Rader), 90–91
"I Have a Dream" speech (Martin Luther King Jr.), 34
In Cold Blood (Truman Capote), 140
International Foundation for Internal Freedom (IFIF), 95
"I Was a Playboy Bunny" (Gloria Steinem), 148–149

Jet magazine, 44
Job, The (Ben Caldwell), 65, 85
Johnson, Luci Baines, 32, 46
Johnson, Lyndon Baines (LBJ), 4, 6, 16–19, 20, 31–33, 44, 66, 70, 72, 75, 93
Jong, Erica, 113, 126–127, 128–129, 131, 133
Joplin, Janis, 1, 69
Junkies Are Full of SHHH (Amiri Baraka), 97–98
Junky (William S. Burroughs), 97, 99–101

Kallen, Horace, 21
Kendall, Willmoore, 22
Kennedy, John F. (JFK), 17, 29, 31
Kennedy, Robert F. (RFK), 93
Kerner Commission/Report, 20, 67–70, 73–75, 78, 83, 103
Kerouac, Jack, 57, 100–101
Kesey, Ken, 5, 96
Killens, John Oliver (J. O.), 46
Kilpatrick, James, 24
King, Martin Luther, Jr., 2, 3–4, 13–16, 21, 26, 28, 31, 32–34, 36, 39, 42, 48, 53, 85, 107–108
Kinsey, Alfred, 127
Kleps, Art, 105
Klute (Alan J. Pakula), 134, 138–139, 144–145
Knapp Commission/Report, 78, 81, 83–84, 143–144, 145, 159n4
Koedt, Anne, 116
Ku Klux Klan, 3
Kunstler, William, 58, 59

Ladies Home Journal, 109, 146, 148
Ladner, Joyce, 117–118, 158–159
Landis, Carol, 121, 122
Leary, Tim, 95–96, 105
Leon, Barbara, 112
Lester, Julius, 31
Leuci, Robert, 82, 95
Levin, Ira, 134, 158n2 (chap. 3)
Lewis, John, 41
Lewis, J. Tarika (Mantilaba), 55
Life against Death (Norman O. Brown), 114–115
Lindsay, John, 73, 75, 83, 103–105, 106, 143
Looking for Mr. Goodbar (Judith Rossner), 134, 138
Love and Will (Rollo May), 115
Lowndes County, Alabama, 35
Lowndes County Freedom Organization (LCFO), 35
LSD, 5–7, 11–12, 95–97, 98

Maher, Bill, 150, 151
Mailer, Norman, 45, 46, 88, 114, 129
Mainardi, Patricia, 112
Malcolm X, 4, 25, 26, 27, 31, 33–35, 37–40, 48, 49, 51–52, 63–64, 85, 97, 158n1 (chap. 1)
Manchild in the Promised Land (Claude Brown), 97, 103, 152
Manson family, 96, 119, 140
Man with the Golden Arm (Nelson Algren), 98
Man with the Golden Arm (Otto Preminger), 98
March against Fear, 34
March on the Pentagon, 92
March on Washington, 14, 34, 36, 37
Marcuse, Herbert, 114, 115
Marshall, Thurgood, 157n1 (chap. 1)
Marx, Groucho, 96
Matthews, Connie, 60
May, Rollo, 115
McCall's magazine, 148
McCarthy, Eugene, 93
McCone Commission/Report, 69–74, 80–81
McGovern, George, 148
McKay Commission/Report, 77–79
McKissick, Floyd, 22, 36, 42, 117
McLuhan, Marshall, 44, 94
"Me and Bobby McGee," 1
Memphis garbage workers' strike, 34, 48
Meredith, James, 34, 35, 42
Merman, Ethel, 122
Merritt Junior College, 48
Metcalf-Volker Bill, 12
Millbrook, 96, 105
Miller, Henry, 46, 88, 128
Miller, Loren, 33
Millett, Kate, 119, 127, 148
Mills, James, 144
Miltown, 121
Minstrel Show, A, 7–8
Miranda rights, 53
Miss America Pageant, 109, 110–112, 146
Missile Crisis (Cuban Missile Crisis), 3
Mississippi Freedom Democratic Party (MFDP), 2, 35
Montgomery Bus Boycott, 15, 28, 34
Moody, Anne, 35–36, 45, 51, 62
Moore, Richard "Dharuba," 60
Moore, Robin, 143, 159n4
Morehouse College, 41, 42
Morgan, Robin, 110, 111
Morrison, Toni, 118
Moses, Robert "Bob," 35
Moynihan, Daniel Patrick, 19, 23, 157n5
Moynihan Report / *Negro Family, The* (Daniel Patrick Moynihan), 17–20, 69, 70, 117
Ms. magazine, 125, 148
Muhammad, Elijah, 39, 40, 117
Mulford Bill, 3, 52, 53
"Myth of the Vaginal Orgasm, The" (Anne Koedt), 116

NAACP, 2, 10, 44, 157n2
National Liberation Front (North Vietnam), 4
National Mobilization Committee (a.k.a. the Mobe), 93
National Organization for Women (NOW), 25, 111
Nation of Islam (NOI), 34, 38–40, 70, 97, 105, 117, 158n1 (chap. 1)
Negroes with Guns (Robert F. Williams), 3
Nembutal, 121, 122
Newark riots, 20, 66, 68–69, 70, 73, 74, 78, 83
Newton, Huey, 8, 10–11, 27, 35, 45, 48–56, 58, 59–63, 89, 91, 93, 158n3, 158n4
New York Radical Women (NYRW), 109, 110, 111, 118, 148
Nixon administration, 82, 117, 144, 157n5
Nowsreal, 9
NRA (National Rifle Association), 2

Oak Room, Plaza Hotel, 25, 147
Obama, Barack, 153
Ochs, Phil, 29
On the Road (Jack Kerouac), 57, 100–101
Organization of Afro-American Unity (OAAU), 38, 40–41

Packard, Vance, 44
Pakula, Alan J., 134
Panic in Needle Park, The (James Mills), 144
Parker, Charlie, 11
Peace and Freedom Party, 10
Phillips, Bill (Patrolman P), 83–84, 143
pill, the (oral contraceptive), 28, 95, 112, 114–118, 120–123, 129
Planned Parenthood, 117
Pleasance, Donald, 107
Plessy v. Ferguson, 22
Polanski, Roman, 134
Poor People's Campaign, 14, 32, 34, 48
Pratt, Elmer "Geronimo," 60
Prayer Meeting (Ben Caldwell), 85
Preminger, Otto, 98
Progressive Labor Party, 55

Quinn, Roseanne, 140–141, 142
Quinn, William, 78

Rader, Dotson, 88, 90–91
"Radio Free Dixie" (Robert F. Williams), 3
Ramparts magazine, 45

Randolph, A, Philip, 15, 16, 32
Reagan, Ronald, 3, 11, 52, 106
Reagan administration/era, 67, 108, 136
Reagon, Bernice, 31
Reconstruction era, 3, 21–23, 24
Redstocking group, 112, 118, 148
Reich, Wilhelm, 114–115
Resurrection City, 32–33
Revolutionary Suicide (Huey Newton), 49–50, 56
riffraff theory, 70
Ringolevio (Emmett Grogan), 92
Riot Sale (Ben Caldwell), 65, 81, 85, 86
Robinson, Ruby Doris, 41
Rockefeller, Nelson, 78, 104
Rosemary's Baby (Ira Levin), 134–135
Ross, Katharine, 136, 137
Rossman, Michael, 5, 88–90, 91
Rossner, Judith, 134, 139, 140, 141, 142, 144
Rubin, Jerry, 7, 27, 59, 89, 91–92, 93–94, 96
Rustin, Bayard, 32, 37, 68, 69, 72

Sanchez, Sonia, 88
Sanders, Marlene, 146
SANE (National Committee for a Sane Nuclear Policy), 57
San Francisco Mime Troupe, 6, 7, 8, 10
Savio, Mario, 2
Schlesinger, Arthur
Scott-Heron, Gil, 94
Seale, Bobby, 3, 50–54, 56–58, 60, 91
Seaman, Barbara, 116, 118, 121, 127–128, 136
Seconal, 121, 122
Second Amendment, 2, 3, 14, 51, 52, 53, 63
Seize the Time (Bobby Seale), 50, 56
Serpico, Frank, 81–84, 95
Serpico (Peter Maas), 98
Sex and the Single Girl (Helen Gurley Brown), 126–128, 134
Sexual Revolution, The (Wilhelm Reich), 114
Shabazz, Betty, 51
Shakur, Assata, 9, 25, 33, 36, 48, 51, 52, 57, 60, 61, 63
Sheehy, Gail, 139, 143
Sher, Louis K., 113, 131, 132, 133
Silliman, Allan, 132
Solanas, Valerie, 107
Soul on Ice (Eldridge Cleaver), 45–47, 49, 56
Sparks, Muriel, 98
Speck, Richard, 140
Spellman College, 151
Sproul Hall, 2
Steinem, Gloria, 93, 111, 116, 119, 146–147, 148–149, 151
Stepford Wives, The (Bryan Forbes), 135–136, 138, 142
Stepford Wives, The (Ira Levin), 119, 134, 158n2 (chap. 3)
Stewardesses, The (Louis K. Sher and Allan Silliman), 113, 131–132
Student Nonviolent Coordinating Committee (SNCC), 2, 4, 27, 31, 34–35, 37, 38, 40–42, 44, 48, 54, 56, 63, 69, 93, 94
Students for a Democratic Society (SDS), 7, 10, 57, 81, 90, 91, 93
Summerhill neighborhood, 42
Susann, Jacqueline, 113, 120–124, 126, 131, 134
Sutherland, Donald, 144
Symbionese Liberation Army, 4

Tabor, Michael "Cetewayo," 60
Tate, Sharon, 140
Ten-Point Program, 10, 41, 49, 61, 91
Thompson, Hunter S., 57
Time to Die, A (Tom Wicker), 77–80
"To Fulfill These Rights" conference, 18
Top Secret (Ben Caldwell), 117
Trump, Donald, 151, 152
Tynan, Kenneth, 99, 103

"Uncanny, The" (Sigmund Freud), 137, 138
Updike, John, 128–129

Valley of the Dolls (Jacqueline Susann), 75, 113, 120–121, 134
Vietnam soldiers/veterans, 6, 11, 132, 133, 142, 149
Vietnam War, 14, 20, 27, 29, 31, 51, 70, 72–73, 89, 93, 108
Vietnam War protests, 5, 69, 89, 90, 94, 110
Voting Rights Act of 1965, 20, 22

Wall, The (Ben Caldwell), 105
Ward, Douglas Turner, 85
Watts riots, 13, 20, 31, 46, 60, 66–72, 76, 78, 83
Webb, Robert, 60, 61
Wedding within the War (Michael Rossman), 89–90
Weinberg, Jack, 2, 5
Wicker, Tom, 76–80
"Wide Open City" (Gail Sheehy), 139
Williams, Mabel, 4
Williams, Robert F., 2–4, 15, 51, 96, 157n2
Wirtz, Willard, 19
WITCH, 146, 148
Women's Room, The (Marilyn French), 120, 123–126, 129

Yazoo City, 42
Yippies (Youth International Party), 7, 57, 59, 89, 91–94, 96

Zero Population Growth, 117

ABOUT THE AUTHOR

JACQUELINE FOERTSCH is a professor of English at the University of North Texas and chair of UNT's Postwar Faculty Colloquium. She is the author most recently of *Reckoning Day: Race, Place, and the Atom Bomb in Postwar America* and *American Drama: In Dialogue, 1714–Present.*